AD WORLDS

Brands, Media, Audiences

GREG MYERS

*Senior Lecturer, Department of Linguistics and
Modern English Language, University of Lancaster*

A member of the Hodder Headline Group
LONDON • NEW YORK • SYDNEY • AUCKLAND

HF
5823
.M93
1999

First published in Great Britain in 1999 by
Arnold, a member of the Hodder Headline Group,
338 Euston Road, London NW1 3BH

http://www.arnoldpublishers.com

Co-published in the United States of America by
Oxford University Press Inc.,
198 Madison Avenue, New York, NY 10016

British Library Cataloguing in Publication Data
A catalogue record for this book is available from the British Library

Library of Congress Cataloging-in-Publication Data
Myers Greg, 1954–
    Ad Worlds : brands, media, audiences / Greg Myers.
        p.   cm.
    Includes bibliographical references and index.
    ISBN 0-340-70006-8. — ISBN 0-340-70007-6 (pbk.)
    1. Advertising.   I. Title.
HF5823.M93   1998
659.1—dc21   98-20774
                                                                      CIP

ISBN 0 340 70007 6 (pb)
ISBN 0 340 70006 8 (hb)

1 2 3 4 5 6 7 8 9 10

Production Editor: Julie Delf
Production Controller: Sarah Kett
Cover Design: Terry Griffiths

Composition by Phoenix Photosetting, Chatham, Kent
Printed and bound in Great Britain by
MPG Books Ltd, Bodmin, Cornwall

What do you think about this book? Or any other Arnold title?
Please send your comments to feedback.arnold@hodder.co.uk

for Alice and Tess

Contents

Preface

Trust me. I'm an advert.
(poster for Holsten Pils)

This book is about analysing advertisements: the written texts, talk, pictures, music, and stories in paid commercial announcements. This analysis may seem unnecessary when people analyse ads so much already. They analyse ads for fun in newspaper columns, academic books, television compilations of funny ads, game shows, stand-up comedy routines, and in talk on buses or in pubs or at parties. They analyse ads in self-defence, trying not to be persuaded and asserting their own independence of mind. Advertisers are painfully aware that their audiences know something about ads, and they try to build this knowledge into ads that refer to other advertising.

The poster I have quoted is one example. To understand it you have to know that it is one of a series in which someone is about to do something potentially embarrassing, such as invite a Bible missionary into the house, pick an inappropriate sexual partner, or join a commune. The quoted text is in the centre of the poster in small red Courier typeface letters against a background that is yellow like the beer's label. There is a text in the lower left that says 'NEW LIGHTER CRISPER HOLSTEN PILS'. The connection between the two messages is made clear by another text in the lower right corner: 'an easier way to change your life'. So the ad is telling us that trusting ads is a stupid move, socially – and yet it is an advertisement that is sharing this joke. The campaign fits within a larger, long-term strategy of positioning Holsten Pils as a different sort of lager (a strategy that also includes television ads mentioned in Chapter 12). The advertiser knows that people will be sceptical about their claims, as they are sceptical (with some justification) about politicians, journalists, scientists, or academics writing textbooks about ads. Yet the agency and client must still be confident that advertising can have the desired effects.

While academics, journalists, and people in pubs do talk about ads, and

approach them sceptically, they tend to talk about them as separate texts –
a Budweiser commercial with a funny line, or a Nike poster showing a
sports hero with a public persona as a rebel, or a Peugeot 406 commercial
with a favourite pop song as its soundtrack. The main argument in this
book that many ads make sense only when considered in terms of the social
worlds around them: the placement of brands in the market; the ways
people interact with each medium; and the ways audiences are defined and
define themselves. Often both critics and proponents of advertising ignore
these processes, and present advertising as a monolithic institution that
makes people want things, buy things, conform to roles, and withdraw into
their own desires. But if we do think of ads in these monolithic terms, we are
left with a number of puzzles:

- How can offensive ads (like some for Benetton or Calvin Klein) work?
- How can boring, repetitive ads (like those for many household cleaners)
  work?
- How can ads stop us from driving when drunk, or using drugs, or having
  unprotected sex?
- How could one advertise anything on the World Wide Web, where no
  one has to watch?
- Who would watch QVC or The Shopping Channel, media that are noth-
  ing but ads?
- Why do ads that are carefully researched and painstakingly crafted by
  highly skilled professionals so often miss their apparent targets?
- How can self-mocking ads (like the poster for Holsten Pils) work?

To understand these puzzles, it helps to look closely at the ads involved,
but also to see them as products that have moved through various worlds –
the client, the agency, the medium – on their way to our worlds. It takes
work to get ads between these various worlds, and make them seem right at
every stage. Often the ad falls apart completely when it reaches us (think of
the inappropriate junk mail you get, or an ad meant to be hip that is just
embarrassing), and the illusion of a monolithic, all-powerful advertising
industry is shattered.

I have used the title 'Ad Worlds' rather than, say, 'Ads in Context' or
'Advertising and Culture' because I want to stress this multiplicity and
tension. John Corner used the phrase 'Adworlds' as a chapter title
(Corner 1995) to suggest how the fantasy worlds within the television
commercial relate to our experience of the medium, and stressed the point
that the contents of advertising texts are not just imprinted on the blank
minds of spectators. I want to keep this focus, but consider a wider range
of worlds. The word 'world' suggests the way people inhabit their systems
of thought, living within their aims, timetables and histories, and assumptions. I have modelled the title on that of a classic sociological study by
Howard S. Becker, *Art Worlds*, and like Becker, I want to use it to
broaden out consideration from the individual work to the activities

around it, and then return to the works. It is worth quoting from the opening of Becker's study:

> All artistic work, like all human activity, involves the joint activity of a number, often a large number, of people. Through their cooperation, the art work we eventually see or hear comes to be and continues to be. The work always shows signs of that cooperation. The forms of cooperation may be ephemeral, but often become more or less routine, producing patterns of collective activity we call an art world. (Becker 1982: 1)

I borrow this use of *worlds* from Becker's work on art, not because I want to enter into the argument about whether advertising is an art like paintings in a gallery or a jazz quintet in a club, but because I see advertising, like art, as a collective activity, in which the co-ordination of efforts is always at issue. A brand manager in the marketing department of a firm has a different world from that of a copywriter brainstorming at the agency, or a director setting up lights on a shoot, or the advertising sales department of a television broadcaster, or a consumer looking at a product on a shelf. Someone who moves from one world of the ad business to another finds the new setting is not just different, it is foreign. But somehow they have to work together in an ad, and work together with us, for it to do as intended, or even for the ad to appear at all.

Once one grants this multiplicity of worlds behind the simplest soap ad, the terrain becomes bewilderingly complex. If we live in a 'promotional culture' (see Wernick (1991) and Chapter 12) and it is hard to see what *isn't* in some way related to advertising. Take a rather banal series for Daz in which the comedian Danny Baker knocks at the door and asks women about their laundry detergent (see Chapter 2). Many people must have asked why the most canny marketers in the world (Procter & Gamble) kept running this much-hated series. The answer could lead us to supermarket shelf space and shop's own brands, research and development (are 'Daz whites' really any different from others?), programmes like *Candid Camera* or *The Big Breakfast* in which television intrudes into 'real life', the serials in the breaks of which the ad ran, people's nightmares (yes, I have heard of it turning up there), jokes, and other ads sending it up ('Guaranteed Danny Baker Free' says an ad for a Fantasy Football video).

That is the main point of this book: detailed consideration of any ad leads us through many worlds. I have divided the terrain into three worlds: brands, media, and audiences. This three-way division is already an over-simplification, but it serves to point us beyond the text of each ad to some of the things it might be doing. In each chapter I focus on one or two main examples: ads, whole commercial breaks, or research projects. The ads are all from Britain or the US over the last 5 years. Most academic analyses of ads, including my own in *Words in Ads*, have focused on print media, just because the examples are easier to analyse and reproduce in a book. Most of my examples here are from television, because that is the medium that is most talked about, but I do discuss other media in the second section. Since it is unlikely that any reader has seen all the main examples, I have tried to discuss them in enough detail so that readers can follow the analysis and apply it to similar ads they have seen. My apologies for losing the full visual and sound impact of the originals.

In an interdisciplinary text like this one, there will inevitably be terms from linguistics, communication studies, cultural studies, or marketing that need definition. In *Words in Ads* I provided a glossary; here I focus instead on a few key terms that call for more extended discussion. I have chosen some terms that may seem to need no definition at all, their meaning is so obvious (CULTURE, POSTER), and others that are specialized academic jargon (DISCOURSE, REFLEXIVITY). My purpose here is not to give *a* meaning, but to show how the term can be contentious, between disciplines and between approaches within disciplines, and to refer readers on to more detailed discussion of these controversies.

This book, like its predecessor *Words in Ads*, grew out of lectures in an introductory course in culture and communication. It is an interdisciplinary course, and I draw on several lines of academic research. Since I start in each case with an example, I draw on those researchers in linguistics and communication studies who provide a basis for detailed analysis. I refer to a number of critics who see advertising as ideological, objectifying, promoting a shallow and limited consumer culture, but as I have already suggested, I think that many of these critics vastly oversimplify the effects of ads. For a corrective to these views, I have often turned to recent work in cultural studies, to research on audiences in media studies, and to histories of advertising in popular culture, all of which suggest that responses to ads are complex, ambivalent, and diverse. Since I do not work in advertising myself, I have found that journalistic accounts, and particularly regular reading of *Campaign* and *Advertising Age*, give a sense of what is important to the practitioners (and they are fun to read, though I find *Campaign* livelier than its US counterpart). I have referred occasionally to marketing textbooks and talked to my colleagues in marketing for the most basic assumptions of the field (especially in Chapters 2, 9, and 12), but this is not a textbook on marketing. Academics in advertising and marketing study society to learn how to sell things; I study the selling of things to learn about discourse and society.

A research colleague of mine says that advertising is my hobby, that I record and analyse ads the way more sensible people might go in for body building, skeet shooting, collecting telephone cards, drinking Californian wines, or growing prize dahlias. Now that people know about my hobby, they send me ads and clippings and dissertations. My thanks to all these people, and especially to my parents, H.A.P. and Pat Myers and to Dan Calef for providing US examples, and Culture and Communication students for bringing in their most and least favourite ads. Legal obligations to copyright and trademark owners are listed separately in the Acknowledgements. My intellectual debts are harder for me to trace, but I must thank Richard Elliott and Ian Kell for sharing some of their marketing perspectives, my research colleagues Phil Macnaghten, Bronislaw Szersynski, Mark Toogood, and John Urry for their insights into current cultural theory, and my colleagues over the years on the Culture and Communication degree: John Soyland, Dede Boden, Jon O'Brien, Rob Shields, Audrey Slight, and Dan Whistler. Lesley Riddle of Arnold encouraged me to write the book, and Elena Seymenliyska chased me up when I fell behind, and chased up advertisers who were slow in responding to requests for permissions. Thanks to those who have read one or more chapters in draft and saved me from various errors and stylistic faults: John Angus, Jonathan Culpeper, Alan Durant, Lester Faigley, Audrey Slight, Mary Talbot, and Mark Toogood. They are not, of course, responsible for any errors or clumsiness in the final version. Thanks also to Alice Myers for calling me over to the TV to see especially good ads, and to Tess Cosslett for letting me watch ads in the movies we record, and for the most part keeping her finger off the fast forward button.

Acknowledgements

The author and the publishers would like to thank the following for their permission to use copyright material in this volume:

BMG Music Publishing Limited and EMI Music Publishing Limited for 'Search for the Hero', words and music by Paul Heard and Mike Pickering © 1994. Reproduced by permission; Broadway Video Entertainment and the National Broadcasting Company, Inc. for the Saturday Night Live 'Bass-o-Matic' sketch; H.P.Bulmer Limited for the Woodpecker ad; the Central Office of Information, Scott Marshall Management on behalf of Dan Ryan and Barry Brown and Partner on behalf of Jacki Webb for the COI Drink Driving poster 'Dave, Christmas 1995'; The Coca-Cola Company for the 'Coke' ad; The Co-operative Bank; Friends of the Earth for their website; General Electric and BBDO (NY) for the General Electric ad; Harlequin Mills & Boon Limited for the reproduction of the bus shelter poster. Mills & Boon and 'Makes any time special' are trademarks of the publisher, used under license; Levi Strauss & Company, Shilland & Company Limited and Bartle Bogle Hegarty Limited for the Levi's ads; NBC for 'The More You Know Campaign' © Courtesy of the National Broadcasting Company, Inc., and The More You Know Campaign. All rights reserved; Norwich Union and Saatchi & Saatchi for the Norwich Union ad; Pepsi-Cola for their website; Peugeot and Euro RSCG Gosper for the Peugeot 406 ad; Procter & Gamble for the Daz ad; TBWA Simons Palmer for the Nissan vans ad; Universal Press Syndicate for the Calvin and Hobbes cartoon © 1995 Watterson. Dist. by Universal Press Syndicate. Reprinted with permission. All rights reserved; Volkswagen and BMP DDB Limited for the VW 'Lampost' ad; and Merryn Williams for the extract from Raymond Williams.

Every effort has been made to trace copyright holders. Any rights not acknowledged here will be acknowledged in subsequent printings if notice is given to the publisher.

PART

I

BRANDS

'Coke'

1

What do ads do?

One of those giant research probes has just been retracted from the consumer core and early samples served up to the national press in sound-bite form. ... A majority of the 8,000 thought advertising was devious. Devious?!! I say, chance would be a fine thing! Most advertising today is not devious enough.

(Gerry Moira, 'Private View', *Campaign* 19/9/97)

The comment by Gerry Moira, Executive Creative Director of the London agency of Publicis, captures a key tension in the study of advertising: people find ads manipulative and powerful, but advertisers themselves find people are sceptical and unpredictable in their responses. We must all wonder at one time or another whether advertising works. We may wonder when we see a particular ad that is particularly banal, or offensive, or clever, or where we remember the commercial but can't remember which brand it advertised. We may wonder about the whole institution when we consider that we ourselves don't believe what ads tell us; everyone over the age of six or so knows that advertisements are trying to sell something, and cannot be trusted as sources of information or aspirations. On the other hand, it seems unlikely that the emperor is entirely naked, and that the marketing directors for 'Coca-Cola', Levi's, Volkswagen, Guinness, Kellogg's, Kodak, Nike, and Procter & Gamble, along with Mr Moira and his colleagues in advertising, have all made some sort of mistake: the ads must lead in some way to sales that can pay for the ads. And we hear all sorts of effects attributed directly to ads: the outcome of an election, the popularity of a movie, a decline in drink driving, the huge sales of one brand of a product composed of water, carbon dioxide, sugar, flavourings, and colourings. One solution to this paradox is to assume that we ourselves are smart (we aren't influenced by ads) and everyone else is stupid (they are influenced). But this assumption, however attractive, is not a good basis for social theory. Another way out of the paradox is to look at what ads do in culture, besides directly promoting immediate sales. That is the aim of this book(see ADVERTISEMENT).

The question of whether advertising works is hard to answer because advertising effects are real but unpredictable. Michael Schudson made the argument most clearly in his classic *Advertising: the Uneasy Persuasion* (1984): some brands sell well with little or no advertising support (such as Marks & Spencer's underwear in the UK), while others flop despite huge advertising support (New 'Coke', or Pepsi Clear). Schudson argues that even the huge success stories of advertising, such as the Volkswagen beetle or Levi's jeans, are matters of demographics and market shifts as well as advertising: the Volkswagen stepped into a market sector ignored by the US auto makers, and Levi's benefited from a large baby-boom generation and a shift to more casual dress. On the other hand, the most stylish advertising in the most insistent media would probably not sell huge numbers of manual typewriters, men's felt hats, watch chains, or nuclear power plants, nor would it make this book the number one bestseller. Or to take more realistic examples, even a very large advertising budget could not, by itself, push a product to overtake the current best-selling toothpaste, canned soup, washing powder, or loo roll/bathroom tissue. The leading brands have advantages that include shelf space, distribution networks, habit, family ties, and even incorporation into everyday language. Advertising professionals present this sceptical view of advertising themselves, when they have to defend tobacco or alcohol advertising; they say they are merely defending market share without increasing the size of the market. Apparently advertising does have effects on sales, but only in combination with other social, economic, and cultural factors.

It is the job of advertising agency managers to play down this unpredictability. The advertising industry does have some remarkably successful campaigns to which it can point. The Institute of Practitioners in Advertising in Britain gives annual awards for Advertising Effectiveness, and I turn to the published accounts of these cases for some of my examples. But these accounts were written by people at the advertising agencies themselves, and we know that other campaigns from the same agencies were not so successful, and that these successes did not always prevent the client going to another agency. And Schudson's arguments apply to these cases of exemplary effectiveness as well, since what is successful in each case is not just the advertising, but the branding and distribution of a product in a complex and changing market. The UK advertising for BMW is admittedly very good, but would anyone want to argue that people buy and enjoy BMWs solely because of the advertising? (If people bought cars solely on the basis of quality of advertising, the whole world would be driving Volkswagens.)

This unpredictability of results is a problem for advertising agencies, but it is also the key to their survival. In every generation, advertisers have offered calculable, reproducible results: Claude Hopkins of Lord & Thomas in the 1920s, with his 'scientific advertising' based on differing ads in split runs, Rosser Reeves of Ted Bates in the 1950s, with his Unique Selling Point, David Ogilvy with various proven rules of thumb such as not print- ing text white on black (the breaking of this rule is the stylistic basis of the current Guinness campaign by Ogilvy and Mather). Celia Lury and Alan Warde (1997) suggest the need to show calculable, reproducible results has led to the construction of an imaginary consumer in advertising research, a construction that is then picked up again in social science research (see Chapter 9). If these rules could actually be codified, then advertising would become a routine, if still important, business task, like inventory manage- ment or delivery schedules. It is because the effects of ads are unpredictable, and the rules of success still uncodified, that want contact with someone who has a personal vision and personal authority, like Hopkins, Reeves, or Ogilvy, or Dan Wieden or David Abbott today. Advertising remains a craft, like neurosurgery, or telling jokes in public, or herding sheep, not a tech- nology like photocopying, word processing, or postal delivery.

So it is very hard to show that any one ad sells products, because the deci- sions of consumers, and the business of persuading them, are highly com- plex and unpredictable. But advertising does clearly have effects in other, broader ways. It embodies in texts a set of meanings and aspirations affect- ing every institution in our society, what Andrew Wernick (1991) has called 'promotional culture', a culture based on the competition of images. So, for instance, if you ask whether an ad for Special K with a very thin woman in it sells more of the cereal than, say, an equivalent amount of money spent on other forms of advertising or promotion, this will be open to debate. If you ask whether seeing the very thin woman in the Special K ad makes other women want to be very thin, this too will also be open to debate, because there would be many pressures on women to be thin even without advertis- ing. But it is a fact that women feel that there are images of very thin women everywhere, and point to these images as the physical form of the daily repeated reminding, and this ubiquity is an undeniable effect of advertising.

The wider effects of advertising are hard to see because it is set in a wider promotional culture, and it is hard to tell where advertising stops and other forms of promotion begin. So, for instance, there are elements of promotion in job application letters, hospital statistics, university course descriptions, brochures from military research labs, covers of textbooks, charity fund- raising events, interviews with authors on talk shows, concerts of classical music, lonely hearts ads, and the building of municipal sports facilities. We know that promotion is everywhere, trust ourselves to discount the hype, and are only surprised when we find promotion in an area where we thought decisions were made on other grounds than images. As a visitor from the UK, I was taken aback in the Louisville airport when I saw a poster for a hospital, showing a surgery team at work, and claiming that this hospital was the best place in town for heart surgery. Of course I knew that American hospitals and health plans advertise, and that this was part of a larger social change in which professional activities are marketed in commercial terms, and that it drew on an American belief in the importance of individual choice. But I had always thought that, faced with a need for heart surgery, I would rather have the decision about where and when made by a professional on professional grounds, not by me on the basis of a particularly striking photo of people who looked very professional. You may have your own moment of shock at the extent of promotion in our culture, seeing a particularly flashy school brochure, a government health campaign for safe sex, or a charity event dominated by the logo of a sponsor. This year the Church of England produced an ad for Christmas. All these are examples of non-commercial institutions taking on promotion.

Promotional culture can be seen moving the other way as well, as advertisements take more and more of a role in areas of life that had previously been associated with other forms of communication. For instance, the cases in this book will consider:

- how an ad for a bank affects concepts of civic responsibility and human rights;
- how an ad for a detergent deals with concepts of the private and the public;
- how advertisements shape the timing of TV comedy;
- how news images are incorporated into advertising;
- how national images are tied up with consumer products;
- how ads try to intervene to reduce consumption;
- how broadcast ads project sincerity.

Other institutions have taken on promotion, and advertising has taken on the roles of other institutions. Seeing this, we can say that advertising certainly does work, but it may not work in any simple way to sell products, and it may not always work in the way that is intended. I will return to the limits of promotional culture in Chapter 12; in the rest of this chapter, I will outline an approach to how we can follow advertising between different worlds.

Branding

In the 1960s, Pepsi advertising made much of a blind taste comparison with 'Coke', in which a higher proportion of participants would prefer Pepsi. But for understanding brands, 'the Pepsi Challenge' doesn't go far enough, since they are only interested in two brands. Each year, I begin my course on advertisements by offering students a selection of half a dozen colas (oddly enough, they are willing to drink the stuff at nine in the morning). The plastic cups are labelled only with letters, and I ask them to identify which brand is associated with each letter. In this experiment, the usual result is total confusion. With a large enough sample, most people can't identify any one brand. So while there are identifiable differences in the recipes of these products, there is nothing about the taste or effect of the product itself that you could advertise. The same point about the indistinguishability of products has been made after experiments with mass-market American beers, or cigarettes, and it would be interesting to try the experiment with sandwich bread, mineral waters, or even compact cars (I sometimes lose our Nissan Almera in a lot full of similar red and rounded little cars of different makes).

'Coca-Cola' is often held up as one of the great triumphs of marketing, because 100 years of marketing have managed to give complex meanings to this mixture of water, carbon dioxide, sugar, flavourings, and colourings. A quick look at these 'Coca-Cola' slogans shows that they have moved away from making any claims about how the composition, production, taste, or other inherent attributes might make it different from other cola drinks.

Delicious and Refreshing (1900)
The Pause that Refreshes (1929)
Things Go Better With 'Coke' (1960s)
It's the Real Thing (1970s)
'Coke' is It (1980s)
Always (1990s)

These slogans don't inform us about the product; they don't say, ' "Coke" is less sweet and slightly more acidic than Pepsi'! They place it in a map of meanings – 'Coke' as a traditional, unique, American, and yet universal pastime, in contrast with Pepsi as a drink associated with youth. Even the no-frill store's own cola lines now promote themselves as brands, so Spar sells something it calls 'American' Cola, and both Sainsbury's and Spar use red packaging with script lettering. But the meanings come, not just from the packaging and slogans, but from the way the product is associated with other people and activities in texts. Daniel Miller (1998) makes this point in tracing the different meanings 'Coke' has in another culture, in his article, 'Coca-Cola: A Black Sweet Drink from Trinidad'. My experiment was strange because it not only removed the packaging, it also removed the social context in which most people drink cola.

The example of 'Coke' introduces two themes of this book – ads associate meanings with brands, and they do so by interactions in and through the ads. The emphasis on associated meanings may seem obvious enough; the point is stressed again and again in advertising agency proverbs such as 'Sell the sizzle, not the steak.' Advertisers stress this view because it presents their business as actually adding value to the product – the products may be nearly identical, but ads give them different meanings. And the meanings are real – a person drinking an ice-cold 'Coke' has a different experience from a person drinking a glass of cold carbonated water with sugar, colourings and flavourings.

It is important to stress, after my introductory remarks on the unpredictable influence of advertising on sales, that ads don't just sell commodities, they give meanings to brands. There is a difference between these two aims. Some tactics that have immediate and demonstrable effects on sales can actually work against the long-term interests of the brand. For instance, cutting the price relative to that of competitors can boost sales while conveying the notion that this brand is a cheap alternative. Changing frequently the style of ads for the product could promote awareness of the advertising and short-term sales but disrupt and weaken the long-term perception of the brand. This is where some ad agencies would see themselves as coming in – as guardians of the meanings associated with the brand, with, or even against, the in-house marketing department that may be primarily interested in immediate sales targets. The UK trade newspaper *Campaign* did an experiment by calling various London agency offices pretending to be a new client. Here are some examples of what they were offered in mission statements:

> Through the boldness of our ideas, together we build brands. (Grey)
> Creativity that builds brands. (DMB&B)
> To be the agency most valued by those who most value brands. (O&M)

(*Campaign* 23/2/96)

It is not just coincidence that ad agencies share this stress on branding. If a company just wants to increase sales, it can spend more money on promotions, or cut prices, or drive bargains with retailers, none of which require an ad agency. If a company just wants the creative expertise to design ads, it can pay its own directors, writers, and artists. Many companies are doing both these things, and spending on advertising through agencies is falling. Agencies hope to keep their highly lucrative niche by presenting themselves as professionals in this broader process of associating meanings and understanding the meanings and practices that are already out there.

Advertisers stress the view of ads as associating meanings with products; so do critics of advertising, especially on the left. When Raymond Williams (1961) calls advertising 'The Magic System', he suggests that this system creates illusory meanings that conceal the real meanings. In this view, a drink of cola cannot provide youth, individuality, the past, or American citizenship, it can only provide water, carbon dioxide, sugar, caramel colouring, and various natural and artificial flavourings. It is indeed refreshing on a hot day – but so is water. This view divides meanings into two categories – true needs, having to do with essentials for survival, comfort, and belonging, and false needs that are created by the ads. But I will argue that the distinction between what we want and what we need cannot be so easily made; the values added by advertising can be real values (see CONSUMPTION).

I want to take seriously this view of advertising as the association of meanings with brands, as a thread that will lead us through the complexities of ad worlds, and of people's interactions with ads. First, a focus on branding can help us understand how ads do things that advertisers want them to do – encouraging people to buy their products. But almost any theory of communication can do that. This view also helps us understand better how ads can fail to do what they were intended to do – how wonderful ads can have no effect on sales, and awful ads can go with increased sales. Finally, and perhaps most importantly, this view of ads can help us see how ads affect the rest of our culture. In associating meanings with brands, we draw on and shift the multiple systems of meaning that make up our culture (see CULTURE). When Spar calls their cola 'American Cola', they are drawing on complex positive and negative associations with the country I come from, and they are also reproducing a sense of what it is to be an American – a sense that includes 'Coca-Cola'.

A 'Coke' ad

Let's consider one ad to illustrate some of these issues about how ads move between worlds. Unlike some I will discuss, it is not a spectacular production that received media attention; it is an ordinary ad that was running on Britain's Channel 4 just before Christmas in 1995. It is easy enough to see what meanings it associates with the unnamed rival product – what is it telling us about 'Coke'?

'COKE' (PUBLICIS)

visuals	spoken words	written text
two boys in kitchen shot from inside refrigerator	'Oh no, Mum's at it again'	
boy holds up bottle	'Urm, sorta looks like "Coke"'	
carefully opening bottle	'Yeah, it sounds like "Coke"'	
one boy drinks	'C'mon Bucks, what's it taste like?'	
facial contortions	'Well, it just tastes like [pause] urm chicken'	
The real 'Coca-Cola' Contour Bottle fills the screen		Nothing Tastes Like 'Coca-Cola'
'Coca-Cola', 'Coke', and the 'Coca-Cola' Contour Bottle are registered trademarks of the Coca-Cola Company.		

The ad shows the disapproval and disappointment expressed by two teenage boys. It features a visual cliché of the commercials, but a rather odd one when you think about it – a shot from the refrigerator, from the point of view of the product. We know that ads show us as embarrassed in front of our friends and acquaintances and lovers – is it possible that we, the consumers, are supposed to be embarrassed in front of our refrigerators? The bottle of 'Coke' that comes down at the end is quite different from that in the refrigerator – larger, brighter, and with droplets of water showing its coldness.

The strategy here is clear enough – they are advertising against the supermarket own brands I have mentioned that threaten to cut into the market share of branded products. It is a real threat in many product categories, because the nationally advertised supermarkets can offer themselves as their own brands, their own guarantee of the quality of products, their own set of meanings. (The case is somewhat different in the US, where supermarkets spend most of their advertising on price promotions of other brands, not their own meaning as a brand.) And in this case, The Coca-Cola Company went so far as to ask Sainsbury's to make changes in the design of their cans. So this knocking campaign is part of that strategy. On one level, it seems to do something I said was hard to do with colas – it focuses on taste. But more importantly, it focuses on meanings – it stresses the embarrassment of the unseen mother – the supermarket shopper – before her son and his friend. 'Mum's at it again.' And it reinforces the vague but persistent promise that 'Coke' is the one genuine cola. The meaning here is genuineness, and it is conveyed by invoking the relationship between shopper and children in the ad and in the home.

Worlds of ads

In this book, I always start with the detailed text of the ads this way. But the approach through brands and through interaction leads us beyond the ads, to the products, agencies, media, and finally to the consumers. Since we have been discussing 'Coca-Cola', we can use their advertisements as an example to show the kinds of dramatic changes that are now happening in each of these worlds.

Brands

First, we need to think about the products themselves, the ways they are distributed and consumed, and the ways they are made into brands. 'Coke' and Pepsi are both nineteenth-century patent medicines that have miraculously survived for 100 years, with changing meanings and marketing. The way they are advertised is linked to the way they are distributed, and to relations in the market. So, for instance, the Coca-Cola Company has changed its advertising slogans as 'Coke' moved from soda fountain sales to 12 oz.

bottles to supermarket bottles and vending machines. Its global advertising has been driven by a strict enforcement of uniformity of both product and marketing, while the independent bottlers remain locally owned. An example of the complex relation of advertising and product is in the 'New Coke' fiasco. In the 1980s, 'Coke' found its market share gradually eroded by Pepsi. It wasn't just that Pepsi used taste tests in their ads – The Coca-Cola Company's own research showed that younger people in particular preferred 'Pepsi's taste. So they developed their own modified 'Coke' taste, intending it to replace the older 'Coke', and they found in blind tests that people preferred it. It wasn't released in the UK, but in the US 'New Coke' was met with howls of disapproval. Still the company pushed on, knowing that the new taste was actually preferred in tests. But finally they had to give way, first reintroducing the old 'Coke' as 'Coke Classic', and finally quietly letting 'New Coke' die.

Various market analysts have pointed out that there were, in hindsight, two major flaws in the 'New Coke' strategy. The first was that, while more people may like the sweeter 'Pepsi' taste than like 'Coke', it is unlikely that 'Coke' would win all these new customers – people who like Pepsi will drink Pepsi, and those who like 'Coke' will leave it. Second, and more important to our theme of branding, 'Coke' had spent nearly 100 years building up their brand as an unchanging product in a world of change. With one wrong move they jeopardized that heritage (though they have recovered market share since then). The change was seen as synthetic, un-American, unfeeling. No amount of advertising could sell the new product against the very meanings created by earlier advertising. The point of this story is that the product itself (and the ways it is distributed and sold) remain important in understanding the ads. We forget this if we focus only on those products that lead to stylish and award-winning ads. I will look at products and their relation to ads in Chapter 2, then consider a different kind of product and strategy in Chapter 3.

In Chapter 4 I will consider some attempts to build global brands, and at the ways the globe and the global are represented in ads. The Coca-Cola Company, which has the quintessentially American brand, was also one of the first marketers to stress the global availability and uniformity of the product. It is now filming commercials to broadcast in Russia, giving the 'Always Coca-Cola' campaign a Russian feel by invoking the tale of the Firebird. '"We had to find a way of allowing Russians to come to terms with liking and accepting the product", Marie-Louise Neill, the agency's [Publicis] planner on 'Coca-Cola', points out' (*Campaign* 6/3/98).

In each of these chapters I also consider the role of advertising agencies, because they play the key role in making the product into a brand. 'Coke' would once have worked through one agency with a team that practically became part of the company – it was McCann-Erickson for many years. That agency benefited from an ad spend that by itself was larger than the gross domestic product of some countries. Now the agency business is changing, and big spenders like The Coca-Cola Company are more likely to ask just what they get from an agency. For a while they tried going it independently, hiring directors to make their films, with McCann-Erickson just getting a fee for placing the ads. Recently, the UK account moved to another agency, Publicis, especially for its pan-European links. The effects when a familiar brand changes its agency are unlikely to be obvious to the consumer – the new agency may keep essentials of the previous campaign, or we may miss a mascot or a star or a tag-line here or there. But the changes and changeability have a huge effect on the ways ads are written. For instance, one worry has been that advertising becomes more research driven, and thus duller, more the same, less idiosyncratic.

Media

The 'Coke' ad also leads us to questions about media – what is appropriate to a television commercial, as opposed to a print ad, a sign outside a shop, or sponsorship of a football game. ('Coke' sponsors the UK professional football (soccer) championship as 'The Coca-Cola Cup'. Can US readers picture the NFL and AFL champions meeting in 'the Pepsi Bowl'?) For decades advertising media kept more or less the same shape, even with the introduction of television, but the general view is that they are now changing dramatically, moving towards more fragmentation. The 'Coke' ad I recorded was shown in prime time on Channel 4. One reason Channel 4 is attractive to advertisers, in comparison to ITV, is that its relatively high-brow programmes deliver a smaller but more affluent audience. The small bit of fragmentation that happened in the UK with the establishment of Channel 4 alongside ITV is now being followed by more radical fragmentation with satellite and cable services, a process which is much further along in the US. Once a prime-time slot on a national network would have guaranteed a genuinely broad audience. But now that people have more channels to choose from, and videos too, and soon electronic links, the once bulk audience is broken up into lots of tiny slices. For an advertiser like The Coca-Cola Company, that means trying to retain some unity in different appeals to different groups. Of course The Coca-Cola Company has had long experience of various media; they not only produce television and print ads, they also produced calendars, wall plaques, signs, and mats – such a flood of objects that there is now a flourishing collector's industry. But it may be they are just too big to play with the kind of interactive approach pioneered by brands like 'Tango', which uses phone-in numbers and a web site along with their consistently bizarre television ads. I consider media in the second section of the book, considering what sorts of changes are made in adapting campaigns between media (Chapter 5), looking at the first medium, outdoor posters, and how these posters define our sense of space (Chapter 6), and at television as an advertising medium and how it defines our sense of time (Chapter 7), and finally at the newest medium, the World Wide Web, and how it defines interaction (Chapter 8).

Audiences

Finally, looking at ads in terms of brands and interaction leads us to questions about consumers and what they do. The 'Coke' ad only makes sense if we think about the way the week's shopping is done – it relates to supermarkets and family buying. It also relates to our daily practices in a more subtle way, because what it pretends to show us is an ordinary daily encounter that just happens to involve discussion of a rival product. This is not so strange as it may seem – people do talk about products, and that talk is far more effective, for most ads, than any paid advertising.

There are several different conceptions of the audience here. One is that constructed by The Coca-Cola Company's market research, identifying the age, gender, socio-economic group, and location of the kind of person who buys large plastic bottles of 'Coke' at the supermarket. This kind of person might be contrasted with the kind of person who gets a 'Coke' can from a vending machine, or a glass from a soda fountain at a restaurant, or a six-pack at a convenience store. Advertisers have developed elaborate methods for categorizing these potential consumers and determining their responses to ads; I will discuss some of these methods in Chapter 9.

Another conception of audience is that projected in the ad itself, showing two boys and talking about a mother, and representing their relations to each other and to the product. The ad makes me cringe, but it was presumably targeted at a different audience; in my reading the target is the absent mother. Advertisers don't try to match the target audience with the people they represent in the ad, but try to make the ad such that it picks out the target. Ulrike Meinhof (1998), in her analysis of the ad, mentions that its last line became popular with another audience; young boys in playgrounds were repeating the line 'Tastes like ... chicken'. Are these boys a target audience? However carefully targeted an ad, it may pick up unexpected responses (Chapter 10).

Another conception of audience is implied in the way regulators protect the public from ads. It might seem that regulations were irrelevant to this ad, but in the UK it might be covered by regulations concerning ads directed at children (depending on when it was shown) and regulations concerning denigration of rivals (Is it denigration to say it tastes like chicken? Is it relevant that the rival is not identified?). I argue in Chapter 11 that regulations frame audiences as passive and vulnerable, in contrast to some of the views we will see in other chapters.

The lads chanting 'Tastes like ... chicken' in the playground are just one case of many in which ads are picked up by popular culture, playing with them (puns and jokes), recalling them nostalgically (old Guinness or 'Coke' ads), sending them up (*Mad* magazine and pop songs), twisting them (in other ads). There has been much debate about whether the knowingness and scepticism of audiences, what some marketing researchers have called 'advertising literacy', is an example of the creative response of the audience, or further manipulation from the advertisers. In Chapter 12 I review this debate, and its implications for criticisms of advertising and for the arguments in the book.

Summary

Advertisements have their effects, but their direct effects on sales are complex and unpredictable. This book is concerned with their wider effects as part of culture, and the various worlds in which people interact with ads. Advertising makes products into brands, so we have to start with the products themselves, and the ways they are distributed and consumed. Advertising only appears through various media, so we need to consider how people interact in different ways with the different media. Advertising does not impose its messages on passive audiences, but provides a text that audience may take up and transform – or may ignore entirely.

Suggested reading: introductions

Journalistic accounts of specific advertising campaigns make a good place for non-professionals to start; they provide the kind of detail that may be taken for granted in textbooks and memoirs. The best is Randall Rothenberg's (1994) account of the Wieden and Kennedy campaign for Subaru; other very readable accounts can be found in Arlen (1980), Mayer (1961, 1991), and Turner and Pearson (1965).

Historians also put ads in a wider context, and give some of the sense of background. Two of the best are Roland Marchand's (1985) well-illustrated account of US industry in the 1920s and 1930s, and Jackson Lear's (1995) broader, more speculative account of the whole development of US advertising. Fox (1990) gives a more detailed chronicle with more anecdotes and less interpretation. Richards (1990) gives a fascinating account of Victorian advertising, driven by the idea that consumer culture is a bad thing.

There are many textbooks on advertising for different audiences. In my view, the best places to start are with Leiss, Kline, and Jhally (1986) for a vast overview of academic approaches, Leo Bogart (1990) on marketing, Guy Cook (1992) on the language of advertising, and Jib Fowles (1996) on the place of ads in popular culture.

Levi's

2

Products, brands, and signs

- A television commercial begins with a scene of a woman in evening dress walking across a polished floor against a Parisian background, with saxophone music, and sitting at her make-up table, applying cream and talking in a soft, husky voice. It seems to be for cosmetics, but it turns out to be for Boddington's bitter.
- A commercial shows documentary-style video footage of a woman stopping to help another woman who is having a dizzy spell – it looks like the ads for charities or Special Constabulary urging us to be Good Samaritans. Only in the last seconds do we see that what has induced the dizziness is her shock at seeing a poster for a Volkswagen Polo at £7990.
- A poster headline says '17-year-olds wanted to serve fast food.' The picture shows relief workers handing out supplies to starving people. In the lower right it says ARMY.
- A bus poster in Seattle shows the masthead of the *Seattle Times* in black and white. Below it, in white on red, the text says 'Great Paper. Lousy Blanket. Give *real* help. Call (206) 722-HOME. Union Gospel Mission.'

Each of these ads depends on our associating a certain visual style and kind of claim with certain categories of products; they can then reverse expectations, make us reflect, and also emphasize something about the product, job, or service actually being advertised (the bitter is creamy, the car is surprisingly inexpensive, the army does humanitarian work, the mission offers an alternative to sleeping rough). These ads depend on our being surrounded by advertising and knowing something about typical ads for cosmetics, charities, job vacancies, and newspapers. I will discuss that knowingness further in Chapter 12.

But why is it funny to sell beer like face cream (or ice-cream or sun cream)? The question is especially important because many analyses of ads focus on just a few categories of products, and apply conclusions drawn from them to advertising in general. In this chapter I want to consider how the product shapes the ad and how the ad shapes the product. First I will consider four factors that marketing textbooks tell us must be considered in selling a brand. But my approach deals with the wider meanings of brands, so I discuss four more factors that constrain the way a brand is reproduced in culture. Then I consider in detail the strategies used in a series of award-winning ads for Levi's jeans, and in a series for Daz detergent, to show how different the strategies, and their realizations in ads, can be.

Products and brands

One of the themes of this book is that brands associate meanings with products. The study of how meanings are associated is a major part of marketing, as branding. It is also a major tradition of academic study, as semiotics, the study of signs. Both marketing and semiotics have been taken up by wider fields, as branding and consumption enter into new areas of our lives; they are no longer of merely specialized interest. Branding, whether of soap or university courses, may seem a simple enough process. An advertiser pays to reproduce their trademark, and associate meanings with it, such as the universality of 'Coke', the genuineness of Levi's, the manliness of Marlboro (see BRAND). Critics point out that these meanings are entirely constructed; Leslie Savan (1994) reminds us that Marlboro was first marketed as a women's cigarette.

The earliest ads just sought to attract attention to the name by repeating it or associating it with some striking visual image: an inflated man made out of tyres for Michelin; the smiling face of a man in an eighteenth-century hat for Quaker Oats; an arm bearing a hammer for Arm & Hammer Baking Soda. These images were chosen to be distinctive and recognizable, not necessarily to evoke the right associations with the brand. Later, as various product areas matured, and a few brands dominated the market, and brands were seen as more and more alike, ads began to use associations with a life the consumer might desire. These associated meanings have become increasingly complex and subtle, and have been translated into the new media of radio, television, and the Internet, but the basic process of associating meanings with brands remains the same. It is a process that is particularly interesting to discourse analysts, because it links particular texts – the ads – to larger systems of meanings, such as what it means to be young (Pepsi), or healthy (BUPA), or a good parent (AT&T), or a Briton (Brooke Bond Tea).

Semiotics is the academic discipline that deals with the ways signs (such as ads, poems, shoes, or cars) take on meanings. In fact, semioticians from Roland Barthes (1977) to Thomas Sebeok (1991) to Gunther Kress and Theo van Leeuwen (1996) have always been particularly interested in ads as examples (and have produced strikingly original readings), because ads use very simple means to convey very complex meanings. However critical these readings are of advertising (and Kress (1987) is critical), I cannot avoid a sneaking admiration for the way that ads achieve some remarkable links, so that the Explorer car stands for the natural environment, Tampax stands for freedom, Häagen-Dazs for sensuality, the Body Shop for political activity, or the Army for humanitarian aid. It may seem that with enough advertising, a product can take on any meaning. This is a common fallacy of both critics and proponents of ads. But these meanings are not infinitely flexible; they have to rely on the way the brand is used, and how it relates to other brands. All the meanings shift when a new sign is introduced or new links are made. To think about those systems, it helps to go back to basic marketing.

The Four Ps

Many introductory marketing courses start with 'the Four Ps' of Product, Placement, Promotion, and Price (Kotler 1983). There are of course other, much more complex models of marketing strategies, but the Four Ps serve to emphasize that marketing is not just a matter of spending more on advertising (included under Promotion) or cutting the price. They are a useful starting point because they lay out factors over which the marketer, for any given product, has some control. Let us think, for example, of a bag of crisps (potato chips, for US readers), and to be very specific, let us say they are Walker's Salt and Vinegar flavour crisps.

Product

It is crucial to have the right thing on offer, and for our example of crisps that means not only ingredients (whole potatoes or reconstituted flakes), processing (what kinds of oils or salt), flavours and cuts, but also the packaging (big bags or small, foil wrapped or plastic), and the presentation (Are most sales in multi-packs or single bags? Can the box turn into a dispenser in pubs?). In what way, however trivial, can the product itself be distinctive? Traditional copywriters were proud of knowing how beans are baked, how beer is bottled, how cars are inspected, or how grains are puffed (see Hopkins 1927/1966; Mayer 1961; Higgins 1965). Advertising may try to make a silk purse out of a sow's ear, but marketers still have to think about the selection of sows and the packaging of ears.

Placement

It is crucial to have the product right there when the consumer wants it. Since crisps are snack foods, so their placement is not just a matter of competitive shelf space for multi-packs at supermarkets, but also displays in newsagents, or at petrol stations, or in vending machines at swimming pools. 'Within an arm's reach of desire' was the goal set for 'Coca-Cola' (Prendergast 1994), and though Walker's hasn't gone that far, they seem to be everywhere. But there may be reasons why a marketer wouldn't want a brand to be sold in some outlets; one might want to keep the image of one's brand as a special treat. We will find in many of the examples in this book that the advertising only makes sense in relation to the distribution network. The Co-operative Bank (Chapter 3) can occupy a market niche without an extensive branch system because of the development of cash machines (ATMs). The expansion of Häagen-Dazs as a premium brand (Chapter 5) required provision of freezer cases to dealers. Benetton (Chapter 11) relies on a chain of franchised retailers, so it has more (though not unlimited) latitude to offend.

Promotion

People have to know about the brand. But there are many ways of promoting a brand besides advertising. The Walker's crisps we have in the house now (not bought for my consumption, I hasten to add) have a Spice Girls tie-in and a chance to win a prize (usually another bag of crisps). The same brand also got lots of publicity with its tie-in with the football player Gary Lineker, and even from complaints about one of the ads (for showing a child talking to a stranger, even if the stranger was Gary Lineker), and went so far as to rename the brand, temporarily, 'Salt 'n' Lineker'. Many of the other brands discussed in this book rely on other forms of promotion, so the Co-operative Bank has various forms of sponsorship to stress its role in the community, and Peugeot 406 has a range of special offers from dealers.

Price

People have to be willing to pay just the amount it says on the packet. Of course lowering prices might increase sales, but it is not always the case that the lowest price is most effective. One of the desired results of branding has always been that people will pay a good price for the branded item, not just the lowest price possible, because of the meanings, the added value, associated with it. Premium crisps are deliberately priced much higher than mass market crisps, to signal higher quality, and it is because of this premium that one can take them, say, to a party as a treat. Pricing was a key issue in a number of the campaigns I discuss; Daz stresses that its price is not much higher than that of store's own brands, while Häagen-Dazs, for instance, starts with the idea of a premium price being part of what identifies it as a high quality product for adults.

Four more Ps

For marketers, the Four Ps are a useful introductory survey of variables; for us as analysts of ads they can serve as a reminder of all the factors involved in marketing besides advertising. What they do not suggest is the way a brand is already constrained by the meanings around it; the marketing strategists are not free to shape the meanings as they might wish (see Schultz 1990 for a treatment of 'Four Cs' from a marketing point of view). To suggest these constraints, I can suggest four other Ps one might derive from cultural studies (and unlike the first list these are just my own list, not a formula memorized by thousands of marketing students), moving from immediate associations with the brand, to its relations with other brands, with consumers, and with the wider system of popular culture.

Past

Brands come with what marketers call 'heritage' and what semioticians might call associative or connotative meanings (Myers 1994). So, for instance, when sales of Adidas shoes were lagging behind those of Nike and Reebok, the UK agency Leagas Delaney knew it still had a powerful starting point in the heritage of the brand. As far as I know, the crisp market doesn't have its classic brands such as Adidas, BMW, Rolex, or Heinz beans, but there are long associations with Lay's in the US or Walker's in the UK. New premium brands like Brick Oven or Phileas Fogg try to project a ready-made heritage, evoking traditional methods and packaging, or a fictional founder. Some companies try cross-branding, carrying the associations of a brand across to a new sector, as Caterpillar has done from heavy construction equipment to clothing, or as Virgin has done from records to air travel to cola and vodka to financial services and now passenger railways. Cross-branding can backfire, as when one is served warm Virgin cola on a delayed Virgin train, and begins to wonder about the airline.

Position

Brands are placed in a competitive position in relation to each other. Walker's crisps must compete, not only with other salt and vinegar crisps, but with other possible snack foods. Being the market leader has its advantages, but many brands (Virgin Air, Motel 6, Co-operative Bank, Holsten Pils lager, Rent-A-Wreck car rental) have built their brands on the basis of not being the market leader, of having instead their own distinctive niche. In a wider sense, the brand is positioned in relation to other brands, most obviously in the car market, but also in soft drinks, beers, or shoes. Some of the

most successful advertising campaigns in history owe their success, not to
the texts of the ads themselves, but to a carefully planned repositioning. But
again the scope for repositioning is not endless. When the agency head who
had just won the new Kia car account said that it would be the Volkswagen
beetle for the 1990s, he was greeted with guffaws from other agencies. One
problem faced by Nike (says the creative director who has the account of a
rival brand) is that the ubiquity of the name and the swoosh make it hard to
continue to market them in terms of rebelliousness and street cred
(*Campaign* 5/3/98).

Practices

Brands are at the mercy of what people do with the product (see CONSUMP-
TION). People eat crisps as an indulgence that breaks a diet, or as minimal
nourishment in pubs, or as sustenance for an all-night session of work, or as
a treat in a child's lunch box (or they rattle them in the cinema, which drives
me crazy). Or they stop eating them because they are associated with fat, or
sodium, or kids. When a politician can call a critic of the Royal Opera
House a 'crisp eater', then there must be some practices that are assumed to
go with crisps and don't go with opera. Some brands can shift the practices
with which they are associated, as Levi's jeans or Doc Marten boots went
from work clothing to fashionable styles, or as Starbuck's coffee moves
from a small coffee-house across from the Pike Place Market in Seattle to a
national chain of counters found in airports, or as mineral water becomes a
style drink rather than a health drink, or as wine replaces spirits at parties,
or as personal computers shift from the business market to the home
market. Marketers rely on research to inform them of these shifts, so they
can counter them or take advantage of them, but one still has a sense that
the marketer is not entirely in control of these meanings.

Paradigms

Semioticians tell us that a change in one part of a network of meanings
affects the other elements. I have used the much abused term *paradigm* to
remind us of the underlying, taken for granted set of relations. Consider the
crisps that come unsalted, with a little blue packet of salt to shake on oneself. The ads for these crisps present this packaging as a matter of heritage,
tracing it back to the first, unpackaged crisps in pubs with salt available in
twisted paper. (A colleague says the blue packet reminds her of the way the
salt always clogged in the damp British homes of the 1960s – a form of nostalgia not yet exploited by the crisp manufacturers.) But the blue packet also
relates to a wider sense that additives can be bad as well as good, that having no added salt, or no added sugar, or no colourings, or being lead-free or

CFC-free or phosphate-free, are further benefits of the product. The removal of CFCs from aerosol sprays affected the consumers of those sprays, but also introduced a kind of phrasing into the language, and a way of thinking that has affected hundreds of other products. The word paradigm can serve for the very broad cultural frameworks that some theorists might call 'orders of discourse' (Fairclough 1992): examples would be ideas about body shape and health, digitization of information, cloning of identical copies, or citizenship (see DISCOURSE). Changes in signs can ripple through the system in unexpected ways. In the 1950s, the 'Radiation' electric cooker signalled modernity and magical ease, but I doubt that the brand name 'Radiation' would have such favourable associations for any product today.

These further four Ps of Past, Position, Practices, and Paradigm are meant to stimulate our thinking, not as marketing strategists, but as analysts of ads. In particular, they focus our attention on wider changes that may affect the meanings of brands as signs. To show these facts at work, we can consider some of the strategies involved in two series of ads, for Levi's jeans and Daz detergent.

Constructing heritage: Levi's 501 jeans

You might think the advertising agency with the Levi's account had an easy job. After all, though the company had a rather disappointing year for profits last year, there remains a huge demand for jeans around the world. In the US they are still reasonably priced as the basic, non-designer jeans; in the rest of the world they carry a price premium and instant recognition. They also carry all sorts of associations with youth, Americanness, and rebellion. But it is just this status as an institution that makes them something of a challenge to advertise. At the moment their market share is being eroded by designer labels and budget-priced own labels. In terms of the Four Ps, Levi's are considering the product (should they market more or fewer cuts?), the promotion (but ordinary advertising or promotions might actually undermine these core meanings of the brand), and the placement (but wider distribution might have its dangers, so, for instance, Levi's has tried to keep them from being sold in truck stops in the US and Tesco supermarkets in the UK). Cuts in price might not be a possibility, since that would run the risk of their being seen as a cheap alternative.

The brief given to the agency that has the account in the UK, Bartle Bogle Hegarty, was that they get across the idea that Levi's were the original but still contemporary jeans. They had to somehow set them apart from the increasingly fierce competition, and show that design features had a tradition behind them, while the style could change subtly. They have done this in a series of ads since 1986, many of which have won awards in the industry and many of which have been discussed by journalists and academics

Table 2.1 Structure of UK Levi's ads (agency: Bartle Bogle Hegarty)

	Belt Loops	Creek	Fall	Washroom	Escape
Setting	California, 1921	Nineteenth-century Yosemite Valley	American West during WW II	contemporary US city	US South 1950s
Look	sepia colour, missing frames like silent films, projector sound (*Little Rascals*)	black and white, (*Ansel Adams*)	aged colour, 1940s film angles (*Nicholas Ray*)	film noir lighting (*Pulp Fiction*)	black and white, frantic editing (*The Defiant Ones*)
Sound	tinkling piano	choral/heavy metal	movie music		metal music
Characters	football players and flappers	Amish family, pioneer hunk, pioneer old fart	oil rig hunk, nurse, doctor and nurse	woman as black/white young black man/ old black man	two convicts/ pursuers and dogs
Begins	football players watched by women and boy	girls watch swimmer and take jeans	man falls from oil rig and is taken to hospital	car screeches into gas station and woman runs into men's room	guards chase two escapees
Change	dog pulls off braces and jeans fall	hunk emerges from water	nurse unbuttons jeans rather than cut them	woman sees man sitting with white cane and buttons her fly in front of his face	one escapee just misses jumping onto a railway car
End	woman laughs, man looks sheepish	jeans belong to another swimmer	another nurse observes her and brings doctor	an older man emerges from the stall and the younger man leads him out	the other pulls him on by his jeans
Text	IN 1922 LEVI'S FINALLY INTRODUCED BELT LOOPS	IN 1873 JEANS ONLY CAME SHRINK-TO-FIT	1943. LEVI'S WERE IN SHORT SUPPLY	ORIGINAL BUTTON FLY FOR WOMEN	RIVETED TOGETHER FOR EXTRA STRENGTH
	Levi's 501. The Original Jean	Levi's 501. The Original Jean	Levi's 501. The Original Jean	Levi's 501. The Original Jean	Levi's 501. The Original Jean

(Corner 1995). If we look back over five of these ads, from a series of more than 30, we can see the outlines of the campaign underlying the particulars of each ad.

Table 2.1 is a rigidly schematic representation of some witty and carefully crafted ads, but it is enough to bring out my point, that while they are strikingly different visually, they keep the same structure and strategy.

- All establish a period and a place, typically America in a not too clearly defined past.
- All draw on lighting, colour, clothing, and especially music to establish a style in the first few seconds.
- All tell a story that involves excitement, voyeurism, and surprise.
- None of them suggests the product advertised until the end.
- All end with a product claim focusing on an apparently trivial feature of the product.
- The logo comes with an assurance of the genuineness of the product.

Now let's look in more detail at how these features work within a strategy.

Textual analysis

The most basic level of this analysis is to look at the signs themselves, the physical form in which you get the message. The signs could be spoken words, or written words, or pictures, sounds, music. With this series, there are no spoken words; it is the music that people remember. It can mark a shift in mood, as with 'Creek', where it is part of the building of tension. The ad opens with a long chord. What is the effect? There is a sense of tension, of expectation. The change in style in the middle marks the shift in structure and mood. Similarly, you may take the rock music as indicating sexual excitement, the choral music as indicating purity. But the association of verbal meanings with music is notoriously variable.

Similarly, the choices in the visual style can have a number of functions. 'Creek' is black and white, while most ads and all programmes are in colour. This choice can be used to link the film to an artistic style (here the nature photography of Ansel Adams, or artistic portraits in the press ads for The Gap), or to suggest a kind of stylized plainness (as in the Co-operative Bank ad in Chapter 3), or to suggest documentary style (as in Peugeot 406 in Chapter 4). In any case, we notice it and try to interpret it because it is different from what we expect.

There are no spoken words in these ads – that in itself is a striking deviation from conventional ads, which nearly always have an off-screen or on-screen voice telling you how to interpret the images. Here you are left with the feeling that you are interpreting them yourselves. Another kind of sign is, of course, the written words. They are simple, as in 'Creek':

IN 1873 LEVI'S JEANS ONLY CAME SHRINK-TO-FIT.
LEVI'S 501. THE ORIGINAL JEAN.

How do we interpret 'The original jean'? For one thing, we are used to having 'jeans' in the plural. Also, the word 'Levi's' is written in the form of the logo. But otherwise it is not itself a striking slogan. There must be something else going one, at another level.

We have seen that the ads have the same basic story, in which we have no idea at the beginning what the ad is for. We get caught up in teasing revelations, and then there is the surprise in which we see, first, what the images meant, and then, second, apply them to the product. Each ad has some new elements of structure; in 'Creek' there is the tension of parents and the daughters, the contrast of the two young women, the contrast of the two men, the contrast of the sensual pool and the cool, pure mountains. But it is the same basic plot. Within this story there is also a visual structure. At the beginning and end are wide shots of the mountains. Then there are medium shots of the family group. There is a black-out, and then the sequence in which the girls watch the bather. Here the shots come much faster, editing together extreme close-ups of eyes and lips with sensual images of his body. His rising body is paralleled by their pulling the jeans over their mouths. But instead of a pornographic climax, there is the joke of the appearance of the man's wet jeans.

The ads, then, establish a stylized past, and position us as voyeurs, before a final joke emphasizing a product claim. Let's see how this structure relates to the kinds of issues I have raised in branding: the use of the Past, the Position in relation to other brands, the Practices associated with it, and the shifting Paradigms of meaning systems.

Past

The key problem for Levi's is to keep the sense of their being genuine American work clothes, while opening them to contemporary associations. John Hegarty explained that with the first in the series, 'Launderette', he wanted a general sense of a mythical America. But America and Americanization can carry all sorts of negative meanings around the world (as I am only too aware). Here is Hegarty's comment:

> I thought it would be more interesting to do the ad with a period look.
> The 1950s idea wasn't in the brief. It just happened, and out of that we established a mythical period for Levi's. *Grapevine*, the music that backed the ad, was a 60s not a 50s song – it came to me simultaneously and there was no real logic to it. The aim was to portray the US without the US being boring – a US no-one could object to.

(*Campaign* 20/9/96)

Almost all the later ads were set in this mythical period America, with elements of anachronism. The music may not be from the same period as the pictures, but they work together to suggest a sort of pastness. This past overlaps with a sense of the past as youthfulness. It is suggested by such devices as jerky film, suggesting the older film with fewer frames per second, or with colours reminiscent of those from now faded technicolor, or with references to styles of photographers or film-makers (see Table 2.1).

Position

Up to the last 5 seconds of these ads, many first time watchers are probably puzzled about just what is being advertised ('Washroom' is a particularly good example). But the ads are not at all unrelated to the product, the ways some clever ads seem to be. Levi's can't afford this – it is in a ferociously competitive market where the competitors make clever ads too. In a sense, the whole ad is a product demonstration of just how good the jeans can look, or rather, just how good the body can look that is under the jeans. Only in the last seconds is the erotic tease transferred to Levi's. Given the success of these ads, other brands have tried similar erotic stories. But in doing so they only reinforce the associations with Levi's. A contrasting approach is taken by the cinema ads for Wrangler jeans, which show awkward, home-video-style interviews with real rodeo cowboys, talking about what they go through in the ring. Levi's themselves, in the current commercials for white tab jeans (also from Bartle Bogle Hegarty), has a zany, Monkees-like 1960s film, that maintains the sense of Americanness and heritage without interfering with the 501 branding.

Practices

Where does one wear Levi's? When I was in college, Levi's were student clothes, manual work clothes, counter-culture. Some time after that, and after I stopped wearing them, they entered into other settings. They were able to draw on these associations with counterculture and informality, and yet be accepted as clothes for older people in more formal situations – such as President Clinton. The company tried to adapt to this shift, recognizing that middle-aged men and women, such as most university lecturers, are different shapes from university students (as you will have noticed). So they sold jeans with different cuts, and developed ads aimed at this market, and developed a new brand, Dockers (UK posters for Dockers showed tough middle-aged men in mock news photos, but the TV ads for Dockers feature the same young bodies as in 501 ads). The original Levi's 501s remained undeniably hip, but part of the appeal was that one could do things to personalize them – shrink to fit, cut, patch, bleach, dye. Some jeans have tried to keep up with these alterations, selling jeans already prewashed. But it is in the nature of such alterations that they cannot be entirely brought within the marketing plan. People are making the uniform commodities their own.

Paradigms

These shifts in the uses of jeans go on against larger shifts in meanings. What it means to be American has changed radically throughout the last 50 years, from GIs to the Beats to Vietnam to the Gulf to Friends; that is why John Hegarty is so careful to set his ads in a mythical, timeless America. Notions of the erotic change too; the transvestite in the ad 'Taxi' and the race-changing woman in 'Washroom' mark current fascinations with boundary crossing. Associations with manual work change as most people are employed in services, The uses of tradition have, if anything, expanded in this period of rapid change; paradoxically, Levi's turns to travellers, drifters, and fugitives for its emblems of rootedness. This is not the place to trace the workings of detraditionalization (see Lash and Dillon 1997); my point is just to stress that this timelessness is the product of a particular place and time.

Constructing ordinariness: Daz Automatic Powder

Levi's ads win awards, more than any other UK campaign over the last dozen years. Just a few categories of products and services account for most of the ads that win awards, get journalist comments, and are analysed in books like this one: clothes, cards, athletic shoes, cosmetics, charities, tobacco, and beer would be examples. I realized how little these categories represented ads in general when I watched all the ads from several 24-hour periods of television. I don't recommend you try this experience unless you are writing a book about ads; most ads make dull, repetitive product claims, with the simplest of appeals, usually for frequently purchased household products. (I developed a particular horror of a fabric conditioner ad; its monotonous repetition made me think of its namesake in Poe's poem 'The Raven': 'Nevermore'.) The producers of these ads might argue that the difference between their ads and the award-winners is not in the quality of advertising, but in the kind of appeal one can make in this product category. Would a shopper would choose a bottle of fabric conditioner from the many on the shelf just because of a witty, ironic, self-mocking image of a brand like Levi's?

Let's take an ad for the category of products known to marketers as 'fast moving consumer goods', one from a series I have mentioned already, in which the comedian Danny Baker approaches 'real people' on their doorsteps or in a shopping mall and asks them about Daz. Daz is a Procter

& Gamble product, and in marketing that means something. It means that the brand manager has a very clear strategy for its place in the market, and keeps the ad agency on a very short lead – the agency has to pass a series of tests, and keep to a very restricted range, and is then rewarded with a loyal and highly consistent client. That is why a Procter & Gamble account is considered such a good training ground for other areas of marketing, even though it is unlikely to win any awards for the advertisers.

This particular Daz ad was repeated many times during one of the 24-hour periods I recorded. It could be argued that all it does is repeat the name, like one of those 19th century newspaper ads that filled the whole column with the brand name of a medicine. But I think more is going on, in the way it uses the interaction between Baker and the ordinary people. The ad focuses, not on the results in washing (as does a typical Persil ad) but on the moment of passing through the check-out.

DAZ AUTOMATIC POWDER (AGENCY: LEO BURNETT)

DB = Danny Baker   OP = Ordinary Person

actions	words	
[supermarket checkout]	DB	You know Daz is good on whites But did you know how good it is on price? Even compared to some shops' own brands.
[puts package through barcode scanner]	DB	We asked people how *they* thought Daz compared.
	OP1	I'd expect Daz to be a lot more expensive.
	OP2	The Daz would be dearer.
	OP3	A lot dearer.
[to checker]	DB	So what is the difference in price Pat? Only 10 pence in some stores.
	OP1	Is that all. 10p.
	OP4	10p.
	OP5	That's a lot cheaper than I thought.
	OP6	10p. You're kidding. I wouldn't have thought it'd be that cheap, honestly.
[tosses coin*]	DB	Check it yourself against shops' own brands. Daz whites cost less* than you think.
Reproduced with permission of Procter & Gamble.		

Textual analysis

How does this ad connect to consumers? It doesn't use the period setting, sexual plots, fancy editing, or catchy music of the Levi's ads. The emphasis is overwhelmingly on the words, and on the way Danny Baker interacts with a range of people.

1. First, it starts with *you*, the pronoun of direct address, the oldest trick in the copywriters' handbook. Instead of telling you Daz is good on whites, it tells you that you already know this. The brand name is used as an adjective ('Daz whites') as if we were familiar with this term of approbation.
2. Then the ad opens with the second oldest trick in the copywriters' handbook – a question. This is to be answered, but only after consulting a version of popular opinion.
3. The strategy of the ad is to reproduce in the vox pop interviews a sense of the kind of talk with 'people' that might go on around a product, outside of ads. The stress on *they* implies, 'Don't trust us, see what *they* say.' This is the main device of the Daz series; they all show apparently ordinary people confronted by the show businessy and confident Danny Baker. How do we know they are ordinary? They are confronted in the shopping mall. They are with other people who look on. They wrestle kids. They don't use the range of intonation in the performer's voice. Most of the ad is spent getting them to seem like ordinary people.
4. Note how the comments are structured. First we start with longer statements, and then we get more and more elliptical comments added to it, as if they were all participating in the same discussion. The effect is to create a sort of universal consensus out of just three responses. Then DB offers the answer (with the rider 'in some stores'). Each of the respondents has to display disbelief: 'Is that all?', 'just', 'cheaper than I thought', 'You're kidding'. Here responses escalate in their incredulity. This is typical of how people state opinions in a conversation, but here the on-going conversation is assembled from several different interviews.
5. Finally DB confronts us, the viewers. Note the last challenge: 'Daz whites cost less . . . than you think.' This is a complex statement that attributes to us beliefs about Daz (it produces white clothes but costs more), then cancels the belief about price – they are not that expensive. (It need not be the case that viewers already do see Daz as expensive). The 10p piece is waved as a symbol of this difference. Then it is used to flip a coin – implying one can't choose between the two alternatives.
6. The name of the competition is 'concealed' with the video technique used to censor obscene pictures or disguise the identities of the guilty – it attracts attention to the competition box. Note that even in this price led ad, the competition is not based on price alone. Instead, Daz is asserted to be not too expensive for what it is, and it is assumed to be a better product.

So here is a different relation of text, brand, and consumer from that in the Levi's ads. The text is not evocatively poetic, but deliberately banal. The ad builds a brand, but it has to build it in a different way, by attributing sceptical responses to people (they would think it costs more) and placing them in a familiar setting, then triumphing over their scepticism. It is a simple but effective little story.

Past, Position, Practices, and Paradigm

The Daz ad might seem to be completely routine, but is shows the same sort of strategic thinking as the Levi's ads.

- Like Levi's, the brand is constrained by its Past: it treats 'Daz whites' as a category already established in people's minds. Brierley (1995) has an account of the kind of disaster that threatened another brand, Persil, when it tried to alter its formula, out of line with its heritage; it was the 'New Coke' story in a box.
- Daz is also constrained by its Position, not only in relation to Persil (from Unilever) and Ariel (also from Proctor & Gamble), but crucially in relation to stores' own brands. As I noted in discussing the ad for 'Coke', these are especially dangerous competition in Britain, where the stores are national, and can serve, in effect, as a powerful brand in themselves. (A much higher percentage of UK purchases are own brand (12 per cent), compared to those in the US (5 per cent).)
- What sorts of Practices are relevant here? Washing powder manufacturers have to think about shifts to 'green' products, or changes in types of washing machines (it's Daz *Automatic*), or in fabrics (the development of non-iron materials and the need to wash them more gently), or patterns of shopping, and perhaps the rise of network selling (the way Amway sells through local distributors coming to the house).
- Finally, though it may seem odd to say so, this ad takes on a Paradigm, one described by Roland Barthes in his essay on 'Soap Powders and Detergents' (1954/1972); he analyses the system of myths underlying ads for laundry powders and liquids, including fighting dirt, cleaning deeply, purifying fire, luxurious foam, and comparative whiteness. (Whiteness remains a bench-mark even when most of the laundry load is made up of fast-coloured materials.)

These two examples, Levi's and Daz, suggest the constraints on marketing strategists making products into brands. They also suggest that the constraints are different for different categories of products, whatever the strategies of the marketers. We can see that a fashionable item of clothing like Levi's jeans will be different from a regularly purchased household product like Daz. What sorts of categories are useful to us in thinking about our analyses of ads?

Product categories

The marketing textbooks divide products into categories such as fast-moving consumer goods (fmcgs), white goods such as refrigerators and ovens, and business-to-business products. But the resulting categories follow the traditional divisions of retailing, so they are not general enough to be useful for our analyses of ads. I will draw on the kinds of issues raised in the marketing and advertising literature to suggest some questions as a starting point.

1. How often does one buy it? One makes a different sort of decision about fmcgs like Daz (a box every few weeks), from that about Levi's (regular users buy five pairs a year) or about tyres (a set every few years). On the one hand, goods bought frequently would seem to leave room for impulses. On the other hand, they may be matters of habit that are very hard to shift.

2. Is it new? Both products in this comparison are well established, and both ads draw on this prior knowledge. A new detergent (as when Radion was introduced in the late 1980s) demands a different, more disruptive advertising (Radion favoured simple, bright, bold layouts); so does a new brand of jeans (such as Guess in the UK) or a new category of casual clothes, such as Dockers. Establishing a new kind of product (for instance, 'green' washing powders) takes much more explanation, as does establishing a new need, such as water purification or computer file back-up. Often these new needs are explained by analogy to accepted needs, so computer utilities, smoke alarms, and credit card protection schemes can all be presented by analogy to household security.

3. How much is it embedded in one's life? Consumers tend not to change banks, sanitary protection products, phone companies, or underwear brands, either because they get used to the product or because it is too much hassle to change. At the other extreme, consumers of pain relievers are notoriously fickle (if one doesn't work, try another), and our cats seem to get bored with any flavour of cat food after just a few weeks. Marketers refer to a category of 'high-involvement' products like hi-fi sets, computers, or cars, to the purchase of which consumers give a lot of thought; these are products for which consumers might compare, do some research, ask around, and go some distance to get a good price or selection. At the other extreme would be crisps, which are always bought on impulse from a wide choice, and for which one's commitment lasts about 5 minutes.

4. Is it visible and significant to others? Levi's can be sold as an image product because they are part of one's display to the world; one's consumption of washing powder is usually private. In fact, most consumption would seem on the face of it to be private, to have no relation to one's social relations or aspirations. It is the brief of most advertising to convince us otherwise, for instance in ads that try (rather unconvincingly) to convince us that the choice of washing powder can have social consequences for ourselves or our children.

5. How is it regulated? Many puzzling features of ads can be traced to regulations; one example is the careful disclaimer that Daz is only about 10p more 'in some stores' (so you cannot complain if you find the difference more at your local store). The rather coy reference to the rival brand is a relic of earlier restrictions on comparative advertising. The sexually suggestive style of the Levi's ads could not be used in US or UK tobacco ads; some Levi's ads are approved only for use in cinemas before 12 or 15 certificate films, or after 9 p.m. on television. As we will see in Chapter 11, the regulations affect not only the obvious categories, such as tobacco and spirits ads, but also toys, pharmaceuticals, cereals making health claims, cars, and financial services.

Summary

The aim of this chapter has been to suggest how products may shape ads and ads may shape products. The key link is the process of branding, the attachment of meanings to labelled products. Two lists can serve as exploratory guides to thinking about how brands are marketed: the marketers 4Ps of Product, Place, Promotion, and Price remind us how much there is to marketing besides advertising, and the further 4Ps I suggested of Past, Position, Practices, and Paradigm, can guide us to ways a brand is constrained by a wider set of meanings in the culture.

I analysed two ads as examples: from Levi's and Daz. In both cases I took approaches that will be used in other analyses in this book:

- Look for similarities and differences across a range of texts.
- Relate choices in various modes: spoken words, writing, pictures, music, etc.
- Look for choices that go against expectations.
- Step back and consider the overall structure.
- Relate details to the overall effect (the transformations in the Levi's ads, the ordinary people in the Daz ad).

I used these ads as a basis for considering what factors might account for some of the differences between ads in different product categories. There may never be a clever, self-mocking, brilliantly shot ad for a toilet cleaner that will sweep Cannes, the British Television Advertising Awards, or the US Clios. But the problem is not a lack of imagination or talent among advertisers winning the toilet bowl cleaner accounts: the marketing manager and advertising team of the toilet bowl cleaner have had to work with a different set of constraints in making their product into a brand.

Suggested reading: brands

In cultural studies, branding is discussed by Davidson (1992) and Lury (1996). For studies of specific commodities, see Prendergast (1994) and Miller (1998) on 'Coca-Cola', Rothenberg (1994) on Subaru, Pasi Falk (1997), one of many papers on Benetton, Frank Mort (1997) on Burton's men's shops, Vidal (1997) on McDonald's, and studies in the annual series from the Advertising Effectiveness Awards (such as Channon 1989). There is an excellent discussion of issues of products, clients, and agencies in Fowles (1996), Chapter 4.

Co-operative Bank

3

Banking, branding, and strategies of address

In January 1996, one could see all over Britain newspaper ads with an object that looked like a helmet with rods sticking out of it. It says something about the increased awareness of this issue between January and August of that year that most Britons were expected to recognize this strange thing as an anti-personnel land mine. But who was the poster for? The Red Cross campaign to help victims of land mines that had been given such a public relations lift by Diana, Princess of Wales? The Land Mine Trust, which won the Nobel Peace Prize that year for its campaign to ban them? The Labour Party, that had promised as soon as it came into office that the UK would sign the international treaty?

People outside the UK might be surprised to find that the ad was for a bank, promising that money invested with the Co-operative Bank would never go to makers of armaments for repressive regimes. And this advertisement was not a one-off, exploiting the prominence given to the issue by the involvement of the Princess and by her death; it was the most recent example of a successful marketing strategy extending over 10 years. The Co-operative Bank's strategy is one of many that not only raises questions about marketing; it raises questions about how we draw boundaries in society, about which institution is responsible for what (see STRATEGY).

In the last chapter I took for my examples ads for major sectors of commodities: jeans and washing powders. The series of Co-operative Bank television ads that I discuss in this chapter might seem a less obvious example of marketing. Ads for financial services were once characterized by understatement and low budgets, but now the major brands are heavily marketed (accounting for four of *Campaign*'s top 100 brands by total spend). The sector is clearly being transformed by deregulation, mergers, new technology, and new brands; for instance, in the UK, major retailers are starting to offer financial services, building on what they hope is consumer trust in their more tangible products. I will argue that the Co-operative Bank has done more than just a branding exercise; they and their advertising agency have asked questions about their company, and have placed it in a new context. By extending their advertising to issues that are usually the terrain of campaign groups, charities, and political parties, they raise questions about where we draw the boundaries between social worlds.

I will link this experiment in branding to an experiment with address, that is, the way they talk to us as consumers, citizens, and people. To show how radical their experiments are, I compare one of their ads to a public service announcement on the US network NBC, which uses a similar sort of monologue, but to an entirely different effect. So this chapter will move from the specific problem this bank had in its highly competitive market, to some linguistic and formal features of its ads, to questions about how we as viewers might respond to these features.

A bank as a brand

The Co-operative Bank campaign raises several issues: how services (as opposed to things) can be branded, how a long-established traditional organization can deal with rapid change, how public and commercial issues are entangled and disentangled. It is an example of successful positioning by a small player (with a 2 per cent share) in a crowded and fiercely competitive market. And at least part of the credit for this must go to the Co-operative Bank's advertising agency Butterfield Day DeVito Hockney (BDDH), which not only made the ads, but helped devise the strategy underlying them. They reaped the reward of a risky strategy that paid off – the Co-operative Bank remains their best-known account. Before analysing the ads, I will review the aspects of marketing strategy that I listed when dealing with crisps, jeans, and detergents in Chapter 2, considering some of the innovations in the Co-operative Bank's strategy.

Product

Financial services ads are, in general, among the most boring and predictable of all sectors. Adam Lury characterized the usual pitch as 'big but friendly' (1994); this is what is put forward by all the main high street banks and the biggest building societies. So though they may be serious or jokey, flashy or traditional, they always make the same sorts of appeals, for the same sorts of services. That means it is easy for an advertiser to stand out, but also very risky.

The success of the Co-operative Bank strategy depends on an understanding of how and why people choose a bank. They bet that there was a small but important group of people who would be interested in how the bank functioned in society. Such people were likely to be fairly well-off, because they could put such concerns ahead of purely financial or practical considerations. BDDH, in their report, noted that, though the bank had a 'slightly upmarket profile', a higher proportion of new accounts in the late 1980s were coming from the C2, D, and E social groups. This meant that these new customers would have less money to save in their current accounts and less interest in other financial services. Their brief was to target new ABC1 customers, while retaining the loyalty of existing customers (IPA 1994).

So the Co-operative Bank has stressed, over the last 10 years, a two part message: it is like other banks in having a range of services and out-lets, but different from them in refusing to support companies that do environmental damage, use animal testing, sell tobacco, or support oppressive regimes. The first ads along these lines struck me very much at the time, because they were insisting on connections that are real but that people don't usually make (Myers 1994). People might see their choice of deodorant or washing-up liquid or car or tuna as a matter of green consumerism, but they probably never thought of how financial services might be linked to environmental damage. It is real information in an ad. And it was all the more striking, because as charities and political parties and unions backed away from making ethical claims, here was an organi-zation that was making just such claims. The message has not changed, but as we will see, the emphasis has changed to stress service at the same time as ethical policies.

Place

The Co-operative Bank's bold stroke would probably have failed if the banking sector had not been undergoing dramatic changes in the late 1980s and early 1990s. Deregulation brought other players into the game, such as the building societies. Reduction of state provision in such areas as pensions created new markets for financial services (for instance, even people on relatively modest salaries, like me, bought an additional pension). Fierce competition and mergers led to reductions in branches. Most importantly, new technology meant that banking could be done by phone or ATM, reducing the importance of branches; new, branchless banks such as First Direct began to take customers from traditional banks. These changes made it easier for the Co-operative Bank to occupy its niche. For instance, I would never have considered having an account with a bank whose nearest office is in Preston, 30 miles away from my home in Lancaster, but I realized I seldom used the services offered by a branch, and with 24-hour telephone banking and cash machines I could do all I needed to do. So this is another example in which the changing distribution of a product is closely linked to its marketing strategy.

Promotion

BDDH, in their presentation to the Advertising Effectiveness Awards (IPA 1994), stress that the new customers were influenced largely by the advertising, not by other forms of promotion. But of course, this new strategy did not just involve 'above-the-line' ads. There were other forms of promotion, such as sponsorship of a contest on the environment for schoolchildren. There were leaflets to explain the ethical policies and the services offered. The ads I have seen came in four media: black and white print ads, television ads that echoed them, longer and more striking cinema ads, and posters on buses and hoardings. The aim of these ads is not to get the reader/viewer to open an account, but simply to have them call a number and get more information. Since changing one's bank is rather difficult and anxiety-inducing, we might expect it would take a much longer process of persuasion, with several stages and media, than it would to get someone to try a soft drink, jeans, or washing powder. It is clear that the Co-operative Bank and other direct financial services brands all decided that potential customers would be best persuaded by having them talk to a live human being.

Price

In all this careful positioning, the bank could not ignore the fact that it had to compete on price: in this case, the interest on savings, the costs of loans and credit cards, and the fees for services. An ad saying 'You can be an ethical investor and lose only 2 per cent of your interest' would lead to oblivion. Though the Co-operative Bank could offer good deals such as a charge card with no fee, they could not afford to develop new financial products that were radically different from those of other banks: they had to pay the same sorts of interest on savings, and charge the same sorts of interest on loans. With the intense competition between banks and building societies, and league tables in the newspapers and consumer press, small differences between interest rates and fees can be used to signal greater efficiency or customer orientation.

So far I have dealt with the headings relevant to basic marketing strategy: Product, Place, Promotion, and Price. But I have argued that the Co-operative Bank is intervening in wider social worlds, so we need to consider how their strategy relates to the meanings around the product, and look at some of the other categories discussed in Chapter 2.

Past

The Co-operative Bank has a genuine heritage pre-dating even 'Coca-Cola' and Levi's. It grew out of the nineteenth-century Co-operative British movement, in which skilled workers set up their own institutions of distribution and services to get themselves a better deal than they were getting from the local merchants who would exploit them. As the skilled working class grew, so did the movement, especially in the North, so that by 1914 it not only provided my smallish town Lancaster with its only department store, it had 20 branches through the local area. It pioneered some arrangements that the big supermarkets are just exploring today – after all, the yearly dividend was the ultimate loyalty card.

So the brand has associations with fairness, joint social effort, progress, work, consumerism – not a bad start you'd think. But it also has associations with a certain dowdy, class-bound style. Just since I have lived in Britain, the last dozen years, the stores have closed nearly everywhere. And much as I admire the ideals of the movement, I admit that I never went into the Co-op shop in Lancaster (before it was replaced by a Woolworth's) without a certain sinking feeling, something like that I felt in the changing rooms at the old public baths or in an under-used church hall. This may not be a fair overall picture, but it is certainly one common perception of the brand, which the Co-op retailing chains have fought against as they tried to convert to superstores. The one undoubted success of the Co-op was the funeral services, still the largest in the country (though as far as I know, the Bank has not attempted any tie-ins with burials). The danger for the bank in this heritage, as BDDH said, was that it would be seen as a working-class self-help fund, 'not a proper bank' (IPA 1994).

Position

Financial services are a ferociously competitive sector, especially after moves towards deregulation in the 1980s, increasingly dominated by the four large clearing banks and a handful of huge building societies (comparable to US Savings and Loan institutions) that abandoned their original mutual status to compete with the banks. Bigger organizations have advantages in this field; with bigger reserves they should be able to offer better deals and more services, and a wider network of expensive-to-run branches. The Co-operative Bank was and is much smaller than the big four, and is largely centred in a few regions such as the north-west and South Wales, and would seem to be a prime target to be swallowed up as other local banks were long ago.

The bank was not swallowed up in this competition and wave of mergers because they found themselves a niche that their competitors could never occupy. The big four banks have a terrible image as public institutions. Whether the issue is loans to South Africa under the apartheid regime, Third World debt, dubious trading, directors' pay, mortgages, or squeezes on small businesses, the banks are the focus, rightly or wrongly, of public mistrust of business. The Co-operative Bank could legitimately claim to be different; their origins in the Co-operative movement meant they already had a different customer base and sense of mission from the big four clearing banks. The big change was not making the bank ethical, but making this the basis of the brand.

Practices

One problem for the bank in extending its customer base was that people don't easily change their bank. I have read that a person is more likely over the course of their life to change their spouse than to change their bank. I can understand that; I have changed my bank, to the Co-operative bank, and it is a messy and time-consuming process, however much they work to smooth it (how it compares to changing one's spouse I wouldn't know). Somehow, the ads have to make promises without making people more suspicious. Two of the promises in the ads I will discuss are that they will open the bank account quickly and not make mistakes in the statements. These promises sound very trivial – hardly more than one would expect of any bank – but they could be seen as aimed at worries about transition periods and responsibility. And since they are small promises, they can more easily be seen as verifiable and believable.

Another problem goes deeper into the ways people feel about handing over their money. Nineteenth-century bank buildings were monumental stone, with cashiers behind bars, conveying solidity and security. Recently these banks have been remodelled to give more of a feeling of openness. Much of the activity is around the ATM machines in the entry-way, rather than around the desks inside. But people may still feel better about handing over their money to a person, with a face and a name, someone who can be held responsible. The Co-operative Bank, and other banks relying on telephone services, had to convince customers that there was a person at the other end, even if they were present only as a voice.

The wider practices around banking do not just involve customers; they also involve the employees. BDDH saw the employees of the Co-operative Bank as another audience for its advertising. They aimed to change their perception of their work from that of participants in a routine bureaucracy to members of a unique kind of institution, an ethical bank. And their own research suggested the ads had this effect, as people started talking about the bank.

Paradigm

The underlying problems for advertising any bank go beyond these issues of service, and have to do with the way banks are seen to function in society. The Co-operative Bank is not immune to the suspicion that affects all other banks, indeed, all other institutions. In our focus groups (see Chapter 9), everyone knew about the Co-operative Bank's ethical policy (that's an advertising achievement in itself), but some people doubted whether it was really any different from other banks.

If the bank does successfully show itself to be different from other banks, it has the problem of working out how a bank can talk about ethical issues, what sorts of words and symbols it can use without the two worlds seeming to clash. It is not that an ethical bank can't offer good services, but that talk about the big global issues makes whatever comes next seem trivial, and talk about the details of services makes whatever comes after them seem distant and irrelevant. The problem then, in a series of ads, was to stress the product claims of the bank while still maintaining the campaigning tone that guarantees that the Co-operative is significantly different from another bank.

Sincerity, authority, and direct address

As we will see, the Co-operative Bank's solution to the problem of combining ethical claims and product claims, in this particular series of ads, involves disrupting the way that a speaker addresses us. To provide a background for analysing this disruption, I will look in this section at how other television ads have addressed audiences (see ADDRESS).

One common form of address is to have an on-screen person speaking and looking at the camera. The advantage of this direct form of address is that it draws a kind of continuous engagement – it is amazingly hard to turn off someone talking to you. The great disadvantage is that it can suggest a kind of bullying authority. So, for instance, Andrew Tolson (1996) has pointed out how earlier British ads (those shown in a historical documentary) used the announcer speaking to camera in a 'product information' format; it was associated with authority figures. Later ads found other devices, including dialogue and voice-over, that worked within a 'personalised' or a 'lifestyle' format (70–79). He notes that these earlier ads are now looked upon 'with amused embarrassment': 'Perhaps, because of its simulation of co-presence, such direct address is particularly vulnerable to historical distanciation' (71). Where direct address is used, it is often in the context of self-parody. I surveyed all the ads shown on Channel 4 in 5 days of prime time in December 1995. About 7 per cent had some form of direct address, but of these, nearly half had some element of send-up. So, for instance, in a BT ad, Bob Hoskins walks through the scene he is describing to us, unseen and unheard by the characters. Sainsbury's has John Cleese parodying the celebrity recipes earlier in the series. Miller Beer has its presenter as a self-important talk-show host, while Holsten Pils has Dennis Leary as an irascible sceptic sending up other beer ads.

To give an idea of how direct address can work, and give a point of

comparison for the Co-operative Bank ad, I have chosen a public service
spot about teenage pregnancy shown in the US by NBC. The spot updates
the conventions of direct address, co-ordinating intonation, non-verbal
communication, and editing to give a sense of earnestness, intimacy, and
sincerity. It features Katie Couric, a woman with short hair in her 30s, wearing a stylish red top. She delivers her monologue with the intonation we
might expect, perhaps slightly exaggerated. Before I give my transcription,
you could get some idea of the expected intonation by marking this quotation of the text, breaking it up into groups as you might do when you read
it aloud, and underlining the words that you would emphasize:

> Babies are wonderful. They're cute and fleshy they wear teeny weeny
> clothes and they smell great. But babies are also real people not dolls.
> And if you're a teenager you can't just say to your baby 'hey see you
> later' and go hang out with your friends. A baby is a job twenty-four
> hours a day seven days a week three thousand dirty diapers a year.
> Babies need a lot of your attention so if you love babies wait to have
> yours. It'll be much better for the baby and much better for you.

In my transcription of the ad I have indicated the grouping of words with
/ marks and the stressed syllables with underlining. The caret marks (^) set
off groups with higher pitch. My point is that the grouping, stress, and pitch
are largely predictable, and are therefore heard as natural. The editing cuts
with the phrase structure, to emphasize key phrases and gestures. An easy
listening music background unifies it, with a saxophone rising towards the
end.

NBC – **NOW YOU KNOW**

MCU: chin on L hand	babies
CU: head at L - pan	are *won*derful/
MCU: R hand comes up and both hands gesture pinched fingers	they're cute and *fleshy* / they wear
ECU: L hand	^teeny weeny^ clothes
MCU	and they *smell* great /
MCU (longer): head forward, hands clasped	but babies are *also* real people/
ECU: hands spreading	not *dolls* /
MCU	and if you're a *teen*ager you can't just say to your baby /
ECU: face pans to waving R hand at face level	^hey see you later^/
MCU: head dipped	and go hang out with your *friends*/

MCU (longer)	a baby is a *job* twenty-four hours a day
ECU: R fingers counting on L hand	*seven* days a week /
CU: face smiling	three thousand dirty diapers a year / *babies* need a *lot* of your attention /
MCU	so if you love *babies*
ECU: hands clasped	*wait* to have *yours* /
MCU: hands opening	it'll be much better for the *baby* /
CU: head nodding	and *much* better for you
animated star turns to NBC peacock	title: The more you know

© Courtesy of National Broadcasting Company Inc.
The More You Know Campaign
All Rights Reserved.

Close-ups of gestures emphasize that the babies are 'not dolls', stress the mocking attempt to leave the baby behind, count the days, and finally stress the need to wait. Alternating with these emphatic shots, we have medium shots in which her eye contact, facial expressions, and head movements all signal engagement with and concern for the viewer. The effect might seem patronizing (or in this case, matronizing) if she were shown in one long take in a medium close-up. Here the constant movement of the camera and constant cutting break up this earnestness. But because the cutting is all logical and the non-verbal cues are consistent, the effect is one of sincerity and concern. As Tolson noted, current British ads seldom use a speaker talking direct to camera like this, unless it is ironicized. I suspect that US audiences have a much higher tolerance for the direct, emotional address of the NBC public service announcement.

The Co-operative Bank advertisement

BDDH and the bank have made various experiments, with differing degrees of success, to try to convey both the sincerity of the Ethical Policy and the details of services. They all work within the 'Creative Solution' proposed by BDDH at the outset:

As well as being provocative and motivating, advertising had to be consistent with values of honesty and integrity.

[The advertising] adopted a simple executional approach in contrast to the 'all singing, all dancing' epics of other banks.

(IPA 1994)

I am looking here at one stage of this campaign, at one of four parallel TV ads, and how they handle this tension. I will argue that what viewers feel as the oddity of these ads relates to the disruption of address, in contrast to the coherence of address in the NBC spot. Then I will relate this disruption back to the overall strategy of promising both ethical commitments and services.

THE AD

secs	spoken words	picture and sound
0	*what's* the *dif*ference between the Co-op*e*rative Bank and the other major *banks*	B/W MS of man sitting behind a table, one arm on the table across his body to the right, face oriented to the left, eyes straight to camera. Stone table and stone textured background
		cut to LS of a policeman kicking a person in a crowd (FX: crowd noises and explosions)
5	*is* it that we have 24-hour *tele*phone banking	CU of man (face distorted by lens) cut to ECU of chin and mouth
		cut to LS of armed personnel carrier on a street, flaming cans in yellow (FX: crowd noises and explosions)
9	*is* it that we have a *net*work of High Street branches	MS of man (blinks)
		cut to LS of man carried out through a doorway by police (pinkish tint)
12	*is* it that we have the use of over *six* thousand	MS of man
	LINK *cash* machines	cut to CU
		cut to LS of riot police attacking students with staves
18	or is it that we promise *neve*r to invest *our* customers' money in countries with oppressive regimes	MCU of man
24 30		Text: The Co-operative Bank [blue logo] 0800 100 555 Why bank with one that isn't?

The monologue

There are two formats in this series of ads, and each of them has two variations, one read by a man and the other by a woman. In each case, there is an interweaving of product claims and ethical claims, with one set treated as given, the other as new. This commercial opens with a question answered with three claims about availability of services (telephone banking, branches, and cash machines), all in the form of rhetorical questions. These questions presuppose the facts within them ('we have 24-hour *tele*phone banking'); they act is if you already know these facts. Then finally there is an ethical claim ('Or is it that we promise never to invest our customers' money . . .'), framed as a rhetorical question about a promise. This last element is a longer group than the others, serving as a kind of conclusion to the series and (as we will see) a resolution to the visual disruptions. The desired action, phoning the bank, is suggested only by the written text at the end. So the general effect of the ad, as a written script, is of very tight weaving together of ethical and product claims, ending with a promise. One danger in this approach, as I've noted, is that the juxtaposition of global political issues and fairly small services can trivialize one or the other.

Forms of address

For readers who have not seen these ads, I should stress that they look very odd. The speakers sit or stand stiffly in uncomfortable and hard to interpret postures, speaking flatly with falling intonation and pauses. The monologues are broken with cuts between medium shots, close-ups, and extreme close-ups made where they would be considered inappropriate by traditional rules of editing. The advertisements are almost (but not quite) entirely black and white, and the faces seem distorted by the close-up lens; the backgrounds are the stone and root textures of Sierra Club calendars, all suggesting art photography rather than any kind of coded naturalism.

In effect, we have a simple monologue, almost exactly the same in each of two pairs of ads, that is distanced, wrenched, and transformed by the way the speakers say it, the way they sit and move, and the way the visuals are shot and edited. The bank modified the style (though not the message) after this series of ads. But I would like to look at this stage, because of the tensions and the way they are embodied in the talk. My analysis is somewhat different from those in the last chapter, because here the words and the way they are delivered are crucial.

Intonation

One way of judging the disruption of address is to do with a Co-operative Bank ad what I just did with the NBC spot, and give you a chance to read the text with your own word groups and stress before looking back to see how it is read in the commercial.

What's the difference between the Co-operative Bank and the other major banks? Is it that we have 24-hour telephone banking? Is it that we have a network of High Street branches? Is it that we have the use of over six thousand LINK cash machines? Or is it that we promise never to invest our customers' money in countries with oppressive regimes.

There are predictable ways of reading such a text, for instance bringing out the contrasting elements in the first sentence by stressing '*ot*her', or stressing '*pro*mise'. There might be a pause after 'promise' to emphasize the act. Or one might expect the variations in pace that could, like those in the NBC spot, signal casual talk. What we find here is a curious flatness and artificiality.

What are the characteristics of this artificiality? There is a sense of slowness, but I think it is more in the unpredictable pauses than in the actual pace. There is a quietness, in one case almost a whisper. There is a level intonation at the end of each of the questions, signalling a list, but a lack of a big fall at the end of each ad, the punch-line, so it is given the sense of an ending only by the written text that appears on screen. This evenness passes up all the opportunities for engagement with an audience through colloquial rhythms. But most important, perhaps, is the way tone groups are broken up in odd places. It is a long ways from the stage performance intonation of some ads, but it is also far from the apparent intimacy of, say, a Dove soap or Tampax ad, in which actresses strive for naturalness in delivery. The sense of oddity arises just because we are so used to the intonation of other direct address ads. It is so odd that it might act as a sort of puzzle, the way many British TV ads work, keeping us to the end by making us wonder why they are doing that.

Non-verbal communication

One can picture the client, on first seeing the ads, saying, 'Real people don't sit like that!' The eyes are on us, but the bodies are oriented one quarter to the left, as if to an unseen interviewer, while one arm is placed across the body to the right. Most oddly of all, the head remains completely immobile, as if fixed in a daguerreotype photographer's clamp. (If you have not seen the ad, this looks as contorted as it sounds.) The bodies are wrenched in the same ways in all four ads, so as with the intonation, it must be intentional. The non-verbal signals are curiously mixed, as if the eyes were engaging us while the shoulders were facing someone else, and as if the whole body were tensed, strained. As with the intonation, there is a break with the formal conventions of performance, but there is no attempt to take on the devices of televised intimacy, the hand to the face or the nod of the head. In this deliberately constricted range of movement, the lightest blink or raise of the eyebrows conveys emotion. The oddity, the tension conveyed by these bodies is heightened by the way the editing forces our attention on the parts of the composition.

Setting

Bank ads have a problem with setting, because the last place an agency would want to set them would be in a bank, the focus of people's anxieties and anger. The Midland avoids the problem by putting their people on over-stuffed sofas; the Halifax builds great sculptures out of customers; Lloyd's has fairy-tale settings; and an Idaho bank shows typical Idahoans with their families. Bank ads usually show customers and what they can do with the money, not employees and what the bank does with it. The setting of this Co-operative Bank ad is a stone textured background and a flat space that serves as a sort of desk. I read these as stylized 'natural' settings, especially stylized as seen in black and white. One effect is to disrupt any sense that this person is speaking as an employee of the bank.

Framing

The disruption of the monologue is most apparent in the framing and editing of the images of the speaker. Even the least analytical of viewers must be startled by the cuts to a big close up of a body part: a mouth or an ear. The CUs use a lens that apparently distorts the faces, so that they do not seem to match the MS. The close-ups of body parts, and refocusing on body parts, draw attention to the symbolic associations of these parts even as they are used by the speaker; embodied voices made to stand metonymically for the bank and its 'listening' (ears), 'actions' (hands), and 'voice' (mouth). It is a very different effect from the frequent use of segmented bodies (pointed out by Goffman (1976), Williamson (1978), and Winship (1980)) when it is the speaker who is segmented this way.

Editing

But it is the overall pattern, rather than the extreme shots, that make for the disruption. Each ad starts with a medium shot, moves in to a close-up, and then to a big close up, before moving back to a medium shot or long shot. I wondered why this had the effect it does; after all, classical film editing techniques involve cuts from medium shots to close-ups, without any sense of a break, and even the more extreme close-ups of the NBC spot seem to make sense. I think the shock arises from several apparently deliberate violations of conventional editing. The cuts come in the middle of phrases ('24-hour/telephone banking' or 'over 6000/LINK cash machines' or 'happy with our/service') instead of emphasizing the continuity of the utterance. The cuts to emblematic events are in colour, so they function as shocking, almost subliminal images, or rather, consciously interpreted images to be read as if subliminal. And the cuts to emblematic events have sound effects, while the monologue has no sounds in the background, except subtly, at the end. In classical editing, continuity of sound would smooth the transition between images.

In simplest terms, the problem for the viewer is that the visual means exceed the meaning. As Karel Reisz and Gavin Millar (1953) say in their classic handbook on film editing, the basic rule is that every cut is there for a reason. A cut in the middle of a noun phrase demands an interpretation, but it is not always possible to provide one. The 'real world' icons of the ethical policy intrude noisily into the hush of the product claims. Viewers who have internalized classical editing techniques will have the vague sense that they are missing something. This is the same feeling we get, by other means, from the intonation.

Spokespersons and disrupted address

These ads do indeed have the 'simple executional approach' planned by BDDH in terms of the scale of the production, but they have complex effects. What is the bank trying to do with its disruptions? There are alternative ways of presenting their message. Many products and services that depend on phone contact (such as mail-order catalogues and telephone car insurance) show a smiling operator wearing a headset to give a sense of a person on the other end of the line. That would be a possible way of presenting the bank, but their chosen strategy is more complex in two ways: the relation of the speaker to the bank and the use of different modes, spoken and written. These presenters are not real people trying to speak for themselves, as in the 'Pampers' or 'Always' ads, where women talk frankly and haltingly to an unseen interviewer, or as in the NBC spot. They are taken as speaking for the bank, even though the setting in 'natural' surroundings is hardly that of a bank. But they are not confident, natural announcers' voices of authority. When each ad makes a promise, the promise is made, not by the speaking voice, but in equally fractured typography, in which the promise is framed in a question and the personality is deliberately suppressed. If the promise works, it is not because we believe in this person and their personal commitment to the corporate promise (one sort of ad, often featuring the boss), or because we place them realistically as clerks or managers (another sort of ad, constructing employees as 'real people') but because they stand for the bank in some abstract way.

In a traditional ad or campaign, the promise is underwritten by the sincerity of the person and trust in the organization. Thus the ad or speech does everything possible to convey them as a coherent personality, and this includes giving their speech the sense of naturalness. This campaign uses specific people to make their case, but keeps the promises separate, written, framed, as if removed from any question of personal credibility. One cannot ask if these people mean what they say; sincerity is not the issue. The unpredictable intonation, the black and white photography, the disruptive editing and odd framing are part of the distancing that keeps us from responding to these spokespersons as we might usually do, examining, questioning, and rejecting them. It also conveys a seriousness that in the Co-operative Bank ad enables them to deal with torture and service charges, global warming and telephone banking, pollution and cash machines, in the same 30-second message.

Such ads contribute to the re-examination of our assumptions in media studies about direct address and spokespersons and our assumptions in cultural studies about trust. Direct address is not a simple manipulative engagement of the viewer; it can be, and now usually is, oblique, distancing, parodic. Spokespersons may not be read as representatives of institutions, but can take up various ambiguous relations to those for whom they speak (see Goffman 1981). And trust is not an all or nothing state, a magic gift, but more like a set of presuppositions that can shift from moment to moment in a broadcast or in other talk.

Summary

These questions about intonation, editing, and address may seem to take us a long way from products like jeans, soap, or banks, towards television as a medium (Chapter 8), the responses of audiences (Chapter 10), and the boundaries of the commercial sector (Chapter 12). But these textual strategies can be seen to follow from the way the Co-operative Bank and BDDH saw the product in a new way. A bank wasn't just an institution that paid interest on savings or loaned money; it was your choice of who should control and channel your money. The choice of banks, like the use of cars, detergents, garden chemicals, or aerosol sprays, could be seen as having consequences for others that go beyond the benefits to you. In this view, money is not just a colourless quantity, but is full of emotion-laden, value-laden qualities. That is not an unusual view for a charity or an environmental campaign group, but it is unusual for a bank. It is a social theory made into a marketing strategy, a theory about how the worlds of commercial enterprises and public choices are linked.

This new relation to the product requires customers to see themselves in a new relation to the bank, so it poses considerable risks. First, as we have seen, it involves juxtaposing images and language that do not go together in most people's minds: images of routine daily business like cash machines, and extraordinary violence and suffering. Second, as politicians and companies have found to their cost, when you stake out the high moral ground you become a clear target for charges of hypocrisy, insincerity, and manipulativeness. The Co-operative Bank and its agency have always been aware of these dangers, and have explored various visual styles and various voices in an attempt to relate the financial and the ethical without ludicrous leaps or a shrill tone.

In this particular series of ads, one part of a long campaign, the main device was the use of a direct to camera monologue disrupted by

- intonation
- non-verbal communication
- the setting
- framing
- editing and composition.

The result in this particular case is odd, distanced, maybe not entirely successful. But it is an interesting exploration of how they might find a new form of address for a new view of the product, not just harking back to reassuring voices. Ads that disrupt address this way are often those that need to make a major shift or self-appraisal, not just a routine purchase. We will consider this problem again in discussing target audiences and drink-driving ads (Chapter 10).

Suggested reading: address

On address in broadcasting, see Ellis (1982), Corner (1995), Thompson (1995), Tolson (1996), and references after Chapter 7. On linguistic features of address in print ads, see Myers (1994). The BDDH presentation to the IPA Advertising Effectiveness Awards (for which they won the Bronze) is in *Advertising Works 8* (Barker 1995), and is also presented in the IPA video on Advertising Effectiveness. The Co-operative Bank web site, at www.co-operativebank.co.uk, has more information on their ethical policy.

Norwich Union

4

Globalization in advertising

In 1971, The Coca-Cola Company produced a television commercial featuring 200 young people at sunrise on a hill, each dressed in some form of national dress, each holding a distinctive bottle of 'Coke', and all singing along with the New Seekers:

> I'd like to buy the world a home and furnish it with love
> Grow apple trees and honeybees and snow-white turtle doves
> I'd like to teach the world to sing in perfect harmony
> I'd like to buy the world a Coke and keep it company
> It's the real thing ...

We have found that people in focus groups still remember this as a generation later. Dated as it may seem today, 'Hilltop' set out a kind of ad that has since become ubiquitous. The Coca-Cola Company was one of the first companies to build its marketing strategy on a single global product and brand image. It was also one of the first to use the globe itself, and the ethnic and national diversity of consumers, as a sign of the brand's universal desirability and availability. And the ad was produced by McCann-Erickson, one of the first agencies to expand into a transnational network. The ad itself is dominated by images and music, and carries a generic message that does not rely on the sorts of complex linguistic play that we saw in, for instance, the 'Coke' ad with the two boys in Chapter 1. Indeed, the music was so catchy that the New Seekers released it as a single and it went to Number 1 in the US charts; the reference to 'Coke' was deleted, but it retained its associations with the advertisement.

One might have thought then that, 25 years later, all ads would be like this: multinational, dominated by images and music, suitable for showing anywhere. Indeed many are: global brands like McDonald's, Fuji film, or British Airways may use the same or similar imagery in a number of national markets, and global agency networks like Saatchi and Saatchi,

Ogilvy & Mather, J. Walter Thompson, or Publicis are there to co-ordinate such campaigns. Globalization seems all-powerful because it provides both a marketing strategy and a set of images. But it turns out that it is rather difficult to market most products at this level of generality. The iconography, typeface, and colours certainly remain the same around the world, but every global brand finally reaches the consumer at a particular time and place and a particular intersection of meanings, so there remains a need for all sorts of local knowledge in the agency and local modifications in the campaign. I mentioned in Chapter 2 that The Coca-Cola Company was making ads to give 'Coke' a more Russian feel. *Campaign* tells us, 'The result is five 60-second blockbuster commercials devised by the London office of a French agency, Publicis, shot in Russia by a British crew for a US company' (6/3/98). Clearly advertising is an international business, but it does not inevitably move towards one monolithic message from central office. Campaigns like this consider local settings, local identities, and talents of specific offices and production teams, and also the personal associations and track record that might lead an Atlanta company to go to a London agency for a Moscow commercial.

In this chapter I will first review some of the pressures towards globalization in the institutions around advertising: the expansion of multinational companies into new markets, the development of global brands, the rise of global advertising networks, and the beginnings of a few global media. Most of the discussion of these changes has focused on problems of translation or cultural difference that might keep an ad like that for 'Coke' from being uniformly effective around the world. I will be dealing instead with the imagery and rhetoric of globalization. The imagery includes photos of the Earth in space (what I will call the Blue Globe), the arrows across the map (like airline routes), the montage of people of different races in diverse clothing. I will call this last kind of montage 'The Family of Man', after the title of Edward Steichen's (1957/1983) collection of photographs from around the world. (I realize that the usage of 'man' to mean 'humanity' would now be considered sexist, but keep the phrase for the kind of humanism it evokes.) The rhetoric is the implied assertion that such globalized brands (such as 'Coke' or McDonald's) or brands contributing to globalization (such as British Airways or IBM) are inherently better. But the messages of such ads are not just in these signs; they are also in the form of the ads, the way they position the company and the viewer. I will be looking at this imagery and rhetoric as they are used in ads for very different advertisers: Norwich Union insurance, Compaq computers, General Electric corporate activities, and the Peugeot 406. I will trace the uses of the imagery in each ad, but I will focus especially on the kinds of movement and language in each ad that position the company, consumer, or product within the ad, and position us as viewers. I will argue that these ads, though global in their rhetoric, are highly localized in their effects.

Globalization and the advertising business: Unilever, 'Coke', Saatchi & Saatchi, and CNN

Globalization assumes, but goes beyond, the globalization of business. The rise of multinational corporations has become a part of our culture, so that futuristic visions such as *Bladerunner* or *Neuromancer* assume a world dominated by a few global companies, their names and logos all around us. Multinationals themselves are not new: the Anglo-Dutch consortium Unilever was formed in the early twentieth century to unite two vast corporations based on food processing and household products that already drew on international networks for raw materials and markets. Ford has been manufacturing in Britain since the 1920s. The Coca-Cola Company started expanding beyond North America in the 1930s. What is new after the 1980s is not the multinationals, but a combination of deregulated capital markets, less unionized labour markets, and extended trading areas that give these companies more power to move production and distribution for increased profits, and give them business advantages over companies based in one nation.

The extent of internationalization is complex: some products are made in one company but exported (Levi's), some retail brands are based in one country but import from all over (supermarkets), some products are made around the world for a company that may re-export them (running shoes, computers), some are made in one country with largely imported designs or materials (cars), some international brands are franchised to locally owned businesses ('Coke', McDonald's, Benetton). Those of us who are not in the upper levels of business are likely to be unaware of such basic organizational differences. We are more likely to become aware of transnationals only when one set of familiar brand names is replaced by another (Ramblers or Morris Minors replaced by Honda Accords, RCA or Bush televisions replaced by Sonys, Wall's ice cream challenged by Häagen-Dazs) or when a brand taken as national is sold to an international corporation (Jaguar to Ford, Rover and now Rolls-Royce to BMW, *The Times* or the *New York Post* sold to Rupert Murdoch's News International, UK electricity providers bought by US companies).

For our purposes, it is important to note that the rise in transnational ownership and trade is not itself globalizing. Most traditional transnationals have prided themselves on responding to local conditions, for instance by presenting somewhat different brands in different countries. Ford made big Mustangs and Thunderbirds and Lincoln Continentals in the US, while in the UK they made Cortinas. Unilever adapted so well to the US market that I doubt that many North Americans realized that Lever Brothers was not a US firm – in the US it sold products with different names from those in the UK, advertised in different ways. Mars is in both the UK and the US, but a Mars bar is not the same thing in the two countries. It would be possible to have a company that was international in its ownership, management, and production, while basing its marketing on national units. Such a company could have huge impacts on local economies, while leaving local meanings intact. (But I admit that I cannot think of one that operates in this way.)

Theodore Levitt (1983) introduced the term *globalization* to present a different view of multinational business; he argued that that there would be a competitive advantage in some sectors in marketing the same product in the same way around the world. If Unilever before World War I is our example of a multinational business, 'Coke' after World War II is a pioneer example of a global brand. A more traditional transnational organization might have given the drink a different name, and even a slightly different composition, in the different markets, as happens with chocolate bars or laundry detergent. Or it might have grown internationally by buying local brands (as The Coca-Cola Company bought the European brand 'Fanta'). Instead they stressed the one brand and maintained a uniform identity for it. There were business advantages to franchising, and to economies of scale in production. But Levitt's point was that there would be what one might call symbolic economies in focusing all one's marketing on one brand presented as the best in the world. There are critics of Levitt's thesis, by marketing analysts who insist that standardization is not required for global growth, and by cultural studies researchers who insist that standardization is not possible, that the same product does take on different meanings in different cultures. But it is useful to take Levitt's simplified statement as a starting point (see GLOBALIZATION).

Levitt's slogan of globalization might have been confined to academic business studies, but it was picked up in the 1980s as part of the business pitch of Saatchi & Saatchi. We can take them as comparable to Unilever and The Coca-Cola Company, as pioneers of another kind of globalization, that of the ad business. The advertising business has long been international in that a big US firm like McCann-Erickson, Foote, Cone & Belding, or J. Walter Thompson would have branch offices in many major cities, including London. Often they would handle the local business for the clients they had back in the US, and leave local business to local agencies. In that way, advertising was parallel with other business sectors dominated by transnationals (see AGENCIES).

Twenty years ago, Saatchi & Saatchi was a small London agency with a big reputation, based on ads for clients like British Airways, Silk Cut, and the Conservative Party. In the 1980s, Saatchi & Saatchi used the high valuation of their stock to buy out old American firms that were much bigger than them, such as Compton and Ted Bates, and within years they were by far the biggest ad network in the world. They ended up with a roster of big international clients, such as BA, Fuji, Mars, and Procter & Gamble. The case Saatchi & Saatchi made to clients was that big international brands needed a big international agency (Levitt was on their board). In the past, a client might have been happy to have a network like McCann-Erickson handle all its advertising, and adapt it in each new location. Or they might try to get different agencies in different places, looking for strong local shops. Saatchi & Saatchi said their network would do ads that could run everywhere, giving a uniform brand image around the world, all through the same agency. So they had a powerful investment in this particular kind of globalization. They could argue that whatever agency was flavour of the month, whichever one had the best local talent, they had the organization and the huge global network. Part of the appeal of this rhetoric may be within the clients' organizations; the promised uniformity and centralization, and the implied comparison to other global brands, may flatter managers even if it doesn't persuade consumers.

One key link in the globalized advertising strategy for globalized clients is that there should be global media for these global ads. Despite the rapid rise and high visibility of CNN and MTV, and their undoubted influence on news reporting and popular music, most media are still organized at the national level, and media buyers must have detailed local knowledge when they buy advertising on television or radio or in newspapers. (I note that one of the sponsors of CNN in Idaho is KIDO, the local news radio station.) Where the new international media are undoubtedly powerful is in reaching a range of national elites (as CNN, the *Financial Times* or the *Wall Street Journal* can claim to reach business leaders); they have not yet developed a new global mass audience (see Sreberny-Mohammadi *et al.*, 1997). As we will see in Chapter 11, different regulatory environments serve as a check on any attempt to develop a single global advertisement.

This brief review of companies, products, agencies, and media is not meant to dismiss the enormous organizational and financial pressures towards globalization around advertising. But it does show that these pressures do not result inevitably in global ads. What it does suggest is that the imagery and rhetoric of globalization may be powerful within business organizations, agencies, and media, in their own branding. In whatever ways they are or are not global in their organization and selling, they want to *look* global, not only to the public but to themselves.

Translating ads

I will give just one example to show some of the textual problems in translating a successful ad campaign from one market to another. A great deal has been written about such issues in the advertising press, because they are related to an important area of competition between agencies. On the one hand, those that are part of large global networks, such as Saatchi & Saatchi or McCann-Erickson, stress their ability to create advertising that will work in many markets. On the other hand, smaller local agencies claim that it is better to adapt campaigns freely through a loose consortium of agencies, each of whom are highly creative in their own market (as Weiden and

Kennedy handled Nike in the US, and until recently Simons Palmer did their UK posters and print work). Otherwise, the local agencies argue, the result is bland ads created by the subtraction of any verbal or visual play that might not work in any one market. The adaptation of advertising is, in its way, as complex as the translation of poetry, for it involves, not just finding equivalent words, but also thinking about equivalent practices and interpretations.

An example is provided in a letter to *Campaign* from Alisdair Ritchie of TBWA International. One of TBWA's best-known campaigns of recent years was a series of posters for Wonderbra, with a picture of Eva Herzigova on the left, wearing the product, and a text filling the right three-quarters saying, in one example,

LOOK ME
IN THE EYES
AND TELL
ME THAT YOU
LOVE ME.

Translated directly into French, this might not convey the right tone of cheekiness (only implying that the man is not looking at her eyes). So the French agency changed the second part of the text instead of translating it directly, implying that the man is looking at her breasts:

REGARDEZ-MOI
DANS
LES YEUX ...
... J'AI DIT
LES YEUX.

As with any translation, the equivalent is a matter, not of looking it up in a dictionary, but of thinking about the effect in another cultural setting.

The new setting here is a matter of the picture as well as the words. The Wonderbra ads won so many awards and so much press coverage because the use in an underwear ad of direct sexuality addressed to men was seen as unusual, just on the boundaries of obscenity. There is a long tradition of *double-entendre* humour in British popular culture, and the suggestiveness here is to be seen in the context of *Carry On* films, naughty seaside post-cards, and nudes on Page 3 of the tabloid newspapers. One wonders if such a campaign would have a similar effect in France, where there is much more nudity in advertisements and there are more frankly sexual appeals. And one could compare it to a famous campaign in America more than 30 years earlier, in which a woman dreams of being seen on the street in her Maidenform Bra (the campaign was originated by Mary Fillius for Weintraub and then developed by Norman, Craig, and Kummell (see Fox 1990: 293 and Mayer 1961: 48). In the Maidenform ad, the nudity was not presented as a sexual appeal to men, but a kind of anxiety shared among women. In the US, the words of the Wonderbra ad might not need to be translated, but the concept would.

Unilever has a reel of films showing how they adapt their ads to different markets. All the ads for Timotei Honey shampoo stress naturalness, but the naturalness is indicated in different ways in Japan, Malaysia, France, or Canada: a mountain meadow for one market, a boat on a pond for another. And as one might expect, the ideas of feminine elegance vary as well, from twirling hair and dress in the meadow, to soulfully dipping the head. At this level of general appeal, the adaptations are clever but always possible. The Wonderbra example suggests how difficult it will be to translate some of the most successful campaigns, which depend on playful or provocative images and words. The brand image can be global, but the words and pictures will usually change from market to market. What I will consider in the rest of the chapter are not global ads, but ads that are in one way or another *about* globalization.

Global images

I will start with an ad for a product that is definitely not global: Norwich Union insurance. The growth in private insurance is dependent on a change characteristic of Britain in the 1980s, the cutbacks in state provision and the need for individuals to provide such insurance for themselves. But though it is limited to one audience, it illustrates several different kinds of globalization imagery: the Earth seen from space, flight across that space, and the survey of differences between peoples.

NORWICH UNION (AGENCY: SAATCHI & SAATCHI)

pictures and sound	voice-over	written words
open vault chord	scientists have spent many years watching the people of this planet	Logo
Family of Man shots (Buddhist monk, Asian city, dervish, tribal ritual ...) blue globe	trying to understand the fundamental things that make us tick	
blue globe more family of man different ages of life	it was when the astronauts looked down at our planet that they saw the answer	
through clouds to the wall	for there was one man-made achievement big enough to be visible from space	

panorama of the wall	something that illustrates what for hundreds of thousands of years has been the most basic instinct known to man: to protect	
chord vault		no other insurance company protects more of the things that are important to you than Norwich Union [disclaimers at the bottom]
Reproduced by permission of Norwich Union.		

We have now become accustomed to the image of the Earth from space (Cosgrove 1994), what some analysts call the Blue Globe. It appears on weather reports with clouds moving jerkily across it, and in posters and postcards of Britain, the Lake District or London, as well as calendars and T-shirts and coffee mugs and PC screen savers. It comes in many forms, but it always has these features:

- the Earth is seen in a black sky, with a bright edge, as a planet;
- it is divided into land and sea, not into political units;
- clouds across it give the sense of movement, change, immediacy.

All these features together mean that we see it, not as a schoolroom representation of the Earth, but as the Earth itself, seen from outside the Earth, as if by an astronaut. It is, in semiotic terms, an icon, resembling what it means, rather than just symbolizing it abstractly (see Myers 1994: Chapter 10). But the Blue Globe is more than just an aerial photograph from very high up. For instance, because we see the Earth as something small, floating in space, it can be seen as showing its fragility; that is how it became an environmental symbol. Greenpeace uses it on the back of its recruitment leaflet, with the heading, 'Think of the Earth as a forty-six year old . . .'. Friends of the Earth used it for many years as its logo. There is an odd contradiction when it is used as an environmental symbol, because it puts humans out of the Earth, and shrinks the Earth to something graspable. From this height, there are no environmental issues or social issues. The image can also suggest global reach of brands, travel, or communications; that is why one sees it most frequently in airports.

But in the Norwich Union ad, we are not just shown the Earth from space; we are shown an astronaut, and the ad uses a series of dissolves through the layers of clouds to link the perspective of the astronaut to an earthbound perspective dominated by the Wall. This sense of flying is another of the images of globalization that one can see in many other ads.

For instance, a television commercial for Compaq shows little spots of light soaring over landscapes and turning, seen by various people below, but giving us, flying with these lights, the sort of view one would have in a flight simulation game. Finally the bits of light fly down into a city where they penetrate into skyscraper-like components of a PC, before drawing back to a globe studded all over with PCs. The flight movement is both visually exciting (think of *Star Wars*) and suggestive of a free, unconfined point of view hovering over a fixed Earth.

In the Norwich Union ad, the Blue Globe and the flying are juxtaposed with travelogue shots of peoples of the world. Depending on one's age, one might associate such pictures with the *National Geographic*, and its artful photography of distant peoples, or with the film *Koyaanasqatsi*, with the fancy shots of human life and the Philip Glass score, or with 'United Colors of Benetton'. I have linked it to *The Family of Man*, a famous photographic exhibition of the 1950s that put together photographs of people from around the world. It stressed by the way they are put together that however different they look they share basic feelings. The pictures of people here draw on that set of readings and visual styles. The people are marked for culture, the sense of culture as the odd things other people do (see CULTURE). There are shots of Europeans, but they are not marked for culture, they are marked for stages of life – Birth, Grief, Age. Each image is exotic in itself, but taken together they are to be the sign of something universal. The textual gloss puts us in an oddly contradictory position. This is the scientists' view of *us*, or *our planet*. We are outside, looking down from outside the world, at our world.

What links the lofty universal view to the particulars of daily life is the cinematic descent through the clouds and a sort of pun – what is universal is 'To protect'. This is very carefully put, an intransitive infinitive, nothing about who protects what from what. Then it is expanded into a highly complex negative comparative: 'no other company', 'more of the things that are important to you'. Everything is vague except the act of fending off this unseen threat. As the Norwich Union logo reappears, we see it is on the door of a safe deposit vault, and that this door is visually paralleled to the porthole from which we saw the Blue Globe. After all the Family of Man introduction, and the Blue Globe stressing the indivisibility of the Earth, what is universal is to build walls, boundaries, divisions. And of course the other thing that everyone knows about the Great Wall of China, besides the fact that it is visible from space, is that it didn't work. Instead of offering solid ground, this offers more anxiety.

Why build this appeal on universality? Unlike other advertising images of the Blue Globe, it is trying to put us back in a sense of the contingent, the risky, the uncontrolled. What is universal, then, is the vulnerability of life at each stage, the sense of threat, and the diversity that leads to this sense of threat. In this view, we buy insurance to divide what is ours from what is not ours. Life insurance ads have often called for this radical change of perspective, this disruption of the everyday – in the everyday world, no one buys insurance. Just as the Blue Globe offers a world in which we see the whole at once, the ad offers us a vision in which we see birth and death. From that great height, we see the impossible: a world without us.

The globalized company

In the Norwich Union ad the various images of globalization were linked by a movement, a cinematic descent through the clouds. Other globalizing ads offer other kinds of unifying movements. The key problem is to link all these images while giving us a point of view, a visual identity for us as viewers as well as for the advertiser. The perspective may be as dramatic as that of the Compaq flight simulation, or it may be a matter of very small movements, as in the corporate ad I will discuss from General Electric.

Much of the imagery of globalization appears in corporate advertising, that is, in ads intended to build the reputation of the corporation rather than in consumer ads intended to sell a product. To understand this we need a brief digression to ask why they spend money on corporate ads at all. This has always been a puzzle in an industry dominated by consumer advertising; there is often the suspicion that the ads make the executives feel good without having much effect on any definite audience. But the fact that corporate ads persist is a reminder that advertising does things besides selling. The ads may be intended to improve employees' morale or focus energies within a company (like employee newsletters). Or they may be intended (like glossy annual reports) to present the company in a favourable light to other companies and to potential investors. Or they may (as with the nuclear power or chemical industries) present a case to the public and campaigners and community groups, who (at least theoretically) have an indirect role in legislation, trade policies, and regulation. Or they may (as with the Body Shop or B&Q) indirectly support a wide range of products by presenting the company itself as a brand. Large companies work in a complex political environment, and selling branded products may be only a small part of their activities.

I do not know the strategy behind General Electric's corporate advertising, but the on-line version of *Advertising Age* (www.adage.com) tells us 'GE plans to spend more of its advertising budget on marketing worldwide, with emphasis on Pacific regions'. Most of GE's turnover is in business-to-business sales, but they are also a well-established consumer brand in the USA. Elsewhere they are surprisingly little known for such a huge corporation, and they may feel they need to improve their name recognition and broaden the public perception of what they do, especially as various countries, like the UK, open public power systems to foreign investment. Or they may need to remind US investors that they make something besides light bulbs. The example I will discuss is from CNN, so I assume that it was intended to be seen by the international business community (I picture them in hotels and airports). The pitch it makes is that GE, a distinctively American company, is a global source of expertise.

GENERAL ELECTRIC (AGENCY: BBDO (NY))

pictures	talk and music	text
	[song in Japanese]	GE symbol
flashing Ginza signs/ dancing women in traditional costume		subtitles: We make your daughters dance
zoom in on model on a TV monitor		We make you pretty
CU plug/ baseball teams at night lined up at home plate and bowing to each other		We make you smile
Tokyo Electric Power symbol / turning page	When Tokyo Electric Power	
meeting behind glass with this symbol/ white-shirted and blue-shirted engineers with plans	turned to GE for its advanced turbine technology	
teams of engineers meeting in plant/ engineers between banks of equipment with plans/ CU: hand throwing giant switch/ panorama of city at night	it gave Tokyo the largest and most efficient power-plant of its kind in the world	
sumo wrestler lifted by boys/ woman in traditional dress	Because people everywhere should enjoy a future	
girl in traditional dress turns to us/ boy in wrestling costume turns to us	full of all the good things their way of life has to offer	
girl in Western dress turns to us		
woman in traditional dress kneeling and bowing to floor	[singing in Japanese] GE . . .	
blue-shirted and white-shirted engineers meeting and bowing		GE (USA) logo We bring good things to life visit us at www.ge.com
Reproduced by permission of General Electric. Copywriter and Creative Director: Al Merrin Director: Joe Pytka		

There are two languages and two sets of imagery here: on the one hand the Japanese song, signs, dances, baseball players bowing, and the children, and on the other hand the English sub-titles, the American English voice-over, and the white-shirted engineers. The opening is disorienting; it is shown as a Japanese advertisement for the Tokyo Electric Power Company (the *we* of the song at the beginning), with sub-titles, and it includes both traditional images of Japan and reminders of its modern (and electricity-gulping) culture. The model is seen on a bank of TV monitors and the baseball game also has the grainy look of a TV on TV, reminding us that Japan is the source of the best-known brands of electrical goods. The baseball teams present a familiar setting – the diamond under floodlights – but with an unfamiliar ritual.

The voice-over firmly places the commercial as American, and it begins by saying that the Japanese turned to GE for help. These two groups are represented as blue-shirted Japanese and white-shirted Americans. The visuals are linked by a set of plans, seen first on the table, then at the meeting, then in the hands of engineers moving through equipment. The voice-over is neatly ambiguous: the *it* that gives Tokyo the power plant could be GE or Tokyo Electric Power. After the lights are turned on, we return to images of Japanese in traditional dress. Where before the images were accompanied by a Japanese song, now the voice-over glosses these scenes for us as a universal right to a particular culture: 'because people everywhere should enjoy a future full of all the good things their way of life has to offer'. Again this is ambiguous about whether this is the motivation of GE or Tokyo Electric Power. There is no need to emphasize here that these 'good things' might be electrically powered; that was shown at the beginning. Finally the two worlds are conflated as the Japanese jingle sings what I assume is the GE slogan we are shown in English as at the end. On the level of sounds and pictures, then, we are to see traditional Japanese culture and American know-how merging unproblematically.

This analysis does not yet suggest how such an array of images and sounds fits together into a whole. The key seems to be in two repeated sets of movements. The linking movement is not flying over the Earth, as in the Compaq ad, or descending to it as in the Norwich Union ad, but the movement of bringing peoples together. In one set of repeated movements, the Japanese people literally turn to us, the camera and viewers, as Tokyo Electric Power is said figuratively to turn to GE. These people are all seen in medium close-up, from head to waist, front on. (Other figures are more distanced: the model, the sumo wrestler, and the kneeling woman are all seen at a distance and at an angle to the horizontal, and each makes a motion that is not this turning to us.) The other repeated movement is a meeting of parallel groups. We see this first with the baseball team, matched players facing each other across a rectangle, with the officials at the end. Because they are seen on a screen, their lines are at a 30-degree angle to horizontal. The same arrangement is used for the two groups of engineers meeting in the plant around the plans, and is repeated more explicitly at the end as they bow to each other.

The parallel presents the engineers from GE and Tokyo Electric Power as teams participating in a friendly and equal spirit, rather than as, say, leader and led, or manager and technician, or salesperson and customer.

These movements position the people in the ad, and they also position us as viewers. We are not in this world, but in front of it. First we watch it as strangers, and then we are brought into it by GE. Their engineers match the Japanese engineers, and allow the two worlds to merge, so that the Japanese world is lit up. Since some of GE's major products (besides power generation plants) are components of jet planes, one might expect them to take on the kind of soaring high-tech perspective we have seen in ads for Norwich Union or Compaq. But there is a danger that such an ad will seem in this context to present the Americans as imperialistic, dominating other peoples. So the ad presents globalization on a different scale, that of teams participating in a ritualized game; we as viewers participate in this game through them.

The globalized consumer

So far we have considered ads in which the viewer participates in a global community by purchasing the product ('Coke'), or by using the product (Compaq), or by following the company (GE), or by participating in universal human needs (Norwich Union). In each case, the imagery suggested a global community, but it was the implied movement in point of view that linked the various elements of the imagery and placed the viewer. Some ads now suggest that consumers have (or should have) internalized this imagery; one example is the UK ad by a European agency, Euro RSCG Wnek Gosper, for a French car, the Peugeot 406.

The ad is famous for two things: the music by M People, which it put in the charts, and for one shot, lasting only a second or so, that shows either a 'gay kiss' or mouth-to-mouth resuscitation. From all the discussion of this one shot in the tabloids, one would not suspect the range of imagery in the ad. It ran in two forms, one running 3 minutes to allow the whole song to be played, and the other version, which was of course the one shown most often, running 1 minute 20 seconds. Both versions begin with the words:

The average person has 12 367 thoughts a day . . .
Here are just a few of them

The only other text is at the end:

There is no such thing as an average person.
Peugeot 406.

The only spoken words come over a graphic of the logo at the end, the slogan 'Peugeot: The Drive of Your Life'. So the ad is almost without spoken or written words; its effect arises from its juxtaposition of a pop song and a stream of images.

PEUGEOT 406 –THOUGHTS

images	song
LS car on bridge	bass rhythms
two title cards, white on black: 'The average person has 12 367 thoughts a day …' 'Here are just a few of them …'	
zoom in on eye of Man in car zoom back on an eye and shaving cut	drums
LS car on underpass MS car headlight MS windscreen	
Man in car glances left	
Girl in red coat running on the bridge	Sometimes, a river flows but nothing breathes
CU truck driver shifting truck	
Man on bridge throws ring, seen from water	
CU Indian applying red face paint	A train arrives but never leaves
Man jumps, camera goes underwater	
MS newborn baby pan to father's face, he faints	
Man giving mouth-to-mouth resuscitation (kiss?), camera draws back	It's a shame
LS of man running to pick up dog as wall collapses in earthquake runner collapsing between crowds of bowler-hatted men	Oh life
LS car from above car from side car reflected in doors (?)	like love that walks out of the door
Man in car glances	
zoom in on photographer and elephant MCU of photographer and balloon CU elephant's brow	of being rich or being poor
truck seen from front, skidding in city street	
naked pregnant woman in room, camera sways	
Girl in red coat in front of truck Girl smiles	Such a shame
bowler hatted men in crowd from behind, Man turns towards us	
CU truck wheels	
man with arms up in front of tank	
Girl with arms up in front of truck Man rushes and grabs girl	But it's then
CU football player does a header	then that faith arrives

Man and girls somersault away from the truck	to make you feel at least alive
Man in car glances	
LS car on bridge	And that's why
Woman in restaurant throws back wine, pulls off tablecloth, climbs on table, grabs tie, and kisses Man CU of kiss and Man's astonished face	you should keep on aiming high
man in front of tank	
troops running towards camera troops drag man away	
Woman in rain points to eye, then hands on heart, then moves hands forward, palms up seen from back of truck drawing away	Just seek yourself and you will shine
LS of car car	
standing Woman and seated Man as priest glimpsed through open doorway as she moves towards him	You've got to search for the hero inside yourself
soldiers at barricade	Search for the secrets you hide
Man emerges from car at office, looks up, astonished	Search for the hero inside yourself
Girl in red coat on the street, zoom in	Until you find the key to your life
'There is no such thing as an average person.'	
'The New Peugeot 406' superimposed on car against office building	
end sequence: animation ending in PEUGEOT: THE DRIVE OF YOUR LIFE	whoosh sound
Agency: EuroRSCG Wnek Gosper Copywriter: Mark Wnek Art Director: Nigel Rose Agency Producer: Geoff Stickler Production Company: Smillie Films, L. A. Director: Peter Smillie Producer: Stephanie Swor Lyrics of the 'M People' song 'Search for the Hero' are by Pickering and Heard, and are used by permission of EMI Music Publishing and BMG Publishing.	

The images are like the Family of Man shots in the Norwich Union ad, but here there are also bits of a personal sexual fantasy (in movie style), news and sports footage (grainy, shaky images) including references to Tiananmen Square, dream images (in surreal, slow clarity), and *Schindler's List* (the Girl in the red coat). They are linked by repetition of some themes, and by the very muted colour (except for the red coat and blood) which allows the car shots to blend with the black and white documentary footage, and by the song, which keeps suggesting oblique connections to whichever images are on screen. They are linked also by the panning, zooming, and dollying in each shot, which echo the smooth movement of the car in the helicopter shots. As in the GE ad, the constant camera movement unifies, transforming the jumble into a stream of consciousness.

When we list the images and actions this way, we see it is a curious vision of action in the world, full of tensions. Everything happens *to* the Man; he is confronted by the need to save the drowning man, the protester, the dog in the earthquake, and of course the Girl in red. The erotic fantasies happen *to* him, as the woman approaches him over a table or across a room, or sends her message across the rainy car park. Meanwhile, he is really, in the linking shots, cruising along curiously empty and silent highways, to the front of a curiously unpeopled office building. In the music, it is a woman's voice (Heather Small of M People) that addresses this man (Andrew Blake (1997) comments on how music by black performers is used in ads with white characters). The emotional power arises, not just from the music, but from the alternation of his calm driving, his eyes glancing around, and the moments of extreme emotion, ending with an ambiguity about which is to be taken as the real. He is imagining heroism, but from a passive position in the car. He is imagining the vulnerability of Girl or protester or drowning man or woman, while protected. Though we see the point of view of protester or girl, his car is also visually identified with the tank and the truck, the machinery moving irresistibly forwards.

How does all this work as an ad? The end-line, that 'There is no average person', is a familiar appeal. It is playing on one of the main tensions in consumer culture. The car gives the buyer distinctiveness, identity. And yet it is a mass produced car; hundreds of thousands can buy this identity (Dyer 1982). For the man (and the target must be a man) who buys this as a company car (it is meant for that market), the message is that this is different from the flashy sports cars that boast of a hero *outside*, of excitement in driving. Instead, if the hero is inside, his turbulent mental life breaking out of the actual time and place of his driving to work. He is both stereotypically English, in bowler hat or uptight at the restaurant, and identified with all men, the falling black runner or the foreign protester. The implication is that an emotional life now is peopled with CNN and news photo images, and with a whole range of possible identities. We as viewers don't have all these thoughts, but we recognize all these images. Oddly, though, the ad is specifically targeted at the UK audience: it is cosmopolitanism as seen from just the point of view of the UK middle-aged middle-level manager, with his stock of images from international news and recent movies. He is (to parody the Intel slogan) the consumer with CNN inside.

Conclusion

Globalization has been a key topic in the advertising industry, because of the rise of multinational corporations, global products, and global agencies, and experiments with a few global ads. These discussions have tended to focus on problems of translating signs accurately, for instance, successfully adapting the cheekiness of the Wonderbra ad, the eroticism of Levi's, the naturalness of Timotei. The picture given in these discussions is one of a world divided into discrete and homogeneous cultural blocks that can be unlocked with the agency's specialist knowledge. These problems can sometimes be resolved in interesting ways, but they are based on a simplistic view of the uniformity of each national culture.

I have turned to ads that are not necessarily examples of globalization (in that they are not meant for worldwide markets) but that are one way or another about globalization. In one ad, for Norwich Union, there were several ways of suggesting global perspectives, for instance through images of the Earth from space, flight over the earth, or juxtapositions of images that I have called the Family of Man. One way these images can be linked is through the use of repeated movement, whether zooming down, or drawing together, or gliding across. I have argued that these movements give a sense of transcendence of one's own position, of global reach. But they also place the viewer in specific ways: as a person from a particular nation and class, for whom this is the vision of the rest of the world, and these are the ways of acting in it: buying insurance, following a huge corporation, or buying a car. We saw how the ad for Peugeot 406 extends the range of advertising in drawing on new kinds of images, bringing in news and documentary as well as pop videos and fictional films. But they assemble these collections in specific ways, as both personal and generally shared. Seeing all this as globalization is itself the perspective of one place and time. As one viewer said after the Norwich Union ad, there is nothing global about the idea of globalization.

Suggested reading: globalization in advertising

A collection edited by Annabelle Sreberny-Mohammadi, Dwayne Winseck, Jim McKenna, and Oliver Boyd-Barrett (1997) has excellent readings on the theoretical background, as well as studies of media, but surprisingly there is little on advertising. On international advertising, see Matellart (1991); for a critique of ideas about the globalization of signs, see Miller (1998). Goddard (1998) has a chapter on the difficulty of translating brand names. A case study of Levi's European campaign appears in Baker (1993), and a study of British Airways advertising appears in Baker (1995).

PART

II

MEDIA

Volkswagen

5

The media mix

Hollywood has always been hard on advertising professionals as over-ambitious, dishonest, and superficial (Cook (1992) provides a useful list of films). But I think the profession reached its cinematic low point at the beginning of the film *City Slickers*, when a man whose job is advertising sales for a radio station is participating in a careers day at his young son's school. The kids are fascinated by advertising, but they have a hard time figuring out just what he does. No, he answers, I don't write the ads, I don't make the ads, I don't make the shows, I don't broadcast radio; I just sell the time in which ads are broadcast. It is significant to the plot that this seems to be the dullest job in the world, selling this empty time, especially in contrast to the great job of the previous parent, a trial lawyer.

But for our purposes, buying and selling media are crucial jobs in under-standing ad worlds. For every ad, someone has decided to buy the time of a medium such as radio, or the space of a medium such as a magazine, and for most ads they have given careful thought to the context in which the ad will appear. Other media buyers note a smart move when:

- a Wrangler's ad parodying *City Slickers* is placed in the first break of *City Slickers*;
- an elegantly simple Boddington's visual pun appears in unlikely maga-zines like *New Scientist* or the *Big Issue*, and always on the back page;
- Volkswagen advertises on the backs of petrol pump handles ('Please assist any Volkswagen drivers who may be inexperienced with the oper-ation of these pumps');
- a Carling ad in *Maxim* happens to have the same shade of blue back-ground as that of the pin-up on the facing page, thus effectively claiming her as part of the ad;
- a poster emphasizing long legs in Pretty Polly tights is placed on hoard-ings rotated 90 degrees to make them vertical.

Critics are also quick to point out a stupid move (and the client is quick to change media buyers) when an airline company gets its commercial slotted into a break in a documentary about plane crashes. And in the context of pressure group calls for media boycotts (see Chapter 12), the media buying is suddenly seen as a key political act.

The assumptions behind such decisions can tell us about the nature of each medium, not just as a channel for a particular advertising message, but also as what Marshall McLuhan called (in the days before use of non-sexist pronouns) 'the extensions of man'. In the best campaigns, the various media are used in effective but unexpected ways, so they dramatize what the potential is for each medium. In doing so, they challenge our vague use of the plural 'media' to blame some monolithic socializing force that makes us do things, and make us think about each medium in its own terms, asking how the sounds broadcast on a radio, or the huge pictures placed on hoardings alongside roads, can possibly become part of our daily lives.

In this chapter, I will review the different characteristics of various media, and show some of these differences by analysing the kinds of changes that have been made as successful campaigns were transferred from one medium to another. Then I will look at the media mix a different way, by considering some of the choices made by advertisers for an industry that has been banned from one medium after another (tobacco), and by considering some of the choices of advertisers who are just beginning to explore media (universities). Then in the following chapters I will look more closely at posters, the first and most basic of media, at television, which is usually the medium people mean when they say 'the media', and at the World Wide Web, a new medium advertisers are scrambling to figure out.

In particular, I want to focus on the role of language in each of these media. There is a tendency, when we focus on images in posters and television, to forget just how central language remains, even when it is cut back to a phrase, as in the Levi's 'Creek' ad in Chapter 2. When I emphasize language, I am in a way reviving an old debate, one that goes back to the first years of the century, between copywriters who favour long copy and those who favour short copy. Long copy ads in magazines would give a whole page of detail on the product. Famous advertising practitioners like Claude Hopkins, David Ogilvy, and David Abbott built their careers on the ability to write pages of material that would grab attention and convey information without ever slipping from the informal and lively tone needed to get people to read something they don't want to read. Others, such as Rosser Reeves, have always insisted that the simple and relentlessly repeated message was dominant. The old debate has shifted ground, as it has become possible to reproduce complex images and sound in a variety of media, and as audiences have come to expect the kind of complexity we have seen in the Levi's or Peugeot 406 commercials. But words still play a key role in holding a strategy together, and defining a relation to consumers, as they do in the Co-operative Bank ads in Chapter 3 or the Norwich Union or GE ads in Chapter 4.

The five media

It might seem that any advertiser would want to reach the biggest possible audiences, and thus that advertisers' discussions of media would focus on the large numbers of the main broadcasting networks and mass-circulation magazines. But they are also interested in cost, so other choices may turn out to be more effective in terms of how much they have to spend for the time or space per thousand viewers or readers. And the discussions of media in the textbooks and advertising press show that they have much more subtle questions about the effectiveness of media:

- How sharply can the audience be targeted by region, socio-economic grouping, age, gender, or other demographic variables?
- Which media reach demographic sectors not reached by others?
- How exactly can the promised audience be measured?
- What are members of the audience doing when they get the message?
- How well is the message remembered?
- What modes of representation can be used, and what associations can be conveyed in these forms?

With these questions in mind, here is a summary of some of the strengths and weaknesses of media as carriers of advertising, to serve as a background for the comparisons that follow. (See MEDIUM for an explanation of why I have chosen just these categories.)

The chart does not begin to summarize the huge marketing literature on

	advantages	disadvantages
press	dailiness of newspapers targetable audience reaches hard-to-reach audiences readers may keep magazines	easily ignored limited formats
radio	link to daily activities (driving, housework, homework) economical repetition narrowly targeted audiences	low recall narrowly targeted audiences
television	broadest audience discussion and press attention range of sound, visual, story	can be ignored by viewers expensive now fragmented
cinema	captive audience high quality image and sound more adult content than TV mostly young audience	relatively small audience mostly young audience
outdoor	visual impact repeated exposure	no way of knowing who sees it seen briefly seen from a distance

media, but it does state the received wisdom on each medium. These are the strengths and weaknesses likely to be raised by the media owners themselves, in their competition with other outlets in their medium, or with other media. Magazines remind us how TV viewers duck out for tea during the breaks, while radio stations stress the importance of routine and segmentation, and poster companies devise a way of auditing the numbers of viewers of sites. These admittedly partial ads aimed at advertisers are worth studying, because media owners have a financial interest in researching and presenting these more subtle aspects of media. In addition to these specific strengths and weaknesses, all media have an on-going tension between availability and saturation. Advertisers want to be able to get the space and time of their own choosing, but when everyone has as much space or time as they want, the message is buried in the crowd, and all the ads are more likely to be ignored (see Chapter 7).

The 'media mix' is the proportion of advertising spent on each of these media, and on other forms of promotion such as direct mail. We have seen how the Co-operative Bank supported television ads with cinema, posters, and press ads. The television ads for Peugeot 406 would have been supported by local press ads for the dealers that stress prices and promotions. Norwich Union would put details of its policies in press ads and direct mail. A company that sells by post like the Franklin Mint may spend all its budget on press ads in Sunday supplements and other magazines that allow for colour ads and reply coupons. Supermarkets in the US rely largely on newspaper ads stressing special offers, where in the UK they have national television campaigns to build the brand. Benetton and Club 18–30 have been successful in putting almost all their advertising into posters, which then receive press coverage that greatly increases their impact. Some products may seem to be naturally suited to one medium, with albums on radio or movies on television or in trailers at the cinema, but the most memorable movie ads have always been posters, and pop and rock albums now rely on the video. And some major marketers may avoid all these media, relying on their own catalogues or posters or sales representatives. Most large campaigns are based on several media (see INTEGRATION). We may understand the differences between media better if we turn from these generalizations to see how several very successful campaigns were extended from one medium to another.

Press to television

One of the key examples of advertising effectiveness in the UK in recent years has been the rise of Häagen-Dazs (Baker 1993). (The example is in no way diminished by the fact that the agency, Bartle Bogle Hegarty, recently lost the account as the owner of the brand unified its European advertising.) Häagen-Dazs was introduced into the UK as a brand that would create a new market sector; it was deliberately priced at £1 more per pint than competitors, even more of a premium than in the US (for the origins of the brand in the US, see Visser (1989)). The UK brief was 'To position Häagen-Dazs as the new gold standard in the market by referring to the immense pleasure of the Häagen-Dazs experience' (Baker 1993). So the advertising had to define the brand as

- a premium product (like other products for which costliness equals luxury)
- for adults (ice-cream was seen as kids' novelty treats)
- associated with sensual pleasure (but the stuff is cold and messy!).

I have discussed the print campaign in Myers (1994). *Campaign* gives the view of the Art Director, Rooney Carruthers, in an article on origins of now classic campaigns. It is worth quoting his story at length, because it is relevant to the difficulty of converting this inspiration to television:

> The idea for the Häagen-Dazs press ads came straight out of the client manifesto document. John Hegarty [creative director of the agency] and Nick Kendall [the planner for this account] kept coming into our office and saying: 'It's about sex! This tub costs £3.00. It's an ABC1 product. People in research groups think it's about arousal, pleasure, fun. It's sex!' Larry picked up a document attached to the brief and read: 'Throughout the 60s and 70s, sales of Häagen-Dazs mounted steadily, relying purely on word of mouth.' I slapped down a photo of a couple kissing and drew in a tub of Häagen-Dazs. I blew up the words 'word' and 'mouth' out of the text. Sex became sensuality. Without the proposition, we would have concentrated on the ingredients which went into making the ice cream rather than on 'pleasure'.

(*Campaign* 20/9/96; for the reference to ABC1 see Chapter 10)

You can see why a linguist like me would like this story: the remarkably visual campaign started with a play on words (I would love to have heard the tone of voice in which the copywriter Larry Barker read these words out). Other executions were developed; in all of them the texts appeared on the left side of two-page spreads, while on the right there was a suggestive picture featuring a tub of ice-cream.

The advertisements were run entirely in print media, focusing on Sunday supplements in quality newspapers and on women's magazines. One reason for using print had to do with the expressive modes of the medium: the pun could be brought out in a witty way by putting words with double meanings in huge fonts. Another reason has to do with the interpretation of the images: the stylized, soft-focus bronze-tone photographs could suggest playful eroticism while moving images might seem closer to pornography. Two more reasons, having to do with the way the images are consumed, are given by the BBH case study:

We wanted to achieve a feel with this advertising that could itself be savoured and enjoyed at leisure, just like the product.

We believed the intimacy of the experience could be better illustrated through personal communication. Television is often a family or social medium. We wanted the communication to be private and not expose it to the comment and reaction of third parties.

(Barker 1993: 197)

The inappropriateness of this sort of ad to television was shown by a parody of the campaign done as an ad for Foster's lager: a couple are eating ice-cream in a sexually charged scene with jazzy music; when the man goes to the refrigerator for more ice-cream, he sees the Foster's lager, drinks it, and instantly turns off the music and turns on football on the TV, while the unsatisfied woman appears in the doorway and makes a comment about men. In the parody, the overcharged images of eroticism combined with ice-cream call for such a send-up (and the beer is associated with lads, not yuppie couples).

Three years later, though, the client Grand Metropolitan did ask for a television ad, perhaps because other super-premium brands had entered the market and it was time to bring attention back to Häagen-Dazs. The wider audience of television would already know about it from the earlier campaign and press coverage, and a wider distribution network meant that the advertising did not have to be so closely targeted as in the earlier days. There was great curiosity about how Bartle Bogle Hegarty would manage the adaptation to a new medium. What they did was shoot an ad in infrared, with the false colours associated with astronomical images, so that the warm bodies showed up in a whole spectrum of colours, while the ice-cream remained deep blue.

Häagen-Dazs (agency: Bartle Bogle Hegarty)

A couple are feeding each other ice-cream in a seductive manner, a spoonful of ice-cream sliding along the skin. On the sound-track, a woman's voice on a scratchy record does a night-club like rendition of 'make yourself comfortable'. Cut to downstairs, a man banging the ceiling with a broom handle, enraged at the presumably noisy antics upstairs. At the end, a thermometer appears at the bottom, with the temperature rising (explicating the colours), with the end-line: 'Dedicated to Pleasure'.

The TV ad continues the witty, erotic tone of the print campaign, while getting around some of the problems with the new medium:

- The oblique reference of the song allows for an indirect connection to sensuality.
- The visual style is distanced and aestheticized, but carries an indirect suggestion of erotic heat.

- The ad takes time to decode and interpret.
- It could be scheduled late at night, during programmes with an appropriate audience (I recorded it during Gus van Sant's *My Own Private Idaho*, a film that has scenes even more suggestive than ice cream eating).

The commercial was the only one made for television, but it established that the campaign could be adapted, if the copywriter and art director thought out the differences in the media.

Television with poster and press

My second example is not a switch in medium but a playful combination of them. Here is an ad from my favourite current campaign; I saw it first in a cinema:

Hiccups (agency: BMP DDB; written and art directed by Andrew Fraser, director Paul Gay for Outsider films)

Most of the ad is done in one stationary shot, done with natural light, and the background sound is strong, as in a fly on the wall video.

A woman is sitting at a kitchen table, reading the newspaper, turning the pages slowly. She has hiccups. As she turns the pages, we notice the sound of hiccups has stopped.

The camera zooms in to show she has stopped at an advertisement that says simply:

VW Polo.
[picture]
£7,990.

Two ads in the same campaign, by the same team, incorporate posters:

Chair

A crowded shopping precinct, seen first from a long shot in grainy video.

A woman suddenly collapses. Another woman helps her to a seat, stands over her, asks her if she needs help, remains and glances around for help. The woman who collapsed says that she will be all right, and the helper leaves her.

The stricken woman, still shaken, glances back over her shoulder at a poster:

VW Polo.
[picture]
£7,990.

Lamp post

Two workmen chat about the weekend as they put red and white striped padding around a lamppost. It is apparently a routine task that requires no thought as they finish this post and pack up to move on to another. Just at the end of the commercial, we see the purpose of the padding when a man walks along the pavement heading straight for the newly padded post, because his attention has been distracted by a poster saying simply:

Polo L,
only
£8145.

In the most recent execution, a grenadier guard at Buckingham Palace impassively puts up with mockery, tourists having their pictures taken, and even a dog pissing on his leg. But when the Polo price goes by on the side of a bus – his eyes move slightly. In all four ads, the surprise comes partly because they have been so well established, visually, in the style of a documentary. We are waiting for some action or comment appropriate to this genre (as, for instance, in the drink-driving ad discussed in Chapter 10). Instead the explanation of the scene is revealed to be the effect of a very simple advertisement within the advertisement.

Why do these apparently simple ads work so well? Car campaigns are often torn between two kinds of advertising: a glossy national television commercial promoting the brand values, and then local press ads for the dealers stressing price or promotions (see Rothenberg 1994). It is difficult to centre the television campaign on price without undercutting the branding, suggesting that the car is just cheap. The claim that people expect one's product to be expensive is a very old one, used by market traders and pedlars long before Volkswagen. But here the price claim is just quoted within the ad (I don't know if any such posters or press ads ever ran, outside these television and cinema commercials). The ads themselves focus on the responses, showing first, before we even see the product or price, that these people consider something enormously surprising. And the ads allow us to put these pieces together ourselves. Gerard Stamp from a rival agency, Leo Burnett, comments, 'Imagine how crass it would have become if an end-line spelt it out for you ("You too will be shocked by our prices")' (*Campaign* 7/11/97). For our purposes, what is interesting about the series is the way it presents the ads in the different media as having different purposes: the press and print ads within the ad tell us what the car costs, while the television ad suggests what kinds of physical response there might be to such a claim.

Television to press, poster, and radio

The examples so far focus on the difficulties and opportunities of relating a television commercial, with the sort of engagement it offers, to a print or poster campaign. Other adaptations have to be made in moving from a successful television campaign to a medium that doesn't have pictures or doesn't unroll in time. I have already looked at the famous TV ads for Levi's that evoke, with great photography and well-chosen music, images and stories of some mythic America. Bartle Bogle Hegarty (again) have tried various ways of conveying this combination of image and product claim in press and poster ads. In one series of press ads, the jeans are worn by older people, elegantly shot with the white background and straight-on framing of fashion photos or portraits. The press ads are like the TV ads in conveying a sense of visual style and wit, while demonstrating they look good, and conveying the product claim, that these jeans have a heritage.

The current series of Levi's posters has scenes that seem to be from *The Incredible Shrinking Man*: a tiny man clad only in jeans stands at the bottom of a huge bathtub using a pin to fight off a huge spider. The only text is 'Levi's shrink to fit'. So there is the product claim of the TV ads, and the demonstration of what they can look like. The sense of retro America is conveyed by the allusion to a 1950s film. An earlier series of posters didn't just shrink the jeans, it eliminated them entirely. Each execution used stylish photographs by the American photographer Bill Brandt, very simple and attention-getting when blown up to poster size, with the Levi's logo and a brief caption suggesting the link to the product. For instance, a close-up of two hands held with interlocking fingers went with the text: 'Zip Front'.

The photographs are marked as art by the unusual framing, the abstraction, and the use of black and white. More subtly, they are associated with a style of art photography dating back to the 1930s, like the abstractions of Edward Weston, so they maintain the sense of retro America. We don't see the product; the claim for it is that we can associate it with the classic style of the photography, while the metaphors stress the product range.

We should not be surprised that BBH can find appropriate adaptations for Levi's in print and posters, the traditional media for fashion ads. But how can it work on radio? One problem, of course, is that we can't see the jeans. A more subtle danger is that, paradoxically, radio might convey too much rather than too little. The TV ads are placed in a vague dream-like America evoked by pictures, styles, and music, not spoken words. An American voice is associated with a race and a time; it speaks too strongly of the various Americas of today, which is not what BBH wants to convey. And yet independent radio is the most likely medium to reach one of Levi's key audiences – style-conscious young people. I have only heard one Levi's radio ad, but it uses a strategy parallel to that of the Bill Brandt posters, leaving out the product entirely (see Myers 1994). An American voice, sounding like someone white, contemporary, and middle-aged, talks for the whole ad about his Leica camera, his loyalty to this old but authentic

(German) product, all in the style of recorded reminiscence. He acknowledges that there are newer models, but 'hey, this is part of me'. At the end,
a different, deeper, voice with an accent associated with African Americans
mentions Levi's, and we draw the parallel between these two classic
brands. It could be that such an extremely indirect approach only works
when the brand is strongly established in other media. For our purposes
what is important is that BBH seized on the brief – the one genuine jean –
and built the campaign in the new medium around that, leaving out everything else about the TV campaign.

Let us consider, then, what we learn about how we interpret media texts
from each of these adaptations:

- They confront people in different ways: Häagen-Dazs read privately in a
  magazine or publicly on TV; Volkswagen showing visible responses to
  private reading; the Levi's poster as something to point at and talk about.
- They embody stories in different ways: Volkswagen requires us to make
  story connections, while the Häagen-Dazs press ad or the Levi's poster
  imply a story, and the Levi's radio ad implies storytelling in the style of
  delivery.
- They establish different time frames for interpretation: the Häagen-Dazs
  press ad lingered over, the Häagen-Dazs TV ad building to a climax, the
  Levi's poster glimpsed from a bus, the Levi's TV ad with its turning
  point, the Volkswagen TV and cinema ads dramatizing people seeing
  posters.
- They each adapt to the medium by leaving something out: no luscious
  product shot in Häagen-Dazs, no voice-over in the TV commercials, no
  colour in the Levi's poster, no product in the Levi's radio spot or the
  Volkswagen commercials.

The key to each of these ads is a decision about features of the
medium to carry the message (the colour, the tone of voice, the story, the
typography), and a decision about what can be left to the audience to
construct.

Exile from advertising: tobacco ads

The tobacco industry, with its declining UK and US sales, ferocious brand
competition, huge ad spend, and tightening regulation, has constantly
explored the limits of media. If they were not regulated, one might expect
tobacco brands to use a media mix more or less like that or soft drinks or
beer, with an especially large spend on television because they are reaching
a large and youngish audience with a brand message based on colour and
packaging. The ban on broadcast advertising, and more complex restrictions in other media, have led them to explore alternatives. Now we are

likely to see a ban on all tobacco advertising, but with controversies over sponsorship of events, the story is not over yet.

Television

When tobacco companies could advertise on television, they did, and their ads were generally conventional and apparently not very memorable. One exception was the famous UK campaign for Strand cigarettes at the end of the 1950s, which had a James Dean like figure out on rainy dark streets, with the end-line 'You're never alone with a Strand'. It was much talked about, but apparently didn't help sales; one wonders if a media strategist now would have put it in magazines that could stylize the dolefulness and reach target audiences who might respond to the imagery. Another exception was a series of ads for Benson and Hedges 100s in the US in the late 1960s; they showed ingenious smokers adapting to the longer length of the cigarette, so in the first half various people would have their long cigarettes bent on windscreens or trapped in elevator doors, and in the second half we would see a man having his windscreen replaced with one that has a bubble-shaped extrusion to accommodate the cigarette end. Hamlet cigars in the UK had one of the best-loved series of ads. Each had the same pattern: a terribly frustrating 20-second situation would be followed by Bach's 'Air on the G string', with the character relaxing with a smoke. For instance, a bald man sits in a coin-operated photo booth, combing just a few strands of hair across his head, and finds himself with an absurd posture or expression for each flash. Finally, the stool collapses, and we see only the top of his head, and the smoke of the consoling cigar rising. In each of these cases, the advertisers turned to the same sort of story (and theme music) to set their brand apart from competitors.

Radio

Several years ago, cigar as well as cigarette ads were finally (and logically) banned from television. That drove Hamlet to experiment with radio ads having the same structure as the television ads. This is trickier than it seems, because the ad had to suggest the same sort of excessive problem, against which the cigar was proposed as a temporary remedy. And of course one couldn't see the person smoking the cigar for the punch-line (what does cigar smoking *sound* like?). But it is a tribute to 20 years of popular advertising that by now, just the Bach tune was enough to suggest the act of smoking a cigar. Here is one example of a radio version:

HAMLET (Agency: The CDP Media Company; writers: Nick Welch and Billy Mawhinney; voices: Stephen Fry and Hugh Laurie)

	horse neighing
Voice 1: OK loves, we're ready for the big scene now. Has everyone got their blood bags?	
Voice 2: [shouting] Blood bags everybody.	
1: Now I want all the Babylonians off the ziggurat double quick so that when it collapses we get a good view right?	
2: [far off] Got that Paps?	
1: That man up there is wearing a wrist watch. Come on, come on.	
All right. Now. Cue the dinosaur.	roar
Ready with the bouncing heads . . .	
and action . . .	sirens
and cue the earthquake . . .	crashing, fires crackling
lower – the mother ship . . .	honking
and CUT. Ohhh, marvellous! marvellous! How was that for you camera?	whoosh of air deflating
Voice 3: Ready when you are Sir Lionel.	
	match striking
	Air on the G String
Announcer: Happiness is a cigar called Hamlet.	

This is the same sort of joke as the television and cinema ads, with a long and puzzling build-up, collapsing into frustration just before the end. As the TV ad worked by using just the camera, this works by using just sound, to suggest a *Close Encounters with the Jurassic Ark* kind of Spielberg epic. But the joke would have been lost in a television ad, where no amount of special effects and extras could quite match the absurd overkill suggested here in a few lines.

Posters and press

We will see in Chapter 6 that, after the UK ban on television advertising in 1966, tobacco companies like Gallaher, Imperial, and BAT transformed poster and press advertising. They showed, more convincingly than any lecture on semiotics, that the core task of advertising was to keep the brand in mind, by associating colour, name, and image. While tobacco ads in other countries still have the clichés of young couples or frolicking in streams with cigarettes or macho men on horses, rafts, or cliffs, the tightly restricted UK posters explored minimalism. Their experiments may have prompted other advertisers, not constrained by the same regulations, to realize the virtues of minimalism in suggesting metaphorical associations.

Sponsorship

Under recent European Union agreements, it is likely that tobacco advertising will finally be banned completely, and similar regulations are likely in the US. It will be interesting to see what the tobacco companies do. But we have already seen their preparatory moves. One strategy is based on the sponsorship of sporting events, such as the Benson and Hedges Cup or Embassy World Snooker. That is why the sponsorship of Formula One racing by brands like Marlboro has been such a political issue in the UK; it has been suggested that tobacco companies are willing to pay far more than alternative sponsors because for them it is one of the few outlets left. The effectiveness of such sponsorship of events, whether by tobacco companies or other marketers, is hotly debated. On the one hand, the product name gets it mentioned hundreds of times, perhaps on the helmet of the driver, to a likely target audience, while that audience is excited and involved. On the other hand, the benefits may decline over the years; one ad executive says that, by now, people may just think that the snooker championship is called Embassy because of the venue, not the cigarette. And identification with an event leaves one open to a kind of gazumping. The Coca-Cola Company was one of the sponsors of the Euro 96 football championship, and Nike was not, but Nike got itself considerable coverage by running its ads with the event. And of course the ban on cigarette advertising could eventually and logically be extended to cover sponsorship of sporting events. One response suggested is that BAT (British American Tobacco), might buy a Formula One team outright, so it would be in the same situation as Honda or Benetton, and it would then have its name mentioned constantly as an owner rather than as a sponsor.

Tobacco companies have also been engaged in a kind of lateral thinking, setting up other, non-tobacco brands. Recently I saw some shoes I liked in the window of a stylish men's shop, but realized they were Camel shoes. They looked good, though perhaps a bit towards the kind of rugged masculinity that befits the models in Camel ads better than me. The current thinking is that Camel can advertise these shoes even after a ban on tobacco advertising. Similarly there are all sorts of Marlboro products that not only perpetuate the brand, but allow it to be advertised. One tobacco company has experimented with extending the brand to a chain of coffee-houses in

Indonesia. You can probably think of some appropriate products to enable tobacco companies to get around the ban. After all, these cash rich companies have to sell something; who is going to forbid them to use their greatest assets, their brand names, in new market sectors? One advertiser suggested the simplest solution would be to allow tobacco advertising, but to package all the cigarettes in plain black and white boxes with the same style of lettering. The colour and lettering are now the one link between the ads and the purchase; without the clearly visible branding, he argued, there would be no point in advertising.

Journey into advertising

Having considered the media choices of a category of advertiser driven out of one medium after another, let us now think about the choices of institutions who are just gradually beginning to think about advertising media: the universities. Traditionally British universities did not advertise, but when the former polytechnics were given university status, they began advertising to attract students in a newly competitive market. They also increased dramatically the number of university places open to students. And they made students' choice much more difficult, for there were now many different kinds of institutions and degrees, all presented on the same form in the same admissions system. It shocks many traditionalists that universities should advertise, at least in the UK: admissions officers are supposed to select, not to promote. After all, universities are not just a consumer service; they also involve the production and transmission of knowledge, and some kinds of marking, grading, and gate-keeping that are not consistent with treating students as consumers.

Universities do have to market themselves somehow, to at least three kinds of audiences: prospective students, prospective users of the research, and prospective donors. But they may not be able to use all the traditional advertising media. There may be some problems in being associated with commercial products, being seen to be desperate for students. And though some universities have tried using television commercials, this seems an oddly broad media choice when the targets are so specific. The target may be people graduating from high school, who are interested only in specific courses, or industrial research and development directors, who are interested only in the most specific technologies, or people with a million pounds or so to give away, who are unlikely to give it on the basis of a television commercial, however slick. These groups, and particularly the last, probably make up a fairly small percentage of the audience for *Coronation Street* or any other popular TV programme. Whatever the solution is, it has to allow for very different kinds of interaction with each person contacted. Universities have tried several different media.

Prospectus

The traditional means of publicizing a university, in the UK and in the US, is the catalogue or prospectus. These are traditionally rather dull documents listing regulations and courses available. But in the last 10 years, in both countries, they have changes their form of address. Norman Fairclough (1994) has compared old and new entries in the Lancaster University prospectus, and shown how the address changes form one of giving requirements, to one of offering choices. The address is now direct to *you*, and with this comes a sense that the student is a sort of customer. The prospectus has also changed in appearance. Twenty years ago it was a plain and formal looking list of requirements; now it has pictures on every page, most of them of students, and has graphic devices such as arrows and coloured boxes organizing the reader's path across the page.

Direct mail

Graduating high school seniors in the US hardly need to be told that their names are worth something on the address lists for mail shots; they get floods of junk mail from universities even if they are not 7-foot-tall National Merit Scholars. Similar mailing services are offered in the UK, but the mailings have not reached the same level of sophistication (as I can testify, having written some dud letters myself). In purely marketing terms, direct mail would seem to be the logical channel, because one can target all and only those people just finishing secondary school, one can include detailed information, and one can tailor the message to what one knows about the candidate and his or her school. But we all know that there are dangers to getting direct mail wrong; the ad that has you wrong may be ignored, but the personalized letter that makes the wrong assumptions about your gender, age, marital status, or interests is offensive. And when this medium is more fully used, in a country with more than 100 universities, the channel will quickly be saturated.

Posters

Graduate programmes have often had recruiting posters; recently these have been seen more often for undergraduate programmes. They depend for their distribution on a model of how secondary school placement offices work. The hope is that, if they are striking enough, they may be put up on bulletin boards in school careers offices. There is still a tendency to try to cram in lots of information; I have yet to see a university use a poster for a simple message with a few words and a picture the way an advertiser would (see

Chapter 6). The only unit at my university that has really had a rethink for this genre is the Management School; their poster is based on quotations from former students. They have made an effort to shift the form of address; the poster is full of questions and answers, and has the busy, colourful layout favoured by the magazines read by teenagers.

Events

The other traditional medium for UK university promotion is the Open Day, parallel in some ways to the trade fairs and exhibitions that are an important below-the-line expenditure for some products. The Open Day is a curiously ambiguous event, between showing off the university and campus to successful applicants, and interviewing and selecting among others. This channel reminds us of the importance of face-to-face, immediate contact (Boden and Molotch 1992). It is crucial, as much for parents as for students, that they see the people involved with the degree, not just the place but us talking. Similarly, I am told that students are more persuaded by their brief hour with a student giving a tour than by my one-to-many talk. This can serve as another reminder, in a time of mediated communication, of the importance of what Erving Goffman (1963) calls 'co-presence', even in such an artificial and brief event as this.

Videos

For a long time, the main promotional material for Lancaster University was a video, 'Welcome to Lancaster'. It is rather like a video version of the prospectus, with huge lists of courses scrolling down the page, and the admissions director talking straight to camera in a way most advertisers abandoned decades ago. It does try to show sunny days and leisure activities, but it is clearly not intended to use the medium fully. The most recent video for the programme on which I teach has more of the devices we saw in the Co-operative Bank ad; it consists entirely of people talking in interview, with a variety of distancing devices, such as shifts to black and white or degraded images seen on a monitor. It may work well or may not, but it clearly shows that universities, as well as banks, must deal with the scepticism of their target audience; one way of doing this, as we have seen, is to break up the presenter.

World Wide Web

It is probably inevitable that universities would be among the first advertisers to use this new medium, since the Web was developed for research exchanges and many academics already have their own home pages and favourite sites. Though it doesn't reach many Britons yet, it is available to many secondary schools, which is where they find many of their potential applicants. But the medium is now used in universities primarily as an aid to teaching: as a sort of bulletin board, work-book, file cabinet, photo-copier, or lecture hall (chapters of this book had an earlier life on the Web). This experience has not prepared admissions tutors (who are members of departments, not full-time recruiters) for the tasks of making web pages attractive so that people seek them out, and making them coherent so that people can move within them. One department at my university has tried to make its pages more attractive by including some bits on the Web that might be useful to teachers. Others have begun the process of channelling out information useful to current students, prospective students, alumni, or people in the community. A clever surfer, looking at all the course materials and administrative documents, could find out all sorts of information about the university, besides what it wants to present. In some ways, these issues apply as well to the commer-cial advertisers I will discuss in Chapter 8.

Conclusion

The different problems of tobacco companies and universities bring out some of the media issues that will be discussed in the following chapters. Here are some themes of these chapters:

Different media convey different information

It may seem obvious to stress that television has movement, posters are seen at a distance, press ads have pictures and text, and radio has sound without pictures. But the ads we have seen have used these simple facts in ingenious ways; none of the best ad campaigns could be transferred to another medium without considerable adaptation.

Different media go with different practices

Media are different, not only in their information content, but in the ways they are consumed. Posters depend on place, TV ads on time, and press ads on where and when they are read. Radio calls for a different kind of involvement, often with other activities such as driving or cooking.

Spoken and written words can limit, link, and extend images

The suggestive puns in the Häagen-Dazs ads both tell us how to interpret the pictures, and make us read them in terms of ice-cream. The lack of words in the Volkswagen ads leave us to go back over the actions we have seen and arrive at an interpretation. Even the warnings in the tobacco ads are used by advertisers; some of the ads wouldn't make sense without them.

Words (including typography) define voice and audience

One of the key functions of the words in these ads is not to convey information, but to set up a sense of relationship. Certainly that is the function of an Open Day, or a prospectus. But it is also a function of the few words at the end of the Hamlet radio ad, or the American voice in the Levi's radio spot, or the typography of the Häagen-Dazs print ads; they suggest the tone and stance of the advertiser and a possible relation to the audience, intimate recollection or elegant irony.

These issues in text interpretation are meant to open up some of the complexities of media choices. Much of the study of media strategies has to do with the audiences reached by each medium: ABC1s, or 18–24 women, or university graduates, or other demographic criteria. For our purposes, we need to think also of how media address audiences, and about how each medium fits in with what people do in their daily lives.

Suggested readings: media

Most books on media are about broadcasting; for references see Chapter 7. More general introductions to media can be found in Lull (1995), and in collections edited by Crowley and Mitchell (1994) and Curran and Gurevitch (1996). Williams (1998) is a usefully broad historical review for Britain. The classic and controversial work of McLuhan (1964) is now having a revival of interest; for a broad overview that puts his work on medium theory in context, see Meyrowitz (1994). Brierley (1995) and Bogart (1990) have overviews of media in advertising. Zenith Media, one of the largest UK media agencies, has an excellent web page with links to hundreds of UK and US media owners, periodicals, and agencies: www.zenithmedia.com. It makes a good starting point for surfing on this topic.

Mills & Boon

|6|

Posters and space

A poster for Mills & Boon® romantic novels recently appeared on the insides of bus shelters. It shows the inside of a bus shelter, almost as if in a mirror, but in black and white. Three people sit bored on the bench, looking into space. In front of them, in colour, a woman stretches out unconcerned in a bubble bath, engrossed in a book. On the back wall of the bus shelter, a poster within the poster says,

Mills & Boon
Makes
any time
special.

('Makes any time special'™ is a trademark)

The poster takes the very place one is standing, waiting for the bus, as its sign of the coldness and boredom and ordinariness of waiting for the bus. The reader inside the poster has been doubly transported, into her book and into the warm comfortable bath it brings. The poster exemplifies the main point of this chapter: when we study outdoor advertising, we study how people interact with visual and textual messages in public space.

Trevor Beattie (best known to the public for the Wonderbra posters mentioned in Chapter 4) may have a vested interest in promoting the creative demands of posters over those of television commercials, but he is also right in tracing the impact of posters to an almost personal encounter on the street.

Posters are about one thing: the idea. I've seen people argue for hours over the merits of a 'beautifully shot', 'fabulously edited', idea-lacking television commercial. Can't happen with posters. With a poster you're naked. There's just you. Stood standing on a street corner with your idea hanging out. Better make it a whopper. The world is watching. And just think ... no excuses, no re-released pop music track to hide behind, no trendy director with an unpronounceable name, not even part two of *Coronation Street* to come to your rescue.

(Trevor Beattie, *Campaign*, 31/10/97, p. 43)

The messages of posters are often simple, but they become complicated when we consider 'the idea' – how people encounter them and what they make of them.

For the purposes of this chapter, I will limit the definition of 'posters' to two-dimensional images posted or pasted for a limited period of time, in outdoor or transit settings (see POSTER for terminology). To define them this way excludes shop signs, window displays, permanent signs, and bulletin boards, but focuses attention on the kind of display most important to advertising agencies. Posters are the oldest form of advertising, and they are in some ways the purest – the statement of what one has to sell, put up on a wall. Unlike all other ad media, they aren't parasitic on some entertainment or information function; we watch commercials because we want to watch the programmes, and we look at press ads between the editorial content, but we see posters because they are there. They were the object of the first attacks on advertising (Richards 1990), and they are still much hated, in principle. But they have also been much loved; if you want a movie, play, or television show to evoke a period now, the quickest way is to use, not its high art, but its disposable posters and packaging – Oxo or Cadbury's or 'Coke' or Brylcreem (e.g. Opie 1985).

Posters make up a small part of the total expenditure on ads (under 5 per cent in both the US and the UK) but they have more cultural impact than this would suggest. The Mills & Boon poster suggests that this impact has to do with the ways we encounter posters in space. For another example, I could start with some very simple, non-commercial messages. As one drives into the centre of Lancaster from the south there is a roundabout (a traffic circle) through which almost all traffic must pass. On one of the four sides is a waist-high railing to separate the traffic from the walkway. On this railing, one often sees, first thing in the morning, that banners have appeared, saying something like:

CONGRATULATIONS
MR & MRS MILLS
FROM ALL AT THE
HANGING BASKET

or

KAREN + STEPHEN
CONGRATULATIONS
ON YOUR
ENGAGEMENT

For a picture, and a discussion of these banners in the context of literacy practices, see Barton and Hamilton (1998: 40).

In some ways this is very simple advertising – paint splashed or cloth letters sewn onto sheets, no pictures, no clever slogans. But the banners are doing what other posters have always done, and still do. Let us think of them in terms of spaces:

- *The layout of the rectangular space of the banner* – As with posters, the size and shape of the space for banners on the roundabout is usually a given: it is limited by the size of bedsheets, the most easily available large plain cloth. As with posters, part of the effect arises from the scale of the message, so much bigger than a birthday card. Banners use the space of a white sheet, filling it with large blocky letters. What they have in common with the most sophisticated ads is that they are using the minimum possible means for their effect.

- *The locality in the town* – These banners don't appear just anywhere, but always here, at what could be taken as the entry into the town. Yet it is also a kind of neutral public place, belonging to no person or institution: the banners aren't hung from the Town Hall or the Priory Church or the Castle. Similarly, commercial posters only occur at particular places in the town, as I will discuss later.

- *The movements of the viewer* – Of course the main reason the banners appear at the roundabout, and not somewhere else, is that a large part of the population of the town passes by them in the morning. But unless the traffic is totally stalled (as it is at rush hour), drivers should be going by rather quickly, and paying attention to other cars rather than personal messages (I find roundabouts tricky even without reading matter to peruse). Most commercial posters don't pose such a threat to driving (the legal sites are regulated to avoid that), but all must find some way to catch the attention of people passing by in the course of their other routines. Though the roundabout messages stay up only for a day, commercial posters are usually at sites people will pass repeatedly and regularly.

- *The public and the private* – Why not write these messages on a card and tuck them under the recipient's door? The same words could be used; but part of the message at the roundabout is that the (usually anonymous) poster-makers want to tell the whole town about this otherwise private event. They are doing the equivalent of announcing it on the radio, or buying a newspaper ad, or having loudspeakers blare it through the streets, or having a plane write it across the sky: the visual equivalent of a shout, as Bernstein (1997) points out. We will see that this boundary between public and private space is an important part of the way people respond to, and complain about, posters (see PUBLIC).

In thinking about commercial posters, it helps to start with non-commercial messages: the preacher shouting in the market place, the messages scrawled in chalk on the pavement or painted on motorway bridges, the banner announcing the church Christmas fête, the floodlit American flag, the Greenpeace denunciation unfurled from the top of an oil rig. Even the non-professional makers of these messages are acutely aware of textual, local, circulatory, and public spaces.

Changing spaces

Posters go back for centuries; Raymond Williams (1961) notes that it is a cliché to begin one's history of advertising with Egyptian announcements of escaped slaves. But the big change came in the nineteenth century with the development of branded commodities. After all, there is no point spending money to say 'buy soap' if hundreds of people make soap, each locally. But if you make Ivory or Pears brand soap, then you need to keep reminding people of the brand name. Any picture of a nineteenth-century street scene is likely to include lots of posters in the background, most of them for patent medicines, packaged foods, entertainments, or newspapers.

These ads were in general quite dull. They just named the product, and maybe showed it, repeatedly, on every visible surface. With new brands being introduced every day, especially in medicines, the only way to get more effective advertising was to put up more and bigger posters.

This is where the first criticisms of advertising arose – not so much from the newspaper ads, but from the intrusiveness of outdoor advertising. For some, the low-point – or high point – of this craze came with the attempt to paint a Pear's soap ad on the White Cliffs of Dover (Niagara Falls was the scene of similar attempts in the US). You may laugh at such disregard for natural scenery. But think of the huge sign saying HOLLYWOOD, high in the hills over Los Angeles, that is often used as the symbol of the city. It was originally built as an advertisement for HOLLYWOODLAND, a big property development. The developers went bust, and the last four letters fell down, but the sign remained, and with age, it has come to be seen as a symbol, not an eyesore. Similarly, the puffing Camel billboard in the Times Square of the 1950s became part of the cityscape.

One way out of the clutter was to go for simple pictorial images that would stand out from the rest. This is the idea behind many of the posters of the first half of this century – Guinness with its pictorial jokes on strength, Bovril with its metaphors for heartiness, Persil with its expanses of flat colour (Bernstein 1997). A typical railway poster for Morecambe, a resort on the Lancashire coast, has three parts, a picture of a small boy batting at cricket on the beach, the slogan 'It'll knock your stumps off', and the name of the place and railway. 'Coke' has a series of posters from the 1940s by Eric Sondblum with women being offered a bottle by the hand of an unseen man, and the single word, 'Yes'. In this period, outdoor ads were distinguishing themselves more and more from press ads. In the press, one could have lots of copy. But in posters, one could have powerful colour effects, simple, bold, and large compositions; that is why they have lasted better as aesthetic objects and items of decor.

We can see the enormous cultural importance of posters in this period by the way they turn up in literature, art, and memoirs. A billboard for an optician looms over the waste land in Scott Fitzgerald's *The Great Gatsby*, the hapless garage mechanic believing it to be the eyes of God. Michael Foreman's memoir *After the War Was Over* fondly repaints his boyhood street with the Brylcreem poster staring across at the upper-class golfer in the Swan Vesta poster. Billboards figure in many paintings of urban scenes from the 1920s, and influenced the style of such Dada-related paintings as those of Gerald Murphy, as well as Pop Art in the 1960s. The movie *Footlight Parade* (1933) has the James Cagney character stopping to paint out his own name as a producer on a billboard; the Fred Astaire movie *You'll Never Get Rich* (1941) opens with titles in the form of billboards, and *On the Town* (1949) is built around the pursuit of a girl known only from a subway poster. From a fairly early date one even sees posters in posters, so the Cadbury Twins play on the seashore in front of a poster of the Cadbury Twins.

The simpler and more carefully sited posters did not just result from a development in taste after the Victorians. There was also a change in the marketplace, as more and more brands were introduced so that the walls were not dominated by patent medicines and toiletries. And there was a change in the media mix, as magazines developed the technology to use pictures and colour, and radio (in the US) became a mass medium, leaving posters for visual branding in public space. Most important, perhaps, living patterns changed, as people moved to the suburbs and began to use public transport and cars to commute to work instead of walking. They then began to travel much further, but along certain well-defined lines of daily routine. So instead of putting posters everywhere you could reach, it made sense to compete for a few well-placed sites, such as at train stations or road junctions.

In the US, dominated by cars, the billboards came to be associated largely with the main highways out of town. A particular form evolved in the long empty straight roads of the West. They were before my time, but here is a remembered example (imagine each phrase on a little sign by the road, spaced maybe 200 yards apart):

DOES YOUR HUSBAND
MISBEHAVE
GRUNT AND GROAN
RANT AND RAVE
SHOOT THE BRUTE
SOME BURMA SHAVE (Bernstein 1997: 103)

Burma Shave jingles drummed themselves into the American consciousness – one hopes they did not have any direct influence on American poetry.

After World War II, posters dwindled in importance in the advertising mix. This was partly due to new media like television, partly due to more careful town planning and regulation. Those that remain are restricted to certain sites, and are heavily regulated. They retain their main function as teasers and reminders: for instance, Bartle Bogle Hegarty used posters for Boddington's to prepare the ground for their famous TV commercials (see Myers 1994), while other advertisers, such as Toyota, use posters to refer back to a TV campaign. (A girl seems to have climbed up on the poster and used a red marker to change 'The new Toyota Picnic easily seats two adults and four children' to 'The new Toyota Picnic *only* seats two adults and *one child*'. I'm told this makes sense if one has seen the story in the commercial.) Some of the largest users of posters have been products that are restricted in their use of other media, such as tobacco, spirits, and the pools in the UK. (I note though that tobacco ads no longer figure in the top ten brands using outdoor ads.)

Now, though, posters may have a new role, in reaching broad audiences as other media fragment. People no longer watch just three or four television networks, or read the same mass-circulation magazines. A poster campaign still offers the chance to reach a range of people, not just those watching football on Sky or reading teen magazines or listening to golden oldies radio. The UK outdoor advertising giant Maiden quotes the agency head John Hegarty saying outdoor is 'the last remaining mass medium'. But to reach this mass audience effectively, advertisers have to adapt their messages to the constraints of the medium, or use these contraints to their own ends.

Rules

Posters tempt advertising practitioners into pronouncing general and definitive rules, the way they would never do for television commercials or press ads. Perhaps this is because posters are apparently so simple and so similar: one large rectangular space to fill with a message. Or it may be because, as Trevor Beattie says in the quotation at the beginning of the chapter, the failure of a poster is obvious to anyone, as passers-by misinterpret it, or fail to connect it to the brand, or fail to notice it at all. The rules of thumb for posters given by different advertising practitioners are generally similar, which may indicate that they are on the right track. I will give two sets to stand for all the others. David Ogilvy, the great copywriter and agency chief of the 1960s, lays down five commandments in his characteristically definite tone:

- Your poster should deliver your selling promise not only in words, but also pictorially.
- Use the largest possible type.
- Make your brand name visible at a long distance.
- Use strong, pure colours.

- Never use more than three elements in your design.
- If you know more than that, please tell me. (Ogilvy 1983; bullets added)

David Bernstein, author of the best book on posters, discusses his rules under eight headings:

- Simplicity
- One dominant message
- Boldness
- Clear, legible type
- Few words (six or seven)
- Big enough type
- Contrasting colours (preferably primary)
- Brand – 'The whole design belongs to the brand' (Bernstein 1997; edited and bullets added).

These rule-makers have nothing to say about the other senses of space I have listed, the spaces of circulation and of public and private, though of course they were aware of these issues. They focus on the spaces of the texts themselves; stressing simplicity of design, legibility of text, and boldness of colour, factors related to the scale and distance of the poster. And indeed, these rules apply to almost all the classic posters included in histories, and most of the posters that win awards. But as we will see in the next section, they are not followed by the majority of roadside posters; to see why we will have to consider specific examples.

But these rules provide only a negative formulation, a check-list of mistakes made by novices and even experienced designers. For a more positive view of the constraints on posters, David Bernstein quotes the classic poster designer Hans Schlager as saying 'limitation produces form' (1997: 101). Bernstein follows this with an aesthetic for poster artists (unfortunately using the masculine pronoun):

Deny the poster artist movement then he has to convey it.
Deny him time and he has to expand it.
Deny him words then the words he chooses not merely have to work harder, they have to grow.
Provide a peculiar or restricted format and he will exploit it.

Of course poster artists are aware of these limitations only by comparison to competing media. But it is probably true that the pleasure we take in posters arises, not just from their simplicity, but from their triumph over the limitations imposed by a 10 foot by 20 foot rectangle on the side of a road.

Posters in Lancaster

Perhaps the best way to see whether these rules work is to imagine you had a roll of film with 36 shots and you had to fill it with pictures of posters in the next hour. Where would you go – walking out to the nearest campus bulletin board, on a drive along the main trunk road (not the interstate or motorway) into town, or to the nearest train station or airport? What I did was drive around Lancaster on a rainy Sunday afternoon. And in travelling around to get to (nearly) every advertising hoarding in town, I began to think about how they are placed, much more clearly than I had in looking at historical examples, or those that win prizes or attract complaints. I will list all the posters I saw, and then use them and other examples to explore some of the conceptions of space that I raised with the roundabout banners.

Since I will be considering their placement, I have arranged the posters geographically from the centre of town to the train and bus stations, and then out along the main roads to the next town and to the university campus.

POSTERS IN LANCASTER

brand	text	pictures/colour	size/location
1. Morrison's Superstore	Open every Sunday. Straight on for value, choice and low prices. Central Drive, Morecambe. Next to Frontier Land 'More reasons to shop at Morrisons'	logo/man arrow white on red, black on yellow	48-sheet on main road in town centre
2. Pretty Polly	If you're not wearing legworks, there'll be a bus along soon Nobody pays more attention to your legs	colour package of tights logo text: white on black	6-sheet bus shelter
3. Royal Mail	This Valentine's Day post your love	Peter Rabbit stamp and kiss mark on heavy stationery text: black on off-white	6-sheet bus shelter
4. Virgin	The Love Album Three simple words... yes! yes!! YES!!!	text: yellow on black	6-sheet bus shelter
5. Rolo Caramel Egg	There's no turning back	woman with caramel strand in mouth and eyes crossed to look at it text: red on yellow (like wrapping of the chocolates)	6-sheet bus shelter
6. Rolo Caramel Egg	Now you're in trouble	woman with caramel strand in mouth and eyes looking down at it	6-sheet bus shelter

7. Lemsip	Someone in Iceland drinking a Lemsip Flu Strength.	blue globe with Iceland glowing yellow and red text white on black	6-sheet bus shelter
8. Shallow Grave	'the first unmissable film of the year has arrived' ***** Empire What's a little murder between friends? [credits] At a cinema near you	shovel in spotlight text: white and red on black	6-sheet bus shelter
9. Whiskas cat food	Fine cuts, fine jelly, fine taste Cats would buy Whiskas	tin of cat food text: white on lavender (like the tin)	4-sheet bus station
10. Our Price records	Eight reasons to be happy grab our book of eight vouchers and get £5 off when you spend £20 or more at 5 Cheapside Lancaster	8 happy faces text: black on purple	4-sheet bus station
11. Harvey's	Sherry with a most distinctive character the best sherry in the world	bottle text: white on blue	4-sheet bus station
12. British Diabetic Association	Always going to the loo, always thirsty, always tired? [much more text]	cupid pissing text: black on white	4-sheet train station
13. Young Person's Railcard	Due to public demand, we've increased the age of consent to 25	b/w couple petting at cafe table text: red on blue	4-sheet train station
14. Intercity	Cross-country travel is now within your reach Driving down prices across the country	hands forming Union Jack text: black on white	4-sheet train station
15. Littlewoods Pools	Forest ... 1 Wanderers ... 1 A bigger draw than ever	couple on elephant text: white on green	48-sheet by carpark
16. King Edward cigars	For king and country. And pub. And car. And garden. And walkies. And armchair. And [health warning]	hand holding pack with NEW text: black on white	48-sheet on main road

17. Granada	Updatable How switched on can you get?	one letter in each television screen, white on blue	48-sheet on main road
18. Rothman's Royals cigarettes	Want something extra? 5 extra for 18p. [health warning]	man combing one strand of hair on a bald head text: black on white and white on black	48-sheet by carpark
19. Rothman's Royals cigarettes	Want something extra? 5 extra for 18p. [health warning]	man in rowboat escaping huge shark fin text: black on white and white on black	48-sheet by carpark
20. Rothman's Royals cigarettes	Want something extra? 5 extra for 18p. [health warning]	traffic warden with clamp faces huge tyre text: black on white and white on black	48-sheet at train station
21. Independent Financial Advisers	With a better financial choice, you can save for the future. Not for the taxman. [more very small print]	b/w woman with logo projected onto her text: small black script on white	48-sheet by train station carpark
22. Royal Mail	[handwritten] Dear Gran, Those piano lessons finally paid off. Airmail makes a world of difference	b/w heavy metal rocker with CD background: light blue and red and blue border of an airmail envelope	48-sheet on main road
23. Royal Mail	[handwritten] Dear Bert, At last! Airmail makes a world of difference	b/w old man in cap and gown with diploma background: light blue and red and blue border of an airmail envelope	48-sheet on main road
24. British Telecom	Five minutes sizzling conversation hardly costs a sausage. It's good to talk.	sausage on a fork text: white on black	48-sheet on main road
25. Foster's lager	Which jumbo will you be on? [much small print]	jets over globe with map of Australia text: yellow on blue	48-sheet by carpark
26. Alfa Romeo	Alfa 145. Surprisingly Alfa Romeo.	blue car text: white on black	48-sheet by carpark
27. Alfa Romeo	Alfa 145. Surprisingly Alfa Romeo.	red car text: white on black	48-sheet by carpark
28. Cancer Research Campaign	Do more for your breasts than any bra can. Examine them. Breast cancer information 0171 224 1333.	text: black on blue; phone number white on blue	48-sheet by main road

29. Royal Insurance	[in cartoon bubble] You'd better ring the Royal. 0800 123 684 One day you'll be glad you belong.	Dog in row of Alsatians, to a cat text: black on white; phone blue on black	48-sheet by main road
30. Hyundai	The Hyundai Accent. When you want everything. The new Accent. From £12,599.	car text: red on white	48-sheet by main road
31. Rover	This Rover 600 is the most powerful and economical car in its class. (By the way, it's a diesel.)	car text: black on white	48-sheet by main road
32. Channel 4	He's a teacher at the school of hard knocks. Hearts and Minds. A new drama from the writer of Cracker. Thursdays 10 p.m.	man with bruised face text: blue on yellow	96-sheet by main road
33. Marie Curie	Marie Curie scientists are only half the story graffiti: *The other half is vivisection* 5000 nurses, 50 scientists, 1 cancer charity	half a man's face text: purple on yellow and yellow on purple black graffiti	48-sheet by main road
34. Folkin Eejits	time and place of performance	black on white	A4 paper taped to pillar on campus
35. Protest poster	Marco's Means Fresh Killed Veal Demo Sat 4th from 7:30 p.m. outside Marco's Restaurant	photo of cows black on white	A4 paper taped to wall on campus

Text and layout

Even with this rather schematic list of the contents of the posters, you can see that some of them follow the rules laid down by Ogilvy and Bernstein, and some don't. So, for instance, in terms of simplicity, most do keep to three elements (e.g. Rolo (5, 6) and Royal Mail (22, 23)), but several are very busy. Morrison's (1) has an arrow, a logo turned into a man, directions, a sales pitch, an address, a location, a banner at the top, and a slogan at the bottom. Traffic on the one-way system will have to be very slow for even the most dedicated searcher for supermarkets to take all that in.

Foster's crowds in aircraft, a globe and map, dates, and other details. Does anyone walk across the carpark to read all this? Presumably in these cases, the client wanted more and more information crammed in, so that the result was finally more like a press ad than a poster.

About half the posters are dominated by a single image, whether a picture of the product (the car in Rover or Alfa Romeo), or a more indirect message (the sausage for British Telecom). There is one interesting exception, in which the Cancer Research Campaign uses only text, with no upper-case letters, and different sizes of the same font to bring out emphasis; in this it contrasts in particular with the well-known exhibitionistic ads for Wonderbra and Triumph bras.

As one would expect, most use clear and legible type, including those for King Edward Cigars (16) and British Telecom (24) in which the text fills most of the rectangle. What is surprising is that some choose type faces or colour combinations that make them very difficult to read; for instance the Independent Financial Advisers choose a script, perhaps because it seems to have the right associations of elegance, that is very difficult even close-up.

A glance over the use of colour contrast raises two points: (1) the advertisers prefer white on black (or other dark colour) to black on white, and (2) despite all the advice on these matters, advertisers often choose difficult contrasts, as with the white on light purple for Whiskas, or red on purple for Young Person's Railcard. In these cases, they are constrained by the colours used on the packaging, or in the rest of the campaign. (See Bernstein 1997: 74–5 for a neat demonstration of legibility.)

In general, then, the posters follow the rules formulated by other professionals, with exceptions. But these rules only guard against common mistakes; they give no hint of the creative devices needed to make a poster work. I see four main techniques in this selection:

> *puns*: 'the age of consent' to sex or to a Young Person's Railcard; Forest and Wanderers as football teams or as describing the safari (Littlewoods); 'for a sausage' as a metaphorical expression of low cost or as a literal sausage (British Telecom).

> *puzzles*: Pretty Polly and Lemsip both require decoding of the text.

> *funny or pretty pictures*: Rolo and Rothman's rely on people looking silly; car ads in general seem to rely on a big picture of the car.

> *reversal*: Rover, Lemsip, and Royal Mail have two parts, with an intended surprise when they are put together.

All these devices work – or don't – because of the layout in which they are placed: left vs. right, top vs. bottom, or centre vs. edges (see Kress and van Leeuwen 1996).

Take the Young Person's Railcard (13) as an example of layout shaping interpretation. There is a picture on the left of two young people embracing,

which suggests 'age of consent' in the text as the age of legalized sexual relation – the poster followed parliamentary debates about the age of consent
for gay sex. But then further reading (well, we're waiting for a train) reveals
that it is BR's consent to a rail-pass that is at issue, not these young people's
consent to each other. The joke depends on our reading picture to text, left
to right, and top to bottom.

There is a similar movement between words and picture in the Lemsip
poster (7), but vertically. The text at the top raises a puzzle (how can we
see someone in Iceland at this scale?) and the picture of the blue globe with
a yellow glowing island resolves it – perhaps the second or third time one
drives past this bus stop. In the Royal Mail posters (22, 23) we see the picture first, showing a type (old graduate, heavy metal rocker) holding a sign
of their achievement. The handwritten message on the left is then the sort
of cliché we might expect in a letter. The outer edge, with its imitation of
an airmail envelope, explains the purpose of this message. All this in the
time it takes for the light to change. This brings out a point that I think
Ogilvy misses in his quick rules: to respond to an ad, the audience must
have a chance to reconstruct it, to be involved, however little, in making
its meaning. The same sort of process goes on when there is no text at all
except a health warning or 'United Colors of Benetton'. We move between
the parts of the layout, looking for possible relevances (see Forceville
1996).

What we see from this survey, and the mixed success of the posters, is
that it is actually rather hard to combine a simple poster with the demands
of attention-getting, new information, and continued branding. Of all these,
only British Telecom and Rolo succeed on all counts, and perhaps the
Cancer Research Campaign by working against the conventions of the other
posters in its use of typography and lack of images. But these criticisms may
be too harsh (or not harsh enough) because we have considered the posters
as spaces but have not yet considered how the posters work in space.

Locality

Posters are consumed in a particular place. That can be a limitation for the
advertiser – if you don't pass by the place, you will never see it. But it also
allows posters to refer to their place, like the Mills & Boon poster referring
to the bus shelter. Many of the posters for stores or fast food outlets just
give directions – for instance the ad for Morrisons is on a busy one-way system before one would have to turn off to follow these directions. The poster
for Pretty Polly, like that for Mills & Boon, makes sense only on a bus shelter; I guess that the consolation 'there will be a bus along soon' is intended
to imply that women wearing Legworks can get a lift. The small bus-station
posters for cat food and sherry are across from a supermarket; the posters
advertising special rail rates are, of course, at the train station. A more

clever use of the setting is the Volkswagen poster on rail platforms, part of the campaign discussed in Chapter 5. It warns:

FOR YOUR SAFETY:
Please stand back from edge of platform.

before telling us in smaller type at lower right:

Polo L £7990.

Some of the cleverest uses of outdoor media involve references to place. Just below the small signs forbidding smoking on the London Underground are equally small signs saying 'It needn't be hell with Nicotinell'. A small ad appears on the doors of telephone booths: 'In emergency open door' – with the number of the Samaritans suicide prevention phone line. (The Samaritans also put their number on bridges where people have been known to jump.)

The ideal of the packages sold to advertisers by outdoor advertising companies is that all one's posters would be as appropriately located as those of Volkswagen or Nicotinell. And there are special cases, for instance when one radio station or political party puts its huge poster across the street from its rival. I recall that Stinker, a local chain of gas stations in Boise, always used to buy the billboard just leaving town, by the State Penitentiary. Then they would put up notices like:

WRITE TO YOUR PEN PALS. THE PAROLE BOARD.

After a string of escapes, they put up a sign saying,

DRIVE SLOWLY. WATCH FOR PRISONERS CROSSING ROAD.

I don't see how these messages sell gas, but they added to the local reputation of Stinker as a funny and characterful and local alternative to the big oil companies. Posters can be linked both to the geographical area and to the particular location of the message.

Posters can be located in time as well as space. They are not dated the way a newspaper is, but the smaller bus shelter posters can be put up for as little as a week, allowing for the references in my collection to Valentine's Day. Other recent posters have had tie-ins to specific football games, elections, or holidays. A Guinness poster appeared in two forms: 'Happy Saint Patrick's Day' with a full pint in the daylight, and 'Unhappy Saint Patrick's Day' with the pint empty, when the backlight came on. And by the same token, posters can be taken down quickly in the case of complaints; but as we will see in Chapter 11, they only have to stay up a day for the press to preserve and reproduce them in scandalized articles.

I have included the campus posters in my survey because, while they are generally unsophisticated as examples of design, they are very careful in their placement. Most of them would make little sense to readers of this book, because they rely on an audience that knows the places, schedules, and calendar of the campus. Most of them are placed along the main walk-way that serves the same sort of function as the main road in town. They are placed in a way to be glimpsed by passers by hurrying between classes, often in repeated patterns. They are typically located near the relevant part of campus (the theatre or sports centre or business school), or attract attention from the centre of the campus to some event off the beaten path, such as blood donation at the Chaplaincy Centre. A sense of an event – whether AIDS Awareness Day or a rent strike – can be created by dangling a banner down the one tall building on campus. In some ways a campus is the ideal laboratory for outdoor advertising, because it retains the completely unreg-ulated conditions and ferocious competition of the nineteenth-century street.

Linked to the importance of specific location is the effect of posters as somehow being really there, in a way electronic media are not. Perhaps the most famous British poster showed a real car apparently stuck on the hoard-ing, with the headline, 'How do they do it?' It was an ad for Araldite adhe-sive. It was followed after some weeks with the same hoarding with a big hole in it, saying, 'How did they pull it off?' The point is that the effect depended on it being a real car, in one place. Similarly, the puffs of smoke coming out of the Times Square Camel poster, or the accumulating grime on a poster about air pollution and lung disease, get their effect by mixing the real with the representation.

Movements

In my survey of posters, it seems that there are just a few kinds of locations: large hoardings by roads or carparks, smaller sites on bus shelters or train platforms, a few very big sites by main roads, and many sites for tiny posters on campus. But my journey around town with a camera taught me that each poster site is different, because of the way people pass by it. Some of the posters that seem simplistic are assuming very brief viewing as the driver moves along the highway. Some of the posters that seem puzzling or inef-fective at first glance depend on repeated viewing by people following their daily routines; this applies to the sometimes baffling British posters for cig-arettes, which are typically placed where a driver will see them once a day. Repeated viewing allows for teaser campaigns, for instance a recent poster that just has words in quotation marks, in different typefaces, against a black background. Only after a week was a logo added for the advertiser: 'The word is Vodaphone'. Two different campaigns have used cardboard boxes in teasers before revealing cars in the final versions of the posters.

The principle of brief and repeated viewing applies only to outdoor advertising. Transportation advertising can work differently; it appeals to a captive and bored audience who, as David Ogilvy puts it, have nothing better to do for twenty minutes or so than to read your copy. So ads in train stations or above the windows of underground trains can have much more text and thus more complex arguments. Here is an extreme example, from a transportation poster for transportation posters:

SO YOU'RE WAITING FOR A TRAIN, ARE YOU?

Boring, isn't it ... Well, you must be a bit bored, else you wouldn't be reading this. You'd think they'd give us something to *do*, wouldn't you. Like giant TV screens hanging down over every platform, or at least a bit of music you could listen to. Imagine the loads of people who have read this in the last week. It must be thousands. Mind you, it's a great way to sell something because people *HAVE* to read posters. There's *NOTHING* better to do. If your company has a product to sell, put it on a poster and get your message across to the thousands of people who, like you, stand on this platform every day. If you don't have anything to sell, we hope your train comes soon, so in the meantime, here's a bit of music ... Dum- dee- dum- dee- diddly- dum- ti- dum.

ADRAIL

This poster, with its plain hand-lettered look, seems to break all the rules, with one long chunk of text. But it displays the effectiveness of transportation posters by working against the poster form, reaching out with conversational cues ('isn't it', 'well', 'wouldn't you', 'mind you') and with pronouns 'you'd think they'd give us something to do'), and questions, and even mock music. It recalls Bernstein's statement that good posters work against their limitations – here referring to the time as well as the place. As delays on British railways become more frequent, advertisers can plan on even longer texts (one bus shelter ad for a radio station even came up with some real music instead of 'Dum dee dum').

Public and private spaces

What is funny about the birthday and anniversary signs on the roundabout is that a private event is brought out for the whole town to see. This was the basis of a campaign in the US (I saw it in Portland, Oregon). Messages appeared scrawled in black on the white billboards, like graffiti, personal and domestic messages such as, 'Carl Budkey – bring home bread.' It seemed someone had gone mad with her partner's forgetfulness, and resorted to vandalism. These notes puzzled the whole town, and led to lots of talk, before AT&T Wireless Services put up their logo, a portable phone, and the message, 'Make it easier for people to reach you.'

The Carl Budkey example reminds us that posters are public in another way as well – we are likely to see them with other people, and if they are striking in some way, they become a topic of conversation, whether the talk is favourable or not. Magazines and newspapers are not usually read with other people, and radio is usually listened to alone. We saw in Chapter 5 that Häagen-Dazs used only press for its sensual imagery; what was witty in private might seem embarrassing in public. But posters can also use this potential public embarrassment and discussion. In the small sample I have considered, Pretty Polly and Rolo play on embarrassing situations, while the Royal Mail situations show someone making a proud announcement (visually) while writing a private letter (textually).

One indication of this sense of what is public is that, though posters make up a tiny part of ad spend, they make up a large proportion of the most controversial, most discussed, and most complained about ads. For example, in 1995 a poster for the movie *Disclosure* received many complaints. Now admittedly it shows a back view of a woman with her skirt hitched up and her thighs wrapped around a man's waist. It had not struck me as a particularly shocking image, compared to what one regularly sees even in women's magazines or mass newspapers, not to mention television or cinema itself. I guess people imagine their little kids asking what that woman and man are trying to do, while embarrassed parents say he must be carrying her over a mud puddle.

Only on this basis, that posters come into public space, can we explain the outcry over the Benetton ads, such as the picture of the baby, or the man with Aids and his family (see the examples at www.benetton.com). They were shocking because they were in public space. Benetton could use this shock – each of the ads appeared only briefly and in a few places, and I imagine more people saw them in newspaper photographs, above disapproving articles, than ever saw them on the streets. Advertising regulators make a distinction between media, so that a Benetton ad that showed three hearts removed from bodies was allowed as a press ad, though not as a poster. The principle was that the press ad could be avoided by people who might be sensitive to it (for instance, families of heart patients) while the poster was unavoidable.

Because ads are public, are in one place, and are open to social interaction, we see people talking back in them in a way we can't in other media, spray-painting graffiti. I have one example in my collection, with the Marie Curie Cancer ad modified:

MARIE CURIE SCIENTISTS ARE ONLY HALF THE STORY

graffiti: *THE OTHER HALF IS VIVISECTION*

Here the graffiti is the same size as the text of the ad. Such a response is not ineffectual like shouting back at a ridiculous ad on the telly or doodling on an annoying ad in a magazine. The spray-paint transforms the message of this particular version of the ad, in this particular place – attracting attention as much or more than the original message, but making it say just the opposite of what was intended. A Renault ad showing a man contemplating the car as art is modified to say,

NOT PRIVATE VIEWING – PUBLIC TRANSIT?

A postcard shows a more artful modification, in which a poster showing a black woman, a white woman, and an oriental baby has the logo 'United Colors of Benetton' replaced with a box of the same colour and typeface saying:

LESBIAN MOTHERS ARE EVERYWHERE

In this case, the postcard spreads the impact of the local modification. An anarchist group publishes a booklet that explains techniques for what they call 'Billboard Improvement'. The same sort of modification can be done, with or without approval, by another advertiser. One advertiser planned to modify the Oasis poster for 'Be Here Now' – which shows a Rolls Royce in a swimming pool – by adding a phone number for car insurance. The wit in this would be in the appearance of 'fly-posting', the unauthorized application of posters. The on-the-spot modification of messages, whether by advertisers or anarchists, reminds us that each poster is exposed in public space.

Summary

I have used posters to show how a medium works in various kinds of space:

- the text and layout
- the location
- the circulation of viewers
- the borderline of the public and the private.

We need to be aware of these spaces to understand the simple rules for posters suggested by advertising professionals: why the type needs to be large, with few words, and why the image is usually dominant. An awareness of spaces also helps us understand the differences between roadside and transport posters, and the relation of posters to the geography of a town, and the kinds of complaints that posters can generate.

Of course all other media transform space in some way. Television projects a circle of people watching in a living room, or a crowd watching a big game at a pub. Radio can be used to define one's private space (for instance, listening on a crowded train), or to fill the spaces of a house (note the effect of having different stations on in different rooms). Even press ads may define a sense of space, as when BBH put its Boddington's ads on the back covers of magazines, where other people in the tube or in a queue would see them. And the issue of what is public and what is private arises with every advertisement that calls out to us as individuals in public. Outdoor advertisements illustrate these constraints and uses of space in a particularly bald and direct way.

Further reading: outdoor advertising

The best starting place for outdoor advertising is David Bernstein's *Advertising Outdoors: Watch This Space!* (1997), which also has an excellent selection of current and historical posters. Irene Costera Meijer (1998) uses the public nature of posters, and the shared response, to argue for a possible relation between advertising and ideas of citizenship. For analysis of layout, see Gunther Kress and Theo van Leeuwen (1996). Of the advertising memoirs, David Ogilvy gives the most consideration to posters, in *Ogilvy on Advertising* (1983). *Campaign's* poster advertising awards appear each year in early October, with the winners beautifully reproduced and credits to the creative teams. For useful web sites of outdoor media owners, see www.maiden.co.uk, and www.abn1.com (for the US). A number of pictures of posters modified to form protest messages are sold as postcards by Leeds Postcards, PO Box 84, Leeds LS1 4HU.

Daz

7

Television commercials, channels, and times

Television watching is so much a part of most of our lives that we tend to take its routines for granted. One way to stop taking it for granted is to switch on the TV to the local or national channels in another country (or to try some unfamiliar angles of the satellite receiver). One may find the same programmes, US sitcoms or BBC costume dramas or Australian soaps around the world, and as I said in Chapter 4, one is likely to find ads for the same brand names. But there may also be some sense of strangeness at the way the programmes are broken up, how they are linked, what sorts of programmes come on when, who speaks to us and how.

Raymond Williams, an influential theorist in British cultural studies, gave a vivid description of just such a disorienting experience more than 20 years ago:

> One night in Miami, still dazed from a week on an Atlantic liner, I began watching a film and at first had some difficulty in adjusting to a much greater frequency of commercial 'breaks'. Yet this was a minor problem compared to what eventually happened. Two other films, which were due to be shown on the same channel on other nights, began to be inserted as trailers. A crime in San Francisco (the subject of the original film) began to operate in an extraordinary counterpoint not only with the deodorant and cereal commercials but with a romance in Paris and the eruption of a prehistoric monster who laid waste to New York. Moreover, this was a sequence in a new sense. Even in commercial British television there is a visual signal – the residual sign of an interval – before and after the commercial sequences, and 'programme' trailers occur only between 'programmes'. Here there was something quite different, since the transitions from film to commercial and from film A to films B and C were in effect unmarked. There is in any case enough similarity between certain kinds of films, and between several kinds of film and the 'situation' commercials which often consciously imitate them, to make a

sequence of this kind very difficult to interpret. I can still not be sure what I took from that whole flow. I believe I registered some incidents as happening in the wrong film, and some characters in the commercials as involved in the film episodes, in what came to seem – for all the occasional bizarre disparities – a single irresponsible flow of images and feelings. (Williams 1974)

Williams brings out the comic scene – the Cambridge Professor of Drama in a Miami hotel room, baffled by the unfamiliar interplay of prehistoric monsters and deodorant commercials. But he uses it to explore an important point about the experience most people have of television, in other countries as much as in the US. People do not necessarily tune in to watch a particular programme, the way one might read a book or go out to a movie, but often just plonk themselves down on the sofa and watch TV, whatever is on, for as much time as they have. If this isn't the way you watch television, think of a child coming home from school, or a lawyer getting home late from work and looking to see what is on, or a retired person after dinner, or someone finishing the washing up. Williams implies that such an experience is passive and even bewildered, but this need not be the case (Fiske 1987); even active, reflexive, critical audiences can start with this sense of 'just watching TV' (see Chapter 12).

Williams's sense that television is experienced as flow is essential to understanding television commercials: he sees them as part of the experience, and the pattern for the rest of the experience, rather than as interruptions. Most analyses of television programmes leave out the commercials, and most analyses of commercials leave out the programmes. But of course when advertisers buy time, they try to buy it for particular programmes with particular audiences. And they assume an experience of television as flow means that, at least for some viewers, it will be easier to watch the commercials than not to. Williams also makes a point about the form of the commercials, the way they imitate the programmes and fit within them. His anecdote makes us aware of something missing in analyses of commercials as separate objects (the way I analysed commercials in earlier chapters): an awareness of the experience as taking place in time. The different times are as crucial to understanding television advertising as different spaces are in understanding posters. To highlight these different senses of time, I will do more systematically what Williams did anecdotally, and juxtapose segments of US and UK television.

Changing times

Williams alludes to an important difference between UK and US television when he notes that 'even in commercial British television there is a visual signal' of a break. The broadcasting system of the USA differs from that in the UK (and most European countries) in that US programmes were sponsored and even made by advertisers, from the early days of radio. In the UK, radio broadcasting was established in the 1920s as a public service, paid for by a licence on receivers. TV was established along the same lines, and commercial television arrived late, in the 1950s (and arrived even later in other European countries). US radio and later television programmes were typically a seamless web of entertainment and promotion, from the *Maxwell House Showboat*, a radio programme in the 1930s, produced by the advertising agency BBDO, on which performers drank surprising amounts of coffee, to the *Kraft Television Theater* and other programmes in the 'Golden Age' of US television in the 1950s. Stephen Fox (1990) quotes the *New Yorker*: 'A girl breaks into song, and for a moment you can't quite pin down the course of her lyrical passion. It could be love, it could be something that comes in a jar.' Sponsorship today may be less blatant, but US advertisers are still so strongly identified with programmes that they can put great pressure on programme makers (see Chapter 12).

In contrast, the UK and European countries introduced commercial services late, and with strict regulation of the timing, form, content, and total amount of advertising (European Union regulations are reproduced in Corner and Harvey (1996)). In general, ads can only come in breaks with specified amounts of programming between them. In the UK, these breaks are signalled by a black frame that, though hardly perceptible, serves to mark off the ads from the programmes. Advertisers cannot introduce any sales message into the programmes themselves, or use actors or settings in a way that would blur the boundaries of ads and programmes. The total amount of advertising allowed in a day and in any hour is restricted; the ads in the US Superbowl alone would use up the allowance for 24 hours. Some national systems were even more restrictive. I am told that Italian television, as late as the 1970s, broadcast all the ads for the day at one time, 9 o'clock; the slot was called 'Carousel' and children were allowed to stay up and watch what they saw as fascinating short films, as a treat before bedtime.

The contrast between US and European flows of television clearly struck Raymond Williams, but they should not be exaggerated. Even non-commercial channels like those of the BBC developed a rhythm of programmes linked into an evening's broadcasting, with advertised schedules (see Scannell 1996). They depended on an experience of flow broken into segments, and people planned their lives around the regular recurrence of favourite programmes or evenings. When they had to face competition from commercial channels, they added more trailers and links to ensure that those who tuned in stayed with them.

The big changes in television experience since Raymond Williams wrote in the 1970s, are the proliferation of broadcast outlets and the fragmentation of the audience. In his bewilderment at the juxtaposition of images, he does not mention that he could have switched channels. In the 1970s, most people in North America had between three and seven channels to choose from, and those in the UK had two. Then terrestrial channels proliferated, and many viewers subscribed to cable or satellite services, so that they could switch at any time between dozens or even hundreds of choices. K. B. Jensen (1996) suggests that these changes mean that analysts need to consider other kinds of flow, besides the *channel flow* discussed by Williams; there is the *viewer flow* as any viewer switches between channels, and a *superflow* of all the possible choices at any one time. The fragmentation of audiences has been widely discussed by advertisers, as both an opportunity and a problem. The opportunity is that new channels can target specific audiences at lower prices. So, for instance, Channel 4 in the UK, with its commissioned independent films, foreign language films, and off-beat documentary series, offers a much smaller audience at most hours than the regional ITV companies with their more popular fare, but the Channel 4 audience tends to be composed of more up-market, higher spending, harder to reach viewers, so Channel 4 can charge premium rates per viewer (and is indeed more profitable than ITV). Similar targeted audiences are offered by some US cable services, or by sponsorship of programmes on the Public Broadcasting Service. New satellite services promise (but have not yet delivered) even more sharply targeted audiences of international business people, young sports enthusiasts, children, or travellers, so that the television market would break up as the magazine market did in the 1960s. The problem for advertisers, in both the US and the UK, is that there is no longer any one channel that can regularly reach a third or half the population of the country at once, just as there are no longer mass market magazines like *Life*, *Look*, or the *Picture Post*.

What is the relevance of these changes to advertising? I have mentioned that advertisers have begun to reconsider other media, such as outdoor (Chapter 6), and new media, such as the Internet (Chapter 8). They have also experimented more with the ways media can work together (Chapter 5). And within television commercials, they have begun to incorporate the viewers' experience into the form of the ads, encouraging the sort of active, playful reading that goes with a broader and more fragmented experience of TV (Chapter 12).

TV channels

Analyses of television forms can focus on the enormous richness of the medium, or on its limitations. The sense of richness arises from the use of several modes:

- speech and written language
- images and graphic icons
- sounds and music.

So, if one looks back to two advertisements analyzed earlier, in Chapters 4 and 3, one sees them making different uses of the modes:

	Peugeot 406	Co-operative Bank
speech	'The Drive of Your Life' at end	monologue until end
written text	'The average person...' cues interpretation slogan at end	promise at end
images	car dozens of symbolic images	face of presenter ethical policy images
graphics	Peugeot lion	colour logo
sounds	door closing	'natural' sound effects
music	'Search for the Hero'	none

Both use black and white images, have one voice, and end with a slogan and logo. But the Peugeot 406 ad makes primary use of music and lyrics juxtaposed with images, with almost no speech, while the Co-operative Bank makes primary use of the juxtaposition of words spoken to camera and written words, with no music. Recall that David Ogilvy's advice for posters was that there should be no more than three elements; even the simplest television ads have more than three elements going at once (one result is that they are very hard to transcribe in print).

In contrast to this richness, some theorists have stressed the physical limitations of the medium. This approach was set out by Marshall McLuhan, who broke from earlier contrasts between the visual and the verbal and instead stressed the difference between high resolution media such as cinema and print or posters (hot), and low resolution media such as TV (cool). The television is made up of many little dots. It is typically small in size (and looks blurred if blown up to movie screen size), and low in resolution. We remain reliant on sound to enable us to interpret these images. McLuhan's conclusion was that these limitations meant we had to work at engaging with the TV image, filling it in for ourselves. From an advertiser's point of view, another limitation inherent in the medium is the clutter with which any ad must contend. So the picture of TV we get from media studies is of a medium that can put out highly complex messages, but messages that must engage the audience immediately or be lost entirely.

Two hours of television

I have analysed specific television commercials elsewhere in the book. Here I want to look at their setting within television as a medium. One way to do this is by comparing the way the ads come across in two different broadcasting systems. I am not interested here in analysing the programmes, so I have chosen two blocks of time with similar programmes: an hour from 6:00 to 7:00 with two episodes of *Friends* on Channel 4 in the UK, and an hour from 7:30 to 8:30 with *Something So Right* and *Frasier* on KTVB (NBC) in Boise, Idaho.

KTVB

time	brand	notes	quotations
7:30	*Mad About You* closing credits		Don't be perplexed, *Something So Right* is next
	Something So Right opening credits and first scenes		
7:40	Rogaine Hair Regrowth	personal testimony	You can interrupt nature, you can stop it
	Inventing the Abbotts	movie trailer	
	Milk Money	TV movie trailer	
7:42	*Something So Right*		
7:48	Hyundai	*Jaws* parody	Look out, it's whole new Hyundai
	1-800-Collect	mother and daughter on sofa	– I was a bit sad when Sarah went away to school but I didn't let on – She was devastated
		stars of show hitting letters of NBC with sledgehammer	You're watching *Something So Right* on NBC
	Frasier	trailer	*Frasier* on NBC next
20:00:00	Coca Cola Classic	Code Red competition	This is not a drill, it's the real thing
	Bon Marché		
	Leeza	trailer	
	US Robotics	Sally Ride	space and cyberspace
	KTVB news	trailer	Is Boise getting too noisy?
7:51	*Something So Right*		
7:59	Ritz Air Crisps	contrast of old lady and wild youths	Inhale 'em
	Rice Krispies Treats	hen	Which would you choose this holiday season?
	Fed Ex	bridal dress from Milan	The Way the World Works
	Kodak contest	Disneyworld tie-in	
	Invasion	trailer	

	NBC	public service announcement	So Now You Know (see Chapter 3)
	Something So Right credits	with trailer for *Just Shoot Me*	
8:03	*Frasier*	trailer	Seattle is famous for more than just rain
36:30:00	Dodge Caravan		*Frasier* is sponsored by Dodge Caravan
	7-Up	drummer	It's an Up Thing
	Boston Market	extra chicken for a dollar	'Don't mess with dinner'
	AT&T	guilt of working mother	When can I be a client? – Girls just want to have fun
	NBC	trailers	NBC Wednesday is new – How new is it?
8:08	Frasier		
8:15	Home Depot	direct to camera	nobody covers more floors
	Dodge Caravan	fish and framing	We thought of everything
	Frasier	trailer	You're watching *Frasier* on NBC
	NBC	trailers	Caroline NBC next
	Federal Flood Insurance	direct address from director of federal agency	Weather experts say your area is subject to flooding
	WBS cable		What Idaho wants to see, WBS shows
	KTVB News	news trailer	
8:18	*Frasier*		
8:30	Avon face cream	personal testimony of 'department store junkie'	Another Avon Lady? Go figure
	KTVB news stand	Canyon County Pet Society	
	Victoria's Secret	Tom Jones	I've had underwear thrown at me all my life
	Bambi video		
	Dodge Caravan	again	
	Dateline	trailer	
	NBC Wednesday	trailer	
1:02	*Frasier* credits		trailer for *Caroline in the City*
	Caroline in the City opening		

CHANNEL 4

time	brand	notes	quotations
	Last Chance Lottery	trailer	Saturdays at 9 on 4:00
	The Big Breakfast	trailer	Channel 4 7 to 9
			This is 4, going back to the top with the first two episodes of *Friends*
6:00	*Friends*	credits over dialogue	
6:14	*Ransom*	movie trailer	
6:15	Terry's Chocolate Orange bar	mock nineteenth-century style	Captain Mikos Theodopoulos, nautical traveller, had an incredible passion for Terry's Chocolate Oranges
	Vaseline Dermacare	woman's body in forest – 10 seconds	Helping dry skin to heal itself
	Clearasil face wash	two boys – 10 seconds	But you're not spotty
	British Meat – Beef	boy going through day – notices spot	Mother: Somebody loves you honey Boy: mmm song: Don't tell me your troubles
6:16	*Friends*	programme identification first	
6:24	*Friends*	closing credits over dialogue	
6:25	Channel 4	trailer for Friday night comedies	
	Channel 4	NBA trailer	Rockin the rim
	VO5 shampoo		What mark would you give the condition of your hair?
	Adidas	black and white except for boxing shots – electronic sounds	Prince Naseem Here on business
	Walker's Crisps	Gary Lineker as priest	Walker's New Barbecue Flavour Crisps are so irresistible, the world can suddenly seem a daunting place
	Here's Johnny	trailer – *The Shining* parody	Something's coming to Friday nights
	ER	trailer	

	Channel 4	identification – characters from *Friends* arguing	'You're among Friends here'
6:28	*Friends*	opening dialogue and credits	
6:30	*Friends*		
6:39	*Love and War*	movie trailer	
	Cadbury's Time Out	clay animation	Put a flake in your break
	Toaster Pockets	Kevin the Teenager	That's so unfair, I hate you
	Quaker Oat Crunch	cartoon penguin – 10 seconds	All the taste of a cold cereal, only it's hot
	KFC Chicken Salsa Burger	young couple watching TV	Kev, we've been going out for two years now. Can you tell me what you really want?
	Elida Organics	Easter Island – slow motion and New Age music	Inner beauty that shines through
	Cadbury's Darkness	young couple in front of fire	song – Fever
6:42	*Friends*	Channel 4 identification	
	Friends		
6:52	*Friends*	closing credits	
6:53	Channel 4	station identification	There's more from the first series of *Friends* next Tuesday at 6:00
	Ant and Dec	trailer	
	Orbit gum	football game – couple	
	Walker's	Lineker as baby, gang member, and mum	Walker's Barbecue Crisps – just make sure they're in safe hands
	Swing Mix album		
	Channel 4	station identification	
6:54	Fresh Pop	Bjork – Miss You – pop video	
6:59	Channel 4	trailer for Howard Jacobson show on laughter	
	Channel 4 News		

TV times

TV commercials make us aware of one kind of time: 30 seconds for most ads (10 seconds for the shorter ones). But they also involve other kinds of time – the instantaneous switch to another programme, the four minutes or so of the ad break, the schedule for the 24 hours, the weekly recurrence of programmes, and the shared memory of other ads and other programmes that may extend over decades. These other frames of time affect our experience of any ad.

Thirty seconds

In both the US and UK ads, the 30-second spot is standard, and many ads are just ten seconds. When an ad runs longer, like the Peugeot 406 commercial in Chapter 4, it is usually a special event, to be followed by shorter versions recalling it. John Ellis, extending Williams's argument about flow, argues that,

> The 'spot' advertisement is in many ways the quintessence of TV. It is a segment of about thirty seconds, comprising a large number of images and sounds that are tightly organized amongst themselves. This segment is found accompanied by other, similar segments: coherent within themselves, they have no particular connection with each other. (1982: 118)

In all the diversity of commercial spots, this compactness dictates a conventional organization of time (see GENRE). Nearly every commercial has set a scene and mood, but hasn't revealed a product, within the first 3 seconds: this is true, for instance, of the Hyundai *Jaws* parody, the direct address of the Avon testimony, the comic caricature of Kevin the Teenager. Nearly every commercial ends with the product name, logo, and slogan; most have some shift of mode (for instance, voice is replaced by text or conversation by voice-over) about 5 seconds before the end. Between these shifts, most ads perform some sort of transformation. A Dodge Caravan ad begins with a fish in a bowl; as the camera draws back we see the bowl is on a self-levelling table in a Dodge Caravan parked on a steep hill, so there is a sudden change in frame. Here are some other common transformations:

- a problem with a solution (VO5 shampoo repairs problem hair, Terry's Chocolate Orange bar keeps the chocolate orange from rolling around the ship);
- a fable with a moral (Federal Flood Insurance can protect your belongings; a mother's shepherd's pie shows her love);
- a riddle with an answer (Fed Ex: how did the woman in Milan get invited to weddings all over the world?);

- a demonstration with a result (the hen chooses Rice Krispies Treats rather than an egg; the boy who uses Clearasil has clear skin);
- a testimonial with a move from person to product (Sally Ride, then the US Robotics logo; Prince Naseem, then the Adidas logo).

In ads we looked at earlier, we saw that the Co-operative Bank ad worked as a kind of riddle, with a series of juxtapositions of service claims and threatening imagery; the tension is resolved by an ethical claim and a service claim, with a phone number. The Peugeot 406 ad raises the question of what all these thoughts have to do with the man driving to work; the riddle is answered with the last card telling us that there is no average person, and then there is a shift to a completely different style for the logo and slogan at the end.

The need for brevity drives all the other decisions about a commercial. The stories will be elliptical, leaving a lot out, and will rely on clear signs of where we are and what these people are doing: the people in the 1-800-Collect ad are mother and daughter, the man in the Kodak ad is asking friends and family questions at a kitchen table, in the KFC ad, a woman watches a man playing a computer game, the crowd in the Orbit gum ad are watching football. Commercials often use classical music – there are CDs of all your favourites from the commercials – but they have to choose bits that establish a pattern within 30 seconds, usually just one bit of a tune. Even pop music tunes are too long for commercials, except for one special showing (as with the first showing of the Peugeot 406 long version). But as Ellis points out, the brevity and completeness of commercials are part of their exhilaration. With some great ads, like those for Levi's in Chapter 2, or the Adidas ad here, the viewer is constructing the settings, characters, and stories of what could almost be a feature film, but with the boring parts left out.

Four minutes

Ads are never seen on their own; they are designed to stand out in a break. They may do this by

- using black and white rather than colour (Adidas)
- using animation rather than live action (Cadbury's Time Out)
- striking opening chords (Cadbury's Darkness)
- having text but no moving pictures (many local ads, like that for Bon Marché)
- disorienting changes of visual style or sound level ('Coke', Ritz).

Advertisers know all too well that many viewers will go and make a cup of tea, or fast forward through the ads in a recorded programme. Media buyers try to assert their control of the break by inserting a short reminder ad at the end. They can also acknowledge their place in the ad break indirectly by parodying other ads. This happens much more in the British ads, where Terry's parodies heritage stories, and Toaster Pockets parodies the kind of demanding adolescents we saw taken straight in the 'Coke' ad in Chapter 1.

John Ellis argues that the commercial break is just the most striking example of the way TV is broken up into segments: 'small sequential unities of images and sounds whose maximum duration seems to be about five minutes' (1982: 112). This segmentation applies to programmes as well as ads. In my table of two hours of television, I have shown the programmes as blocks of 10 or 20 minutes, but these are further segmented, depending on the genre, with title sequences, news stories or interviews, pop videos, or games within a game show. In a dramatic programme or film, one might think of all the segments as closely linked in one plot, but in a soap opera, a characteristic TV genre, the different strands, focusing on different groups of characters, make up short segments that do not depend on each other. In Ellis's view, we take the length of the commercial break as natural because the 3 or 4 minutes of ads fit within a broadcast output that also consists of units of about this length. I was surprised at what a difference it made to these same episodes of *Friends* when I watched them on a videotape collection without ads; there were no longer the breaks to punctuate the episodes and set off the sections and the final joke.

Twenty-four hours

Part of the skill in media buying is in choosing the right programme and right time of day. One aim of the television network is to provide viewers with identifiable strands in the hope that they will continue with the flow rather than hop to another channel. So the NBC trailers stress comedy evenings on Wednesdays; similarly, Channel 4 strands US sitcoms one night, and on another night UK comedy programmes appealing to lads. The audiences, and ads, also change during the broadcast day, repetitive ads for fast-moving consumer goods (fmcgs) from 9 to 5 giving way in the evening to more stylish ads for cars or financial services. But the sectioning of TV time is not so simple; media buyers are also aware of viewers beyond the groups for whom the programmes are primarily intended, so, for instance, there are ads directed at women during children's programmes.

Could you tell from the ads alone the kinds of programmes between the ads in my sample hours, and the kinds of intended audiences? There are a number of ads intended to be funny (Hyundai, Terry's chocolate, Cadbury's Time Out) and a number that base their humour on character types like those found in sitcoms: mother and daughter in 1-800-Collect, obsessive middle-aged man in Kodak, officious aunt in Ritz, working mother of cute kids in AT&T, hapless teenage boy in Beef, sexually mismatched couple in KFC, as well as the Kevin the Teenager ad for Toaster Pockets, in which

Harry Enfield recreates a character from his comedy programme. There are ads aimed at men (Rogaine Hair Restorer) and at women (Avon), but no ads that could not be directed at a youngish audience, no ads for business services or health insurance, and no ads for the kinds of products so heavily advertised during the day: pain-killers, cleaning products, washing powders, or toothpaste.

Occasionally a media buyer gets clever or lucky and places a commercial at the exact break at which it will relate to a movie or sports event, such as a Ford Fiesta ad that draws on *Edward Scissorhands* being shown in the first break of the movie itself, or a football player's endorsement of film being shown during a football game in which he plays. Sometimes a media buyer gets unlucky and puts an ad where it will have unintended readings: Peugeot would be unwise to put the 'Search for the Hero' ad in Chapter 4 on during *Schindler's List*, where it might seem to trivialize the events in the movie. But in most cases the relation is not so direct. Raymond Williams, after an analysis of the ads during the news, complained that there was no sense of connection between a news item on drug claims, and the ads for painkillers that followed. In our UK example, there is no connection between the ad for an acne cream, and the story in an ad for meat, about the boy obsessed with his pimple. But Williams was assuming that if no connection is made by the television, the audience will be unable to make the connection. From listening to people talking during ads, we know they can make all sorts of links between ads and programme and ads and ads. Or they may just ignore the whole break and make a cup of tea.

One week

One important unit of TV time is the flow of programming over part of the day, whether sitcoms in the evening, soaps during the day, or Saturday morning cartoons. Another important unit is the week, because most programmes come in a series that is broadcast weekly. It is this repetition that builds up the sense of involvement with characters (even where there isn't an on-going plot), and a sense that the programme is part of our own routines for, say, Saturday night after dinner. How does this affect ads? They too can build on a sense of recurrence and familiarity. Sometimes this is done with a serial imitating the soap operas, as with the long-running saga of the couple who drink Nescafé Gold Blend. But more often, the links are by association, alluding to earlier ads rather than following them. So, for instance, the Walker's Salt and Vinegar crisps ad on Channel 4 only makes sense if you know that there has been a series of ads in which Lineker, a notoriously nice footballer who was never sent off for penalties, steals crisps from a kid. In this ad, later in the series, the boy sees Lineker in disguise in a passing priest or lady. We only need to be told, 'The world can seem a dangerous place' to recall the earlier ads. In other long-running series of ads the link is provided by a spokesperson (Bob Hoskins for British Telecom) or a character (the puppy in ads for Andrex loo paper or the Eveready bunny), or a structure (as when American Express did a series in which the name of the person doing the testimonial was revealed on the card at the end).

What advertisers cannot rely on is the regularity of viewing. If one watches enough television, one will see the new Boddington's ad, but (with a few exceptions) one cannot tune in at a specific time to see it (or I would do so). In this unpredictability, in which particular ads come on unscheduled, while the breaks themselves are absolutely predictable, ads are in a sense more typical of television's flow than are regularly scheduled programmes.

Years

Some programmes rely on memories longer than a week. Viewers of long-running soap operas know a whole history of a community, including events that happened to characters long departed. Fans watching the Superbowl or the World Cup recall a long succession of previous games. These experiences tie television, not just to our daily routine, but to our sense of the shape of our own lives from year to year. Ads sometimes try to draw on this longer sense of time by evoking much earlier ads. For instance, an ad for Rennie indigestion relief tablets incorporates a black and white advertisement from decades earlier; a younger woman laughs at the corniness of the ad while an older woman assures her the product still works. Sepia-toned ads for Hovis bread consciously evoke, not only an imaginary Britain of generations ago, but a nostalgic advertising campaign (directed by Ridley Scott before *Blade Runner*) of 20 years ago. A 'Coke' ad at Christmas evokes the 'Coke' print ads of 60 years earlier, in its painterly colours and its Haddon Sondblum Santa. People are surprisingly nostalgic about old ads, just because they evoke the ordinariness of a past time.

Different times

In my comparison so far, I have treated the UK and US ads together. But there are some obvious differences in the way they relate to programmes. First, of course, there are many more ads in the US; there is more time devoted to them, and more of them are very short 10-second ads. There are also many more trailers in the US, and the trailers are used strategically to link to the upcoming programme. But the most important difference goes back to Raymond Williams' sense of missing, in the US, a gap between programmes and ads. In the UK, ads can only be shown three times in an hour, with specified gaps, and trailers are only shown between programmes. US television integrates the trailers of one programme and the credits of another, and includes the sponsor over the beginning of the programme, and separates out the credits with a block of ads. These differences may seem rather subtle, but the effect is immediately noticeable; US television is (and apparently always has been) perceived as a constant flow, while UK television (and other European channels) retain a sense of separate programmes with ads between them.

There is another contrast that has to do with the kind of channel I have chosen, rather than with a difference between the UK and the US. There are no local ads on Channel 4, as there would be had I chosen Granada, the regional ITV station of north-west England, for comparison. The economics of US broadcasting are based on local stations making their profit by selling some spot time in the network programmes. This makes for another difference in the experience of watching these hours of television; the local ads may be cheaper and less interesting, but they also tie the transmission to local names and places, for instance a show put on by the Bon Marché, a local department store, or the Canyon County Pet Society, or trailers for the local news. Indeed, local broadcasters, whether Granada in the UK or KTVB in Boise, have an interest in marking off their broadcasting region as a geographical space that becomes real to their viewers, so that KTVB is one medium creating 'the Treasure Valley' that stretches from south-west Idaho into eastern Oregon, and the north-west of England, what used to be Lancashire and Cheshire, become 'Granadaland'. Advertisers often think in terms of TV regions even when they are buying other media, such as posters. The locally sold television spot started as a business arrangement in the US, but has become an important part of the way Americans imagine their local communities.

What is a television ad?

Guy Cook has pointed out (1992: 18–19) how any definition of advertising as a discourse type throws up many borderline cases. This is perhaps more apparent in the print media, where advertorials and competitions blur the distinction between a magazine and its advertisements, but it is true as well in broadcast advertising, even where there are strict regulations on sponsorship. Consider these cases:

- Sponsored events like Embassy World Snooker and the 'Coca-Cola' Cup (a UK football championship) give a mention of the sponsor's name even in news reporting.
- Miller Beer promoted this American lager in the UK with a series of long ads in the form of 5-minute parody talk shows with real guests (such as James Belushi) and an egotistical and not very bright host. The times of the ads were advertised in the newspapers, and trailed earlier in the evening.

- MTV moves from pop videos, to advertisements for albums featuring bits of the videos, to station identifications featuring 1-minute films, so that at any moment it is very difficult to tell whether one is watching an ad or not.
- The Public Broadcasting System, the non-commercial network in the US, has expanded the announcement of financial support for programmes from a simple acknowledgment of the name ('broadcast of the Prairie Home Companion was made possible by a grant from the XYZ Corporation') to a longer message indistinguishable from an ad ('broadcast of the Prairie Home Companion was made possible by a grant from the XYZ Corporation, makers of high quality bicycle parts including toe clips, caliper brakes, and alloy seat posts . . . ').
- Broadcasts of Formula One racing and other events can now electronically alter the posters around the track, visible in the background, to provide only advertisements appropriate to the audiences and regulations of each country.
- Several rather envious advertisers have noted in *Campaign* that the best ad currently running on British TV is running on the non-commercial BBC: it is an ad made by Leagas Delaney for the BBC itself, featuring more than twenty musicians, each doing a line from Lou Reed's song 'Perfect Day', so that the last chorus of the song becomes a comment on the way the richness of BBC music depends on the Licence fee: 'You're going to reap just what you sow.' The promotional film was then released as a CD and a video, for the benefit of Children in Need.

This blurring happens because advertisements take on the form of talk shows or pop videos, but also because other television forms take on the structure of advertisements: acknowledging support, promoting commodities, and packaging the message within a very short, concentrated segment, starting with a puzzle and ending with a message. One aspect of this blurring has become particularly controversial, in the debate over whether sponsorship of sports events should be covered by the ban on tobacco advertising; the debate focuses attention on the logos that viewers may treat as just part of the design of cars and clothing (see Chapter 5).

Conclusion

I have stressed the context of TV commercials in the overall experience of TV as a flow and as segmented. Even simple commercials make complex use of different modes: spoken and written words, noises and music, images and graphics. In fact, some sophisticated ads will draw attention to themselves just by having no music, no images, or no spoken words. These short, intense messages are set within several time schemes:

- the 30 seconds of the ad itself, which the advertiser structures to emphasis a message in the closing seconds;

- the 3 or 4 minutes of the commercial break, in which the ad must stand out against other ads;
- the 3 hours or so of potentially continuous television watching in an evening or day-time period, with the scheduling of programmes in slots;
- the routines of the TV week, with the recurrence of programmes;
- the memory over the years of earlier programmes and earlier ads, and their associations.

The flow of television is often presented as a problem for advertisers, a kind of clutter that makes it difficult for any one message to be heard. But it also provides patterns that the advertisers use to their advantage. Indeed, careful attention to the flow, segmentation, and recurrence of ads in the commercial breaks may help us understand the rhythms and appeal of the programmes, the pleasure, not of some particular show, but of 'just watching TV'.

Suggested reading: television

Of the many books on broadcasting, few say much about the advertisements. Exceptions are the books by Raymond Williams (1974) and John Ellis (1982), cited throughout the chapter, and John Fiske (1987), John Corner (1995), and Andrew Tolson (1996). Allan (1997) provides a sophisticated commentary on Williams's argument, in terms of his other work. Of the books on advertising, three pay special attention to television as a medium: Guy Cook (1992), Leslie Savan (1994), and Robert Goldman and Stephen Papson (1996). Michael Arlen (1980) and Randall Rothenberg (1994), which I have mentioned earlier, are both excellent journalistic accounts of the whole process of producing particular ads, ending with the broadcast. Richardson (1997) analyses talk on QVC, the UK satellite shopping channel, and the whole issue of *Text* is devoted to broadcast talk. Paddy Scannell's *Radio, Television, and Public Life* (1996) has nothing about ads (he is studying the BBC) but has profound comments on the experience of broadcasting.

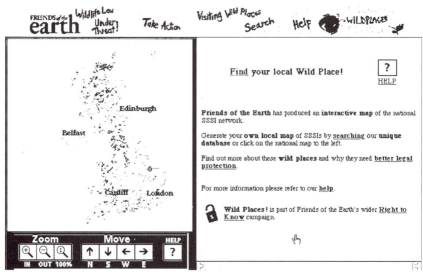

Friends of the Earth

Pepsi

8

Advertising, interaction, and the World Wide Web

Colin Clark and Trevor Pinch (1995) tell about a rainy day when they found themselves in a small market town in the north of England joining the crowd around a market trader selling toys consisting of a motorbike for a Barbie or Sindy doll with a little baby already on the back. The market trader attracts a crowd, apparently fascinated and horrified by the way he insults his assistant; then he displays his product, threatens to take it away, keeps them laughing, and keeps them watching, building up to the sale with a skilful patter. His routine draws on the weather, the time of day, the space around his table in the market, the expressions of people in the crowd, the assistant, references to common knowledge, all carefully timed, gauging the crowd's reaction at the moment. And, to the initial surprise of the sociologists Clark and Pinch, it works; by the end of the performance the people in the crowd push forward with money in their hands.

This rainy market-place in Yorkshire may seem centuries away from Java, Shockwave, frames, push media, and the other new technologies involved in advertising on the World Wide Web. But this trader has what the advertisers want; his pitch is selling at its richest, using all the visual and verbal modes, in real time, with constant feedback from potential customers, and it remains the model for what marketers from Proctor & Gamble or Pepsi or Compaq want to do in all media. Advertisers dream of a medium that will multiply the selling power of personal face-to-face. They want the ability to respond to a glance or a nod, and they want the involvement this responsiveness brings, and also the richness of information that suggests two people are paying attention to each other (Boden and Molotch 1994). But of course they want to do it on a grand scale, reproducing this scene in some way around the world. That is why they have always explored ways of getting feedback from audiences, and why there is now so much fascination with potentially interactive media.

Advertisers are fascinated with the Web, even though it still accounts for only a tiny fraction of their spending, because of the way it seems to breach limitations of other media.

1. The audience is distributed in space – While print journals and broadcast channels and posters are geographically limited and locally regulated, it is just as easy for me to access a web page located physically on a server in California as it is to access one on my own campus.
2. The audience is distributed in time – While TV broadcasts are transmitted on a strict schedule that, as we have seen, defines the experience, web pages are there so anyone can log on when it suits them, at lunch or in the middle of the night or before getting down to work.
3. Hypertext encourages a web-like set of connections – So while print ads are seen in relation to the editorial content around them, and broadcast ads seen in a break, a web page can be put in all sorts of new contexts, without constraints of linear ways of reading.
4. Space and time are cheap – While advertisers buy expensive space or time in other media, there are no constraints in the total space or time available on the Web. The constraints, as we will see, are in the ways users come to and move through the medium.
5. The Web provides information about users as it provides information to users (Rothenberg 1998).

All media can be interactive media. A student who wants to sell last year's course textbooks (perhaps including this one), who does not want to stand out in the rain hawking them like the market trader, may put up a photocopied poster on bulletin boards where this year's students on the course might see it. The poster becomes interactive when the student puts her phone number on twenty little tear-off strips at the bottom. If she is very clever, or a marketing major, she may give a slightly different form of her name on each poster, and thus find out which posters where get a response. Other media allow for other kinds of responses, but the issues remain the same; we need to consider, not just the technology, but how people relate to each other and to what they are doing (see INTERACTION). All this means that, whatever the confusions about what the Web is, who uses it, and for what, it remains fascinating both to advertisers, seeking new ways of marketing, and to students of media trying to understand what sorts of interaction are possible.

In this chapter, I will use two examples of sites that use the Web in different ways, to introduce basic features of the Web as a medium, and different ways of thinking about it. My third example will be an account of one brief session on the Web, and what this can tell us about the processes involved. It is in these processes of searching and browsing that we need to look for the possibilities of interaction. Finally I will consider web designers' criticisms of other sites, their lists of what not to do, as a way of telling what designers think about users.

One preliminary note. If you have read any of the flood of journalistic and academic comment on the Web, you will have noticed that writers divide rather sharply between enthusiasts and sceptics. I am an enthusiast.

Example 1: Pepsi

The first page one sees when one links to the Pepsi site (www.pepsi.com) starts with Pepsi branding, but then goes on to instructions about how to receive the site (in yellow and red on black in my browser).

'Welcome to the official site of Generationext'

[Pepsi World logo]

To fully enjoy Pepsi World, your browser should either be

Netscape Navigator 3.0 [or higher full release version]

or

Microsoft Internet Explorer 3.0 [or higher full release version]

This site is shocked, so if you don't have it, go get it. [Shockwave logo]

[animated Pepsi logo and Generationext button]

AOL users may get specific instructions on how to view the site

by clicking here

Clicking on the Shockwave logo takes one to another site (with other banner ads). Then the user goes through routines to download the Shockwave software, and the software goes through various routines to figure out what sort of machine one has, and to put the software in the right folder. When one exits and re-enters Netscape (with more ads), and goes back to Pepsi, the first page of the actual site offers the following choices around a graphic of a basketball player with the Pepsi symbol for the ball (the illustration is a later version):

	THE VAULT	HOLIDAY	ECARD	
		POWERPLAY	CENTRAL	
MOVIES				MUSIC
		BASKET		
BACK		BALL		FORWARD
		PLAYER		
GAMES				SPORTS

One can register for this competition (one used to have to register before entering the Pepsi site, but now they seem to think they get the information better through a competition). If one doesn't want to play the game, there are other options represented by icons on the margin of the page: movie reviews (with clips to view), music, or sports. What the page looks like is a kind of arcade game in which one moves through various levels.

What does all this do for Pepsi? It serves as a kind of branding, associating Pepsi with youth culture by associating it with the Web and with arcade games and entertainment. And why do people come to the site? They may find it on a list of hot sites, or may see the URL in Pepsi's other advertising. Once they find it, the site encourages them with constantly changing content to bookmark it and come back. Other competing brands may use the Web in different ways; for instance Tango (www.tango.co.uk) has had a series of completely puzzling little features (such as one on 'How to Hide' giving an illustrated guide to hiding in dustbins or behind posts). What they have in common is that the overall feel of the site embodies something of the brand as conveyed in other advertising: youthful Pepsi or wacky Tango.

Example 2: Friends of the Earth

The home page for Friends of the Earth UK (www.foe.co.uk) gives a range of choices:

[FOE Logo that leads to a leaflet on the organization]
England, Wales and Northern Ireland

Latest Press Release...... 23 Dec 1997
FESTIVE FARE FOUL? FOE TALKS TOXIC TURKEY

Climate Change
Climate for change, or just
hot air?
FOE's view on the Kyoto deal
    and more ...

Wild Places!
On The Web
Help protect wildlife sites
where YOU live ...

The Chemical Release
Inventory
Find the Pollution in Your
Backyard

Cars Cost The Earth!
Test drive our Virtual Java Car

Wild Woods!
Stop the Destruction of
the Snowforests

Tomorrow's World
Friends of the Earth's blueprint
for a sustainable future.

We rely almost entirely on concerned individuals to fund our vital work. Please join in & help us today – the Earth needs all the Friends it can get!

- Environmental Campaigns
- Find out about Friends of the Earth
- FOE's Publications Catalogue
- Jobs at Friends of the Earth

- Press Releases
- Internet Information and Environmental Hot Links
- Friends of the Earth Local Campaigns
- FOE Needs Your Views
- Friends of the Earth International

[Friends of the Earth] Clicking on the FOE logo will return you to this home page, from any other page.

This World Wide Web system is running on a SPARCserver 20 kindly donated by Sun Microsystems.

Copyright © Friends of the Earth / webmaster@foe.co.uk / Support FOE!

Compare this site to a Friends of the Earth leaflet, which has to put the work of the organization in general terms. With the Toxic Waste and Wild Places pages here, the user is given a map to click on the nearest emitters of wastes, and their records, or the nearest Sites of Special Scientific Interest, with current threats to them. And users can submit their own information on local sites that may not have reached the official records.

All this is useful if one is already involved in the environmental movement, but why would any user come to this home page? They might come via a search engine like Excite or Infoseek, using a search term such as, say, TOXIC WASTE. (I first found many environmental sites by searching for GUINNESS and getting sites related to a protest group occupying Guinness land in London.) They might come via links from other environmental sites (such as www.envirolink.org). Or they might come via a review in one of the many awards for hot sites (The Friends of the Earth site was recommended by the magazine *New Scientist* and had a link from their web site). These people browsing could be attracted by the Virtual Car. Or they could have been attracted a couple years ago by the chance to download a cinema ad that had been banned in the UK (see Chapter 11).

I compare this site, one that is full of information but visually rather modest, to the all-singing, all-dancing Pepsi site because FOE uses the medium so well for its purposes. The full list of reports on toxic waste sites would fill a whole shelf of reports, while here the user can just look up areas near his or her home. The map used as the starting page for Toxic Wastes and for Wild Places also identifies Friends of the Earth UK as being particularly concerned with these islands, down to the most local setting; users can place themselves on it, the way they mentally place themselves on television weather maps. (I'm not sure a map of the US, in the US Friends of the Earth site, would have the same effect of showing grassroots concern.) The list of SSSI's offers the chance for the organization to gain information as well as give it. The Kyoto reports can be updated daily. What would in any other form be a daunting pile of information is here reduced to manageable, searchable, local form. It gives the audience things to do on the screen, but it also gives them places to go for further action, joining local groups or writing protest letters or filing complaints. Friends of the Earth uses the Web largely as linked texts, not as multi-media, but it gives the user a sense of involvement.

What kind of medium is the Web for advertisers?

The Pepsi and UK Friends of the Earth sites raise questions about just what sort of medium the Web is. Such questions arise whenever a new medium is developed, and advertisers, who have a great deal of money to gain or lose, are often the first to ask them. It took decades before magazines began to earn more of their income from advertising than from sales or subscriptions. In the first years of US radio in the 1920s (Fox 1990), it wasn't clear what sort of medium it was, or more practically, who would pay for it; it was not obvious that it would be paid for by sponsorship, or how this sponsorship would work (see Chapter 7).

The same basic issues have arisen with the Internet. For instance, why would anyone see one's ad? No one logs onto the Web and thinks of searching for a Pepsi advertisement to find out that they now have blue cans rather than red, white, and blue. In the jargon of media studies, what uses and gratifications are involved? Users may be looking for specific information such as flight times, or passing a lunch hour with a game, or checking on news, or pursuing sexual fantasies, or finding a sense of community. In trying to understand these uses, advertisers turn to analogies between the Web and existing media and places with which they are more familiar.

- They can treat the site as a *poster*, with banners, small rectangular ads, in places people are likely to see them, as Business week says, 'much like a billboard on the Info Highway' (Himelstein, Neuborne, and Eng, 1997). The difference is that this poster can lead people to link to another site with much more information.
- They can treat the Web as a *bulletin board*, a place for lots of people to put messages. This is one way Benetton uses its site, contributing to the sense of controversy and suggesting a sense of openness on the part of the company, and a shared community between its customers.
- They can treat it like *sponsoring* a programme, the way Playstation co-sponsors the PepsiWorld site, or Apple sponsors the page of the Excite search engine that I use, or Adidas sponsors a site on World Cup football. This obviously costs more than just a banner, but it can allow for branding, associating the values and impressions of the site with the advertiser.
- Many paper publications have experimented with developing *on-line magazines* and newspapers (see the list at the end of the chapter). But for the most part the only ones that have funded these ventures in the traditional way, by charging a subscription fee, are business journals, which

can claim there is a commercial value for access to up-to-date information and archives. For instance, I was willing to pay a small charge for access to all the recent articles on advertising on the Web in *Business Week*, and *Campaign* is planning an elaborate on-line version (with a very high subscription charge). Other on-line publications include services that currently come free with registration, such as Go2, the *Guardian*'s web experiment, and the excellent service offered by *New Scientist*.

- Advertisers can take on the role of the *broadcasters* themselves, and put together lots of different kinds of content. Sites like Oneworld, devoted to development and aid issues, collect articles and links on a particular theme. MSNBC and CNN sites both present themselves as general news channels. A different approach is taken by *Wired*, with its excellent site 'Hotwired'. It does not just provide a web version of some articles from the print magazine, but uses 'Hotwired' as an entry point linking various lifestyle and technical features, and a powerful search engine Hotbot, with subscribers receiving regular e-mail updates on the contents. Search engines such as Excite and Infoseek encourage this analogy to broadcasting by calling their offerings such names as 'The Business Channel' or 'The Sports Channel'.

- Some providers of web material see their role as different from that of broadcasters, and talk of *pointcasting*. The new word is meant to suggest the way that the Web can tailor information to the individual user, so that, for instance, I can set up my Apple/Excite home page to greet me each morning with just those stocks, sports results, and areas of news that interest me (which would also make it possible to send me only advertisements that fit my particular profile).

- Web providers can also treat the Web as a sort of *club*, a space with different kinds of entertainment, constantly changing to encourage repeat visits. They may ask visitors to register, in return for further access. Pepsi promotes this sense of a club, as does Disney, and the children's magazine *American Girl*. Amstel Light has a parody version of such a club in 'Garrison Boyd's Homepage of Decency' telling us to 'Wake Up America – Avoid Amstel', with a conservative middle-aged man telling us about various recent Amstel-sponsored events – supposedly so that we can avoid them.

- Another possibility is to see the Web as an interactive *catalogue*. Whether customers buy directly from the Web or not, the site can hold almost unlimited information about, for instance, CDs in stock, or technical specifications of computers, or versions of software, or reviews of plays currently playing in London. This is how car companies such as General Motors or Toyota use the Web; one is unlikely to buy a car electronically, but one may certainly use it as part of one's research before going to any dealers.

- A further possibility for marketers is to see the Web, not just as an ad or a catalogue, but as a *shop*. There have been pioneering efforts at selling books, CDs, software, computers, chocolates, flowers, and of course pornography over the Web, often running losses while they establish themselves in what is seen as a potentially lucrative market. One advantage of such channels over conventional mail order is that the Web is so easily searchable. And web providers can store information about customers, for instance offering them suggestions of new books that match in some way their previous purchases. Until recently web retailing was held back by the lack of secure encryption for credit card numbers, so most buyers preferred to order by post or phone after they found the information on the Web. Now that that hurdle seems to have been overcome (I knock on wood, having just given my card number), a number of retailers are hoping to expand from pilot projects to real competitors. For instance, the on-line bookstore Amazon is one of the 25 most-consulted sites on the Web, up with the major search engines, CNN, and Disney.

One reason advertisers see the Web in so many different ways is that it serves several different marketing purposes. For Amazon it is a matter of direct sales, and building a loyal customer base. For Toyota or GM it is a matter of stimulating visitors to local dealers, who will do the direct selling. For Pepsi, Tango, Guinness, Amstel Light, or Miller Lite it is part of branding their products, especially in relation to a specific young, largely male audience. For almost all advertisers a web site can also have market research functions, telling them something about who has consulted the site, whether just recording numbers of hits, getting registration information, or tracking the movements of their browser (see Chapter 9).

Statements about which functions the Web can serve are seldom disinterested. For instance, web advertising consultants have an interest in showing that the Web can be used for branding, and thus can do the central work of advertising in other media. The market research possibilities are promoted by web site providers, as a way of attracting advertisers. The possibilities of on-line retailing are promoted by makers of servers, because customer service in real time, though it may seem simple enough, requires big, fast machines.

Example 3: links

With posters and television, I emphasized that one advertisement cannot be taken as an isolated text, like a poem or a painting, apart from the way people experience it in space and time. This is even more true of web advertisements, where each section brings the user dozens of pages, and each page consists of many parts. The key to the Web is the interconnectedness suggested by its name (Barbules 1998). We may be especially aware of the fragmentary, interlinked quality of the Web in the current state of technology, when we see each image load, painfully slowly, and see each URL, instead of having everything appear as a whole. Let us consider an example of a 20-minute session on the Web.

Suppose I want to look for some background to this chapter. I launch Netscape (which dials my link to the university) and start by searching on the Excite search engine using 'ADVERTISING and WEB'. There are hundreds of possible responses listed, in the order that the search engine thinks approximates what I am after. There is also a banner for NEC Notebook computers:

> Built like a [picture of a tank]
> Funny, it doesn't look like one [notebook computer with tank treads]
> But it will blow you away.

This is the sort of banner that could have been sent to me because of my choice of search term, in this case 'WEB'. Different terms might trigger different banners.

I click on Microscope, a review of banner headlines on the Web (www.pscentral.com). It reviews five banners this week, with the examples there. My favourite, of those reviewed in the week before Christmas:

> How do you find a partridge in a pear tree?
> [Types in the box of a search engine three possible phrases]
>   creative fruit baskets
>   pet shops – domestic, exotic birds
>   poultry farms
> Big Yellow. Tis the Season for shopping on the Web.

Besides the reviews of banners, the Microscope site also has a paid-for banner ad for 'Thunderlizard', a company offering seminars on web advertising, with a link to further details on the next seminar. Microscope has other information on other pages, for instance a page of awards it has received, archives of past ads featured, a page for submitting one's own suggestions for advertisement of the year, and a hot link to the editor for asking permission to quote (but as far as I can tell, no identification of who sponsors the site).

Microscope also has a page of links, including one to Channelseven, another site on web advertising, with its own awards (www.channel-seven.com). Channelseven has its own banner ad, for Infoseek, a search engine, as an advertising medium. This banner has changing caricatures of someone trying to look like Groucho Marx, Marilyn Monroe, and Elvis Presley:

> We don't just deliver impressions.
> We deliver results.
> Once you know you know.

Below the banner, a message from Channelseven says 'Please support our sponsor'. I go back to the Microscope links and try a wonderful site of

'Advertising Quotations', offered by a Professor of Advertising at the University of Texas (advertising.utexas.edu/research/quotes). Finally, my connection crashes.

If one focuses on the information delivered, this constant movement and distraction may seem a trivial side-effect of the Web. But it is crucial, both to web users and to advertisers. For most uses of media, I need to know what I am looking for and how the medium is organized – whether it is the categories and alphabetization of telephone book yellow pages, the indexes and pagination of academic journals, the gate folds of pornographic magazines, or the sections and features of a daily newspaper. In most uses of the Net, I don't need to know what I am looking for, or how the pieces of the medium fit together; at each stage, I can just go from one page to another, and back (see WORLD WIDE WEB). On the one hand, this may seem to make the advertiser's task hopeless, placing a needle in a haystack. But if the advertiser has the right keywords, or the right links, or puts the URL everywhere in other media, they can have huge traffic passing through, even if only for seconds. More importantly, the users are people who, potentially, have a different sort of involvement from those glancing at the page of a magazine, or stepping out to make tea in a commercial break.

Using the Web

In the example I have given of one session on the Web, I have done several kinds of actions: searching, browsing, reading, inputting, downloading, and (don't forget) crashing. Each of these actions is important to advertisers using the Web.

Searching – This is typically the first action of a user looking for a particular site or particular information, so search engines are very heavily used and are themselves the most expensive sites for banner ads. If one has in mind a keyword, one can use an index, like Excite or Infoseek, that consults an automatically compiled index of words, or if one has in mind a topic, such as theatre listings, one can turn to a directory, like Yahoo or Yell, that has a tree of sites chosen and arranged by humans. (The difference is shown by an example in which I look for the RSPCA for information on pets; Excite gives me hundreds of pages of advertising, organizations, and individual résumés that mention the organization in some way, while Yahoo gives only the RSPCA home page.) Searches can be much more sophisticated than what I have shown here, two words linked by AND. I could, for instance, have used a site that assigns the search terms to a number of different search engines. And I could use terms to narrow down the huge number of possibilities the search engine turns up, and put them in an order more useful to me. We have seen that advertisers can have their banners turn up with the responses containing certain search terms; *Business Week* tells us that the use of the term 'beer' on Yahoo triggers an ad for Miller Brewing, while 'laptop' triggers an ad for IBM.

Browsing – My sessions are seldom a simple matter of seeking and finding. Instead I try several sites that look interesting, and follow leads from several of them onto others, often sites completely unrelated to what I was originally looking for. So, for instance, I found Channelseven, not by my first search, but through Microscope. Links work both ways: the links from a page can make it worth finding (see the Zenith media site), while links to it make it findable (a page without links is invisible both to browsers and to search engines). Browsing means one can glance at many sites, but it also means that one's commitment to any one site can be very slight. It also means users have little patience with sites that slow down their browsing with complex graphics. The Miller Lite site opens with a simple text message: 'Don't be in a hurry. Let this page load. It's worth it.' This acknowledges the impatience of the browsing user, though I am not sure the message keeps them hanging on.

Reading – Once I get to a site, I read it. But how? Guides for web authors stress the relative importance of images compared to text, and the reduction of each textual unit to a size that can be easily scanned on a screen, and the replacement of linear text by a sense of multiple paths through a set of texts. All this is less of a surprise for advertisers than it might be to journalists, novelists, or academics; advertisers have been producing short-copy, strong image texts for decades. The visual design of the page is important, but this is to some degree out of the Web producer's hands; they specify what is heading and text, but different browsers will give these headings and texts different fonts and colours (the very elements advertising art designers would want to control). In studies that stress the openness of hypertext, it seems that the user, rather than the writer, is in control. But there is another aspect of web reading in which the user has little control. Web texts typically tell very little about who made them and why. I know that an ad in a magazine is paid for by the advertisers and is trying to sell me something; I know that an academic journal is refereed; and I know that the prospectus of a university is an official publication subject to legal requirements. Web pages typically give much less information, and fewer clues that would help interpret why they say what they say. In the case of advertising, the boundaries between advertisement and content are blurred in a way that is less possible in other media.

Inputting – I keep this unlovely word because it includes different ways of putting in data: typing one's name or postal code, clicking an icon, clicking a point on a map or diagram, or pulling down a menu. Users quickly learn that there is a crucial difference between the mouse being represented by an arrow moving around the screen, and the same pointer when it has turned into a little hand that can make choices. All these are ways of giving information, and however trivial the data seem, they can be collected to give some picture of the user. Users also leave information at some sites unwittingly, in the form of cookies that record the paths they have taken (see discussion in Chapter 9). Both the conscious giving and unconscious leaving of information can be crucial to advertisers. The same sort of information about readers of magazines or viewers of television programmes is gathered indirectly, and at great cost per subject. The data can be used for market research purposes, but also for targeting users with appropriate ads and offers.

Downloading – This is another unwieldy word that covers a range of similar actions. If I could only read what was on the screen, my experience of the Web would be limited to the time I was actually logged on. But the Web was originally designed for sharing large amounts of scientific information, and it allows for rapid transfers of large files. One could make these transfers before with other file transfer programs, but the Web presents them, not as complex codes one has to know, but as simple buttons to push. For instance, one can download the following:

- pictures of pop stars from their official and unofficial sites;
- articles from the archives of *Business Week* (even including the cover art and pictures as separate images for downloading);
- the text or video of Earl Spencer's eulogy for Diana, Princess of Wales, from CNN;
- controversial ads from Benetton;
- forms for applying for research grants, from the Economic and Social Research Council;
- software from Shockwave or RealAudio to use on other sites;
- games from Pepsi;
- television ads from Miller Lite;
- critical parodies of television ads from Adbusters;
- upgrades of systems or utilities such as QuickTime;
- and even the browsers themselves.

For advertisers, these downloads may be premiums to attract users to one's page (even Friends of the Earth offers art for kids to put on buttons they can make and wear), or they may be ways of extending one's ads, as screensavers or wallpaper. So, for instance, the Guinness ad, downloaded as a screensaver, or a still from a Disney film, downloaded as wallpaper, will keep working every time the user turns on their computer.

Waiting – I mentioned at the end of Example 3 that my Netscape connection crashed. Other users may have more reliable connections than my modem at home, but all users have frequent problems: service providers down, URLs unavailable, software conflicts, inadequate hardware, and for 20 hours of the day incredible slowness in connecting and loading. Sceptics stress these problems; enthusiasts for the Web seldom mention them. To be fair, the Web presents complex problems, providing pages that work in more or less the same way for different operating systems running different browsers on hardware of various ages with different sorts of connections.

Sceptics call it the World Wide Wait. Enthusiasts claim the problems will be solved with new browsers, faster chips, new plug-ins, lines that carry more information. The importance of the problems to advertisers is that problems break down the sense of message and response. If a page takes 10 minutes to download, we focus on the recalcitrant machine instead of imagining interaction. The problems make us aware of how much advertisers rely on the predictability of other media.

The actions I have listed do not represent different kinds of users or different styles of reading; they are all involved in any routine session on the Web. They call for different kinds of strategies from advertisers:

- searching – linking banners to keywords
- browsing – trying to get relevant links
- reading – designing banners to stand out through colour and movement
- inputting – persuading users to give up information, knowingly or unknowingly
- downloading – providing goodies as premiums
- waiting – anticipating problems of software conflicts, memory and speed, hardware limitations, over-use.

As with other media, advertisers have been quick to respond to the new possibilities for interaction, and have also shaped these possibilities as the medium has developed. Shockwave, frames, cookies, and elaborate browsers were all developed because commercial web sites would use them.

How to wreck a web site: what advertisers say about web ads

One way to see how advertisers view the new medium is to look at the criticisms of specific ads. There are several such critiques on the Web, such as Adland, *Advertising Age*'s 'Cyber Critiques', Microscope, and Channelseven, as well as in print publications such as *Campaign* or the *Independent*. No clear consensus has emerged on what makes for a great Web ad the way it has, for instance, with posters (see Chapter 6). But there is some consensus about what *not* to do. The complaints about ads can be thought of in pairs:

- The site is too boring (all text and dull pictures)
- OR it is too busy (with too much on one page).
- The site gives no opportunities for interaction (just reading and watching)
- OR it is too complex and unfocused, with meaningless games.
- The software used is out of date (no frames, Java, Shockwave)
- OR it is too reliant on users having the latest browsers and plug-ins and a fast connection.

- The ad has no relevance to the Web as a medium
- OR the site is relevant to the Web, but not particularly related to the brand.

The fact that these complaints come in pairs suggests there are inherent tensions in trying to adapt the medium to the needs of advertisers. It may surprise boosters of the new technology that these complaints tend to parallel those about ads on posters or on TV. The rules in all three media are to keep it simple, reduce text, emphasize the brand identity, think of the user's context and interests, and leave the audience something to do.

Summary

In the 'keywords' I outline three ways of looking at interaction: (1) an exchange of message and a sense of *response*; (2) a message that gives the receiver choices about what comes next, and a sense of *participation*; and (3) a sense of *presence* of another person paying attention. The Web excites advertisers because it offers new ways of thinking about response and participation. For the rather narrow audience who uses it now, it can do things no other advertising medium can do. But what is promised, usually in news articles and science fiction, is something more like simulated presence. It could be that this is not the logical extension of the first two kinds of interaction, but a kind of experience opposite to them. Eventually advertisers may give up trying to do on the Web what other media do, and use it instead for what only it can do: incorporate audience responses and choices into the experience of the medium.

The Web is important to analysts of advertising even if they do not accept all the claims for it. It gives us the chance to see a medium emerging, and a chance to see how a new medium forces advertisers to re-think what each medium does. It may settle down, the way TV did, into a stereotypical role (branding for mass market products) and a stereotypical form. Or it may not.

Suggested reading: advertising on the Web

There are a number of books with titles like Jim Sterne's *World Wide Web Marketing* (1995), but they tend to date very quickly. Academic studies of the Internet, such as Rob Shields, ed., *Cultures of Internet* (1996), have so far tended to focus on usenet and e-mail, but see Snyder (1998) and Faigley (1998), and the references they contain. The best print commentaries on web advertising are in the trade press, such as *Campaign*'s monthly section *Campaign Interactive*. The most up-to-date information is on the Web itself, but of course each source must be read with some thought about the sponsor's interests: they are software developers, consultants, publishers, or manufacturers. Here are some good starting points:

http://www.adage.com (the US advertising weekly – see CyberCritiques)

http://advertising.utexas.edu/research/quotes (an entertaining collection of quotations on advertising – perfect to liven up an essay – including some from Jef I. Richards, who put the site together)

http://www.blipp.com/adland/debate.html (Adland has many links to discussions of ads)

http://www.channelseven.com (reviews of web advertising)

http://www.fallon.com (Fallon McElligot, a hot US agency, with links to Miller Lite and other sites)

http://www.hhcl.com (a hot UK agency, links to Tango and news)

http://www.hotwired.com ('We waste our time so you don't have to')

http://www.microscope.com (reviews banners and provides useful links)

http://www.wilsonweb.com/wmt (Web Marketing Today)

http://www.zenithmedia.com (an excellent list of links to media/marketing sources)

URLs of other sites mentioned in this chapter:

http://www.adidas.com (in four languages)

http://www.amazon.com

http://www.americangirl.com

http://www.benetton.com (no longer has all their posters, but does have discussion of their communications, and lots of pictures)

http://www.cnn.com

http://www.disney.com

http://www.envirolink.org (links to many organizations)

http://www.foe.co.uk

http://www.g-boyd.com (Amstel's mock 'Legion of Decency')

http://www.gm.com

http://www.greenpeace.org

http://www.go2.guardian.co.uk (the *Guardian*'s on-line version specializes in news of science and technology)

http://www.guinness.ie

http://www.msnbc.com

http://www.newscientist.com (news from the magazine and excellent links)

http://www.pepsi.com

http://www.tango.co.uk (consistently bizarre – currently 'The History of Shopping Bags by May Beal')

I checked all the addresses the day the book went to press, but the Web changes rapidly. By the time it reaches you, some of these will have changed or disappeared, and many more will have started. As the chapter suggests, searching for them is part of the fun.

PART

III

AUDIENCES

Calvin and Hobbes

by Bill Watterson

Calvin and Hobbes

9

Constructing the audience: advertising research

In a room in Seattle, chairs are arranged informally in a circle, and a group of women, strangers to each other, are talking about cars. Behind a one-way mirror, a planning director from Weiden and Kennedy, the Portland advertising agency, is looking on, trying to find out something they can use about the image of their client, Subaru, in relation to those of competing brands. The discussion is being led by a facilitator, Lisa, who has the women playing a game. They are given a brand name, and they give a description of the stereotype of the owner of that brand. Then the others have to guess the brand.

> Jenny took a card. 'Single woman,' she offered. 'Educated. Modern. Conservative in dress. Has a medium-small dog. Healthy. Has quite a social life and used the car a lot.'
>
> Helen, the chatty one, responded. 'Sounds like me. Sounds like Honda.' And it was.
>
> Cheri went next. 'Great family car. Outdoor activities. People who insist on buying American. Bigger people. People who go camping. Bacon and eggs for breakfast. Middle-aged. Financially secure.' The answer came back severally: Ford vans.
>
> Helen took a turn. She looked at her card and launched into a stereotype: 'They're outdoorsy. They're interested in fuel economy. They're athletic – they like to ski and bicycle. They could be a teacher or an engineer.'
>
> This time, Cheri leapt in with the answer. 'That's easy. Subaru. That's the person they target in the ads.'

The story is from Randall Rothenberg's (1994) fascinating account of the Subaru campaign from start to finish. This particular exercise may seem like an after-dinner entertainment at a rather dull party, rather than research. But they are finding something – not just that these women know the stereotypes created in the ads, but they know they are stereotypes, created in ads.

Table 9.1 Methods of advertising research

Questions and techniques	Uses	Problems	Subjects	Actions	Interactions
Who sees the ads?					
Audits of circulation and audiences	– detailed quantitative information on a representative sample	– may not reflect actual practices or differences in practices	– organisms responding to stimulus – situated in homes	– subscription or tuning in taken to stand for attention	– interaction through interview or automatic monitor
Web cookies	– detailed information on every user's choices	– privacy issues – can be blocked	– assumption of consistency over time	– paths stand for preferences	– most users unaware of the cookie
How do they respond?					
Surveys of consumers	– can cover a careful and broad sample	– saying is not doing – the survey constrains possible responses	– bundles of traits – situated in public	– accounts stand for actions	– one-to-one contact in question and answer format
Depth interviews	– more complex responses about underlying meanings	– researcher control – tied to psychological models	– divided selves without access to their own motivations	– talk stands for underlying motivations	– interaction modelled on therapy
Focus groups	– complex responses – link to everyday talk – effect of realism	– not generalizable – moderator control	– role players – situated in public, group interaction	– guided talk taken to represent informal conversation	– interaction of facilitator and subjects mediated by group dynamics
Does the ad sell?					
Mail order	– directly confirms effect of the ad	– not usable in all media	– behaviourist models – situation is the point of sale	– sales stand for ad effects	– interaction only via sales data
Coupons and responses	– shows action – sense of involvement	– only a small part of the actual audience	– behaviourist models – situation is the reading of the ad	– responses stand for ad effects	– interaction only via response data
Retail surveys	– direct evidence of sales	– only indirect evidence of effects of ads	– behaviourist models – situation is the retail outlet	– stock stands for ad effects	– interaction only via stock data
Bar code scanner data	– sales data linked to specific customers	– subject to local and temporary fluctuations	– behaviourist models – situation is the point of sale	– sales stand for ad effects	– interaction only via sales data

As we will see later in the chapter, this kind of focus group research, and other forms of advertising research, play a crucial role in constructing what audiences are, and how – or whether – they respond to ads. In Chapter 1, I discussed the difficulty of showing that any particular ad causes an increase in sales, because ads have a range of possible effects, and because there are many reasons why people buy things at a particular time and place. Research seeks to reduce the uncertainty that is so much a part of the advertising business. But the research carries its own uncertainties.

Advertising research has been part of the business since nearly the beginning, because all the participants – advertiser, agency, media owner – have an interest in showing advertising effectiveness. There are, of course, different aims for different users of the research: the client may want to know how the brand is seen in relation to others, retailers may want to know if it will move a specific product at a specific price, agencies may want to know if a headline or concept sticks in people's minds, media owners may want to demonstrate their ability to reach a target audiences, policy-makers may want to know if ads contribute to public health or reduce energy waste, academic researchers may try to show how their analyses of ads in terms of cultural theory relate to readings given by various groups. The approaches of marketers, advertising researchers, and cultural and media studies researchers each have their general models, their stereotypes, and their favourite examples (see Suggested Reading).

In this chapter, I will review some of the methods that have been used to study advertising audiences and effects (see EFFECTS), then compare the assumptions of these different methods, and finally look in more detail at one method, the use of focus groups. I will not provide a definitive approach to audience effects research (if I could do that I could get rich quick), but suggest a set of questions we should ask of any approach, academic or commercial:

- How do they conceive of the *subject*, the person who is part of the audience, on whom the ads are to have an effect? (For instance, do the subjects themselves know what effects the ads have?)
- What *actions* stand for other actions in their research? (For instance, sending in a coupon may stand for having read an ad and having been convinced by it.)
- How do the researchers and people *interact* in the research? (For instance, do they meet face to face, or are responses recorded automatically?)
- What *kinds of questions* does the client (or reader or user) of the research ask? What questions don't they ask?

Of course we could ask these questions of any social science research. One reason to stress the questions with audience research is that the various approaches come from different groups with different interests (for instance, commercial audience size measurements vs. effects experiments, or academic media studies analyses focusing on attitudes vs. cultural studies analyses focusing on practices). The different approaches may have different strengths and weaknesses, but they may also be studying quite different things that they all call 'audiences' and 'effects'.

Methods of advertising research

The market trader described in Chapter 8 doesn't need to buy any research, because he is doing it himself all the time. He has his stock in the van, so it is too late to change the product. His pool of potential customers consists of all the people who walk past his stand, and only them. There are no other ads for these pen sets or towel sets or necklaces (though he may refer to print ads to confirm higher prices and to build up his bargains), and there is no word of mouth or brand heritage to build on. The trader makes his pitch, and it either moves the goods and he makes a tidy bundle, or it doesn't and he returns home with a van load of towel sets. In Clark and Pinch (1995), Colin Clark describes the painful process of learning about audiences in this direct and often humiliating way.

But as soon as the pitch is separated from the seller, and various media are used, this direct contact is lost, and advertisers have to ask:

- if people are seeing the ad;
- if they are affected by it; and
- if there are enough additional sales as a result to justify the advertising.

Who sees the ads?

In the nineteenth century, newspapers would inflate their claims of circulation, and out-of-town advertisers were in no position to check. Just as advertising agencies were beginning to form, Rowell and Company in the US offered a service of checking these claims, making themselves highly unpopular with publishers, but essential to advertisers. The Audit Bureau of Circulations was founded in the UK in 1914, and continues today. An ad for their services in *Campaign* warns that the advertiser who doesn't know enough about a publication and its audience finds out, 'How to turn a powerful, persuasive advertisement into wastepaper'. They offer their detailed profiles of publications that will avoid this happening. Recently a similar service has started to provide audited data on the rather difficult problem of who sees each poster; the owners of outdoor advertising sites need such data to compete with other media.

Even with decades of experience in circulation auditing for press advertisers, there are constant disputes between rival publications, not just about the total size of their sales, but about how they were sold (newsstand, subscription, special offers), who reads them, how they are read and passed on. Leo Bogart (1990) notes such complicating factors as whether subsequent readers are as attentive as the person who first paid for a magazine, and whether someone seeing a magazine in a dentist's waiting room counts, and whether specific issues of *Sports Illustrated* might have quite different kinds of readership with a golfer or a basketball player on the cover.

Equivalent kinds of auditing of audience numbers arose as radio and television had to demonstrate their reach, in competition with newspapers and magazines. A. C. Neilsen started in the US in the 1930s phoning people and asking them what they were listening to. (Scannell and Cardiff (1991) point out that the BBC did audience research around the same time even though they did not yet have any advertisers to impress – they had to justify the licence fee.) But there are problems with the survey approach, as there are for audits of circulations. I might claim to be listening to a classical broadcast when in fact I am listening to Country and Western, or vice versa, or I might claim to be listening when I was not, just to oblige the researchers. So Neilsen set up a panel of homes, chosen to be statistically representative, and then attached black boxes that would record just what people were listening to. In the 1950s, as applied to television, these ratings became hugely important – not just advertisers but programme producers and programmers responded immediately to the results, and there was a Congressional investigation into their influence. More sophisticated versions of this viewing survey exist today; with technology called the 'People Meter', users have to press a button to indicate they are in the room, and presumably watching, not just leaving it on for the cats. But even these highly technological surveys have huge weaknesses. The viewer or listener could turn it on for the programmes they felt they ought to be watching, rather than just those they usually do watch; or different people could be in the room, some of whom detest the programme. The box tells us what the set is doing, but not what the people are doing.

In Chapter 8 I argued that part of the fascination the World Wide Web has for advertisers is that it provides similar information about readership, even if the potential audience is, at the moment, rather small. It is as if every ad came with a coupon. Sometimes sites require a visitor to register, giving various kinds of personal information, before searching for information or playing a game. (I recall that the menu at the Pepsi site asked me how often I drank Pepsi; I was unable to give a true figure because the pull-down menu didn't allow for anything less than 'once a week'.)

More recently sites have begun to send out 'cookies', routines that lodge in the user's browser, and automatically download information to the site's server when one returns to it, information about the user's movements from page to page (see 'Suggested Reading'). One of the largest commercial firms collecting this information, DoubleClick, explains on their home page the advantages to their clients:

> DoubleClick, the internet advertising solutions company, is the leader
> in building on-line, one-to-one relationships between brands and con-
> sumers. A unique combination of media and technological expertise
> and the delivery of a quality network of Websites enables DoubleClick
> to hit an advertiser's desired target, every time.

They can claim to hit the target because they have gathered, automatically,
detailed information about each consumer's preferences, not what the consumers told them on some survey, but what they showed by their own
choices of routes through various pages.

Some uses of cookies are innocuous; they allow Amazon to keep track of
what books you have ordered before, so that they can suggest new ones that
might interest you, they retain your personalized set-up of your chosen
search engine, and retain password and user-name data. But they worry
some writers on the Web as a public forum, because they allow for sharing
of data about where you have gone on the Web. DoubleClick says they
scrupulously guard the confidentiality of their data, but industry self-
regulators are drafting standards to have the design of cookies restricted so
that they can only go back to the domain the user sees, not on to other
domains. Some marketers say this restriction would make cookies useless for
their purposes. When I read the discussions of these and other issues at
Cookie Central (www.cookiecentral.com), I set my browser to alert me
whenever a site wanted to send me a cookie. Although I haven't refused any,
I'm amazed at how many I get in the normal course of browsing (eight the
first time I visited MSNBC), and how much information they must be
collecting. Whether this information leads, as DoubleClick claims, to a one-
to-one relationship between brand and consumer, is another matter.

How do audiences respond?

The circulation and audience surveys and the cookies just tell the
researchers who was potentially exposed to the advertisement; they don't
tell whether anyone looked at it, read it, remembered it, or acted on it. So
commercial organizations have developed surveys of media consumption
and purchasing habits, again starting in the 1930s. You may have been
involved in one of the tens of thousands of market research surveys every
year about brands and consumption habits. Similar surveys are done specifically on advertising. The researcher might ask subjects, unprompted, if they
remembered any ads for cars, or might prompt them with some names, or
some ads. But of course this does not reproduce the situation in which
readers see ads, so the Magazine Audience Study Group developed a
method that involved showing the subject a whole magazine, having them
leaf through it, asking them about the articles, and only then asking them
about the ads (Bogart 1990). Later, in the 1950s, there might be a quasi-

experimental set-up, in which consumers would be brought together, asked about probable purchasing preferences, shown some television commercials, and then asked again (Haskins and Kendrick 1993). Or researchers might take longer, with fewer subjects, and explore their feelings about a brand or associated practices in a 'depth interview' (Mayer 1958). Here the assumption is that the subject doesn't really know and can't tell their underlying, subconscious responses to brands; they must be drawn out by more careful and indirect probing, almost like therapy.

Surveys and interviews may seriously constrain their results by setting up a situation highly unlike reading a magazine or watching a commercial, and by considering only the questions the researchers can think of as relevant. I recall a market research interview about motor oil that recorded everything I could possibly think about the various brands, their logos, and the places I could purchase motor oil, without having a way of registering on the questionnaire the important observation that I was completely indifferent to the whole topic. Many market research programmes try to cover themselves for this kind of tunnel vision by combining some narrow and directive form of quantitative research with many respondents, such as experiments or questionnaires, with some broader, more qualitative forms of research, with fewer respondents, that could suggest unsuspected links and problems. In a focus group, the researcher recruits a group of people who share some characteristics, and leads them in a tightly focused discussion of a topic. The idea is that people talking to each other will say more, and more unpredictable things, than they might talking directly to an interviewer, or in response to a questionnaire. I will consider the uses and limitations of focus groups with some examples later in the chapter.

The problems of determining audience effects parallel those of determining audience numbers. As one pollster put it after the 1991 UK elections, faced with his inaccurate predictions based on polls just before the elections: 'People lie.' But it needn't be so simple. If you asked me what I was going to buy at Sainsbury's, you would get a shopping list that for many reasons doesn't match the receipt I get at the check-out at the end. I might be trying to impress you, or to cover up my purchases of large amounts of expensive salad leaves, or I might see some cheeses that I hadn't noticed before and buy them, or there may turn out to be an offer in the wine section, or I might not get to Sainsbury's at all because of the traffic. Such problems of talk and action occur in all social science research; they stand out in marketing research only because the intended action – taking an item to the check-out – seems so simple and unequivocal. It isn't.

Does the ad sell?

Faced with the difficulties of interpreting indirect information about inclination to buy, advertisers may look for increased sales as direct evidence of effectiveness. The connection between ad and sale is most direct with mail-order ads: readers must have been moved by the ad or they would not have sent in their money. But not everything can be sold by mail (it is unsuitable in different ways for cars, bananas, and loo paper), so advertisers may use coupons, premiums, and offers that prompt some response to the ad, even if the response isn't a purchase. This cuts out layers and layers of uncertainty about the placement of the ad – every single person who responds read at least part of it. Claude Hopkins developed in the 1920s a system he called *Scientific Advertising* (see INTERACTION). The approach was simple – a good ad is the one that gets the most coupons sent back. The intuitions of client and copywriter should be ignored. Every part of the ad should be tested. So one could, for instance, print half the run of a major magazine with an ad headed:

THEY LAUGHED WHEN I SAT DOWN TO THE PIANO, BUT THEN I STARTED TO PLAY.

The other half of the print run of the same magazine would have exactly the same ad in the same place, but headed:

TEN PERSONALIZED PIANO LESSONS FOR LESS THAN $5.

Each version of the ad would have a coupon to send for further information. The version that drew the most coupons had the best headline. Hopkins points out that the same could be done for the picture, the claims, the length of copy. Bogart (1990) tells of a similar experiment by a major motor retailer, who had his company's magazine ads left out of 100 000 copies of a mass-circulation magazine, and then at the end of several years compared auto registrations among the people who took the magazines with the ads to those who took the magazines without the ads. There are surprisingly few such large-scale experiments (Schudson (1984) describes a few others), perhaps because they are highly risky to the experimenting marketing director. If there is no difference between sales with and without ads, why do we need the ads, and if the ads work, why did we pay for them and then cut them out of 100 000 magazines?

Claude Hopkins' 'scientific' approach based on copy testing using coupons was much favoured by such advertising gurus as David Ogilvy. And it survives today in the familiar mail-order ads, direct mail ads, and the phone response ads on television, some of them serious (buying compilation albums or kitchen products) and some of them spoofs. Recent phone-ins have involved reporting 'counterfeit' cans of the soft drink Tango (the ads by HHCL), or choosing who one would like to put extra cheese on McCain's frozen pizza, (HHCL Brasserie), or reporting someone you think needs to be beautified before they can drink Martini vermouth. The point is that even if the phoning back has little to do with sales, it gives the advertiser information about who was watching, information it can then use in dealing with the agency and the media owner, and also use in planning its own campaigns.

The problem with such response ads is that the people who decide to send in the coupon or dial the phone number may not be representative of all those who saw the ad, or of those who are inclined to buy. Direct and representative information about sales was, until recently, surprisingly difficult to get. The producer knew how much of a product they had manufactured and shipped, but didn't know if it had sold. The retailers knew what they had ordered, and their overall total sales, but stock-taking on any particular product had to be fairly infrequent. They could not say what they had sold, when, at what price, or to whom. Shopping baskets of individual purchasers could be monitored only by elaborate pre- and post-shopping surveys. A. C. Neilsen, the same organisation that later produced the TV ratings, began conducting retailer surveys of product stocks in the 1930s. They recorded their information from a number of representative stores, such as pharmacies or grocery stores, and then sold it to all the companies in that industry. The surveys were labour intensive and expensive (an academic researcher can hardly imagine the cost of gathering social data on such a scale, over years), and they provided a powerful bargaining tool to producers.

In this kind of research, as with audience measurements, there has been a very important technological change. Now supermarkets generate vast amounts of data from records generated by the computerized bar code scanners. Mayer (1991) quotes an advertising researcher, Ben Lipstein, saying there were two critical events in the history of marketing: 'The first was in the first decade of this century, when we discovered we could ask questions. The second was in the eighth decade, when scanner data taught us that we didn't have to ask questions' (21). These data potentially give retailers an understanding of market processes beyond what the producers or media researchers could have. They not only know just what they sold; combining the information with their loyalty cards (which give my address and other data), they know who bought exactly what, with what. But there are still complexities of interpretation, partly because there is now so much information with which to deal. With data so detailed, there are problems of local fluctuations in sales, seasonal and weekly variations, effects of special offers and tie-ins. So even this remarkable source of information, which would have been seen as the holy grail of marketing research just 20 years ago, does not necessarily answer the question of whether a specific ad led to sales.

Assumptions of research on audience effects

I have traced some changes and continuities in advertising research over the years: from circulation audits to web page hits, from consumer surveys to focus groups, from store stock audits to bar code data; an overview is given in Table 9.1 at the beginning of this chapter. Now let us return to the questions I raised at the beginning of the chapter, about the assumptions about the subjects and the researchers underlying each of these approaches.

- How do they conceive of the *subject*, the person who is part of the audience, on whom the ads are to have an effect?
- What *actions* stand for other actions?
- How do the researchers and people *interact* in the research?
- What *kinds of questions* does the client (or reader or user) of the research ask? What questions don't they ask?

Subjects

All studies of audience effects imply some idea of the self, the subject who is buying things at the end of the process. Jonathan Potter and Margaret Wetherell (1987) provide a useful overview of some of the ideas current in psychology and cultural studies, making us aware that we cannot take even something so basic as the self for granted. Audience and circulation audits assume a simple model of stimulus and response – if the audience-member was exposed to the ad, then it has an effect. Some marketing surveys assume a model of trait theory, in which people in various categories possess bundles of traits such as adventurousness or caution, self-reliance or other-directedness. They try to divide the population into people with bundles of traits, assuming they will act in other ways consistently on these traits. On the other hand, depth interviews assume that true motivations are hidden both from the researcher and from the subjects themselves, and can be released in extensive talk the way the Freudian unconscious shows itself in therapy sessions. Focus groups draw on theories of roles and role-play, in which people will reveal themselves by their social interactions. For instance, a group of women in one group I attended looked around the room, saw that all the others are also mothers of toddlers, and talked that evening as mothers of toddlers, rather than in terms of all the other identities they could take on, as nurses, teachers, environmental activists, or Christians. The parallels between advertising models of consumers and psychological models of the self are no coincidence – advertising theory has developed along with social psychology (see Lears 1995).

Some advertising researchers cling to a model in which potential consumers are moved through a 'hierarchy of advertising effects' (outlined and criticized by Bogart (1990: 372):

awareness → comprehension → conviction → purchase

This hierarchy is useful in reminding us again that merely seeing an ad doesn't lead one to purchase the product. But in any complex case, the stages and links break down. First, the hierarchy assumes a blank slate of a subject, for whom 'awareness' of the ad is the first exposure to the possibility of purchase (thus, as Bogart points out, it works best for completely new products). Second, 'comprehension' can be at all sorts of levels, from careful reading to the vague humming of a jingle, from positive associations with the provider of an entertaining ad to misidentification of the ad as that of a competing brand. And as we have seen in earlier chapters, interpretations of ads can go in many different directions, not all of them favourable. 'Conviction' too can come in many forms, and in relation to other experiences besides advertising, such as discussions with other people, or existing habits of use. The intended effect of the ad may be immediate purchase, or it might be a shift in the associations of the brand that would have long-term effects. Finally, the 'purchase' of the product is, as we saw in Chapter 1, dependent on a number of factors, of which the advertising is just one, and seldom the most important one. The problem is not just that the steps are oversimplified, but that the person assumed here is more coherent, controlled, and compartmentalized than anyone I know.

Actions

In each research approach, one action that the researcher can get at stands for other actions about which the researcher would like to know. For instance, in circulation research, subscribing to a magazine is taken to stand for reading it and its ads. In survey research and experimental research, accounts of how one has responded or will behave are taken to stand for one's response and future purchases, and statements of one person are taken to stand for those of other people in their category. In focus groups, the conversation with strangers is taken to represent social interaction with a group, and the exercises are taken to stand for choices one might make in other situations. In Hopkins' 'scientific advertising', the sending in of a coupon is taken to stand in for reading, comprehension, and an increased willingness to buy, when it may not mean any of these things. In stock audits and scanner data, the assumption goes the other way: the fact of sales is taken to stand for the influence of ads. In each case, the researchers have made a model world they can control, and have projected other actions from it.

Interactions

Researchers in each approach intervene in and modify the results. This is most obvious in survey and experimental research, where the researcher meets the subject face to face. Interviewers are trained and questionnaires are designed to reduce the effect of interference. But one must recall that a survey is a strange sort of interaction, and at each moment the subject is not just answering a question (often an odd or apparently trivial one), but making a guess about why it was asked. Researchers on media audiences have gone to great efforts to try to leave themselves out of the study, by registering automatically that the set is tuned to a channel, that a person is in the room, and that the person is watching. We must assume that even with such indirect, electronic monitoring, subjects want to project an image of themselves in an interaction. One advantage of focus groups is that the technique starts with the fact of interaction, and observes the interaction instead of trying to reduce it. But this interaction is highly constrained, not only by the researchers' topic guide, but by the dynamics of the group. These problems are not necessarily matters of bias, trying to get one result rather than another, but they may none the less result on the researchers spending a great deal of time and money to get results confirming what they thought beforehand.

Kinds of questions

All this research is done for someone. This doesn't mean it is necessarily biased or dishonest, but it does mean that one participant or another has control both of the research and of the results. When you read commercial advertising research, you will seldom read studies of how ads didn't work, because most of the research is done by groups with an interest in that particular campaign (as in the excellent case histories in a series like *Advertising Works*). All research will be focused on the researchers' questions. An advertiser wants to know if a given ad leads to increased sales of mascarpone cheese, or perhaps to less direct benefits like a change in perception of Sainsbury's as a brand. A social scientist might be interested as well in the way the ad affects other practices and beliefs, besides just purchasing and brands. For instance, Sainsbury's ads might be studied for their influence on or reflection of ideas about food, gender, shopping, nationality, health, the environment and the self, in relation to current social theory. Both advertising researchers and social scientists will be constrained by the sorts of questions considered important by their colleagues and the users of their research.

Why does it matter who does research on what? Information about the preferences of consumers can bring power in negotiations and money. Media owners had great power when only they knew who read their publications, before Rowell produced independent information with their audit. A. C. Neilsen had power when it could provide an independent audit of who watched which programmes and which stock lines moved fastest. Agencies or clients would do research on advertising effectiveness, and use the results to negotiate their contracts, or take the results to develop to new links to other clients or agencies. Now the power could be shifting again. Sainsbury's has huge amounts of data, in-house; it knows what lines are moving much better than the manufacturers, and can use this information to make decisions about, say, shelf space allotted to a brand, or the geographical distribution of new products. New media like the Web could shift knowledge to the media owners again, with companies like DoubleClick collecting huge amounts of data from cookies.

It is important to ask about the assumptions and interests of any research, whether commercial or academic. But the link to interests does not mean that the research should simply be rejected. All research makes some set of limiting assumptions; advertising research is different only in that the field is so divided, with different kinds of researchers doing different kinds of research for different ends. It still has the potential to tell us something new, or at least to shake up the platitudes constantly repeated by advertisers, academics, and members of the public.

Example: focus groups in commercial and academic research

I will take focus group techniques, those used in the example at the beginning of the chapter, as a more detailed example of the assumptions I have been discussing. I choose them partly because they are a method used by both commercial and academic researchers, and partly because they are a form of research I am doing myself. In a focus group, researchers choose about eight participants who fit the criteria in which they are interested, and have a trained facilitator, following a topic guide, lead them in a group discussion. The results are usually taped and written down, and the facilitator or another researcher analyses, summarizes, and reports the results for a client (see 'Suggested Reading' for guides and critiques).

Here the place is a front room in a village in Lancashire, and the participants are middle-class people between 50 and 65, four men and four women. The topic is public attitudes to genetically modified organisms (GMOs) and food. The research was funded by Unilever, the huge food and household product company, but conducted by an academic group, the Centre for the Study of Environmental Change, with the help of environmental and consumer organizations; it was intended to help policy-makers making decisions about regulation, trade, and consumer information. At this point in the session, the facilitator, Phil Macnaghten, has shown the group a card with a picture of Sainsbury's tomato puree, and the words 'These tomatoes have been genetically modified to soften more slowly. This makes processing into tomato paste easier.' It reminds some of them of a television documentary they have seen about genetically modified tomatoes, and they have been talking about not knowing what is in the food one buys. The facilitator turns the discussion to whether they would be put off by the information on the box of puree:

Genetically Manipulated Organisms

PM   Okay, so that's fine. So would people buy this then?
M   With that I feel there's a problem of image because I'm so used to tomato ketchup, tomato soup, the word tomato puree suddenly doesn't ring ...

PM   You just wouldn't buy tomato puree?

M   No, it doesn't, it's not something I ...

F   It sounds safe, are you saying, it sounds safe?

M   It's not one of my conventional tomato ...

F   Oh, I see. But you'd use it in a recipe wouldn't you?

M   Well, I probably wouldn't but my wife would.

F   My two vegetarian daughters use a lot of tomato puree but also they look at every label that is on the supermarket shelf to see what's in and how it's made before they actually buy anything.

PM   And how do your vegetarian daughters respond to the genetically modified tomato?

F   Well, I have one that's a bio-chemist and I think she would be suspicious before she'd looked to see why and how and what, and whether it gives any indication on the label what's used in order to produce this.

M   I think the other point is as well that any new line of products or new method, the actual marketing people have to be very careful how they introduce it to the public and if they were to introduce the right tomato, first and foremost, and say this is your tomato that has been modified, or this is your orange, people will immediately stand back and take guard and be suspicious. If they put it in a paste which is perhaps not the main product sale and it's in a tube and it's in a box, people are a lot less susceptible to what they're actually buying. If it doesn't appear to be a fresh product, it's camouflaged to some degree and then several months down the road the advertiser and manufacturer says well this has been on the shelf for the last two years and you've been buying it and people say oh, yes, but we hadn't realised. It's a subtle way of introducing it onto the shelf.

PM   And is that alright? Does that mean it's alright?

M   No, no, I just say it's a subtle way of introducing it onto the super-market shelves. (Grove-White, Macnaghten, Mayer, and Wynne 1997)

This is a rather more straightforward set of questions and answers than in the Subaru focus group described at the beginning of the chapter. But here too the topic guide and the cards on specific products were carefully planned so as not to steer the participants. The responses are different from what one might get if one simply asked in a survey whether the respondent would buy food made from genetically modified organisms. In this section they raise all sorts of complications: one wouldn't buy puree anyway, because he doesn't recognize it as an ingredient; another notes that her vegetarian daughters read labels more than she does, and could understand the scientific implications; and a third says that there is less resistance to modification of a product in a paste, in a tube, in a box, than there would be to buying whole tomatoes. From there the discussion shifts to the labelling and introduction of such products, seen as part of the strategy of the supermarket.

In this string of comments, the participants respond as much to each other as to the facilitator. The facilitator probes, often reformulating what they have just said, but lets them pursue their own directions. They often linked their responses to genetically manipulated food products to issues such as chemical additives, 'tampering with nature', or food contamination as with BSE. A scientist working with biotechnology might argue that these are quite different issues, but the purpose of this research is to determine the contexts these people use to think about these new technologies and their possible risks. In their final report, the researchers used the passage I have quoted to highlight people's scepticism:

> The suspicion with which people generally viewed the intentions of companies was related in one group to speculation about whether the innocuous sounding tomato puree might be the first stage of a master plan to get consumers to accept other products.

> (Grove-White, Macnaghten, Mayer, and Wynne 1997: 9)

This is a different kind of conclusion from what one might find in commercial report. One kind of research, like that Wieden and Kennedy were doing for Subaru, quoted at the beginning of the chapter, uses people's views of society to tell us about their probable purchasing choices. The other kind of research, like that being done at the Centre for the Study of Environmental Change, uses their comments on purchasing choices to explore their conceptions of risk, trust, expertise, and responsibility, and to present these conceptions to policy-makers. But as in the Subaru research, the GMO researchers found people were already reflexive about advertising and marketing (see Chapter 12).

Let us consider how our check-list of questions might apply to these examples of focus group techniques. *Subjects* in focus groups are seen as part of a group, and they come to see themselves this way, looking around the room and wondering why they are here. They are likely to be strangers at the beginning, but they soon start speaking as representatives of their kind of people, whoever they take that to be – middle-aged working women, older churchgoers, secondary school students. In these groups, the participants are asked to do something unusual – play a game, guess about the source of a statement – in the hopes that these *actions* will stand for their first, unconsidered response to a brand, or their underlying assumptions about large issues. The *interactions* between researchers and participants involve them displaying their opinions. They show they are well aware of the tape recorder and the public nature of what they say, but they also draw on their experience of informal conversation in groups. The *questions* that underlie these two pieces of research are different, but both are looking for something new to them, beyond what people typically say in market research interviews about Subaru, beyond the bland and general acceptance of environmental slogans.

One can imagine an academic standing behind the one-way mirror at the Subaru research wanting to probe further the irony in the way the participants take the stereotypes of car owners. And one can imagine marketing researchers in the front room in Lancashire wanting to pursue the specific implications of their comments on the label (Who reads the labels? How much of a deterrent is it to sales? How does the perception of risks relate to that for additives? Should there be a symbol or a label?). But in each case, the facilitator leads the discussion to the kind of talk needed for the researchers, to talk about perceptions of brands of cars as they are relevant to marketers, and about general issues of risk and trust as they are relevant to policy-makers. Focus groups do not, then, replace other forms of research on audiences, but they can explore areas missed by more direct methods such as surveys and more individualistic approaches through experiments or interviews.

Summary

In this chapter, I have outlined a number of different approaches taken to audience research, by commercial advertising researchers and by academics. I have raised a set of questions about each of them:

- How do they conceive of the *subject*, the person who is part of the audience, on whom the ads are to have an effect?
- What *actions* stand for other actions in their research?
- How do the researchers and people *interact* in the research?
- What *kinds of questions* does the client (or reader or user) of the research ask? What questions don't they ask?

A brief review of the emergence of different approaches (summarized in Table 9.1) shows how audits of circulation, consumer surveys, and sales analyses can be seen in relation to each other, each emerging to satisfy needs for information that was problematic in the other approaches. Technological innovations such as People Meters, cookies, and bar code scanners have made much more data available for analysis, but they do not resolve the underlying issues of advertising research. I have argued that these approaches make different assumptions about consumers, and construct different kinds of audiences as bundles of traits, respondents to stimuli. Research on effects is worth analysing in this way, because it is not just of interest to advertisers, but to researchers dealing with effects of ads on children, regulators interested in the relation between advertising and smoking or drinking, and social activists resisting the images offered of women, ethnic minorities, the disabled, or older people. We need to know about advertising effects even if we have nothing to sell.

Suggested reading on advertising research

This chapter has relied heavily on three views from different perspectives: Michael Schudson (1984), a classic of cultural studies analysis responding to very general and inflated claims for advertising effects; Randall Rothenberg (1994), a very readable journalistic account that, unusually, devotes detailed attention to research, and Leo Bogart's advertising textbook (1990), especially Chapter 11, which gives a surprisingly sceptical and reflective view of audience research from an experienced practitioner. Brierley (1995) has an excellent chapter on research packed with good UK examples. There are a number of more conventional and detailed textbooks on the subject, for instance Jack Haskins and Alice Kendrick (1993). Accounts for general readers can be found in two books by Martin Mayer, *Madison Avenue, USA* (1961), which is not as dated as it might seem, and *Whatever Happened to Madison Avenue?* (1991), which deals in detail with the uses of bar code data. My argument that advertising research constructs audiences draws on Celia Lury and Alan Warde (1997), as you can tell from their title: 'Investments in the Imaginary Consumer'.

Cookies are relatively new, and I found little about them in print publications. But there was a great deal of discussion about them on the Web. A good introduction is in an article I got from the Business Week site (Himelstein, Neuborne, and Eng 1997). There are many comments on what they do and how to beat them at Cookie Central (www.cookiecentral.com), and a running commentary on the regulation of cookies, with links to the regulations themselves, at Web Marketing Today (www.wilsonweb.com/wmt). The DoubleClick site (www.doubleclick.com) also gives useful background, and a defence of their procedures.

On focus group research, see Morgan (1988), Krueger (1994), and the collection edited by Barbour and Kitzinger (1998), and for detailed linguistics analysis, Myers (1998). *Campaign* had two pages of commentary on focus groups in its 26/9/97 issue, with some funny comments on 'focus group groupies'. For more general overviews of qualitative social research, see Robson (1993), which is a useful and broadly based handbook, and Silverman (1993) and Alasuutari (1995), which are more selective, theoretically informed, and critical.

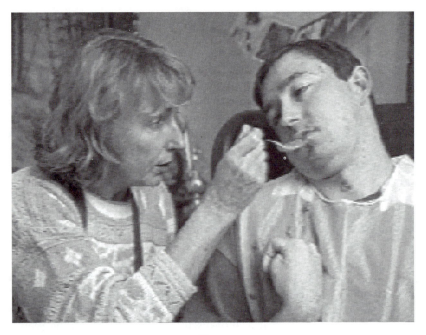

Dave

10

Projecting the audience: drink driving

A couple of years ago, the UK travel company Club 18–30 ran a series of deliberately offensive ads promoting the connection between sex and their holidays with posters like the following: 'Girls, can we interest you in a package holiday?' (over a picture of a man's bulging boxer shorts) or 'I saw, I conquered, I came'. When a group of students doing a research project interviewed their marketing director, she said that the ads worked fine with the target audience – the people between 18 and 30 that are referred to in the name of the company. The target audience was a group that considered itself young, free, adventurous, maybe a little rude and unconventional. People outside this age group did not matter to them. And if some people inside this age group were offended, then they were the sort of person who wouldn't, and probably shouldn't, go on a Club 18–30 holiday. Though the marketing director did not say it, the fact that other people would be offended, and complain, only helps with the target audience, who would be confirmed in their own sense of humour and lack of prudishness. Even when the posters were banned and taken down, they helped Club 18–30 establish a niche for itself as offering identifiably different holidays with an implicit promise of sex and booze.

When people outside advertising talk about its effects, they often underestimate the degree to which advertisers are aiming at some groups and not at others, projecting an audience in their ads. For instance, those who thought the Club 18–30 campaign would hurt the company, or thought Benetton's ads would alienate its customers, or who find safe sex messages too explicit, are imagining that advertising is aimed equally at anyone who can see it. Advertisers may make the other mistake, and overestimate how much advertising can be, or needs to be, targeted at a particular group, as when DoubleClick promises that their network allows them to 'hit an advertiser's desired target, every time' (see Chapter 9). They may overestimate the accuracy and the possibility of targeting just because it is their particular professional skill, part of the expertise they offer clients.

The 'target audience' is that part of the potential audience who are intended to act on the ad's message. It does not include all the people who encountered the ad but were not intended to act on it, but it does include all the people the advertiser intended to reach who did not happen to encounter the ad, as well as those who did. The idea of a target audience is crucial to understanding many controversies in advertising. For instance, there has been much criticism of negative advertisements in political campaigns (Kline 1997). If they work, it is because the campaign managers have identified a group of undecided voters as their target, and have addressed them rather than the committed supporters of either side. Tobacco ads are another example of targeting; the advertisers claim that their target audience is existing smokers, and that they only try to make them change brands, not to get them to smoke more, or to get others to start smoking. Any target audience is a fiction, like the other conceptions of audience we considered in Chapter 9, but it may be a useful fiction. Even if there is no coherent group out there corresponding to the target audience, an identity may come across strongly in the ad (as it does in those for Club 18–30).

In Chapter 9, I was looking at ways of finding out about the responses of real audience members by using surveys, experiments, and focus groups; here I am interested in what is projected about the audience in the ad itself. My argument in this chapter is that ads do not necessarily find (or miss) a target audience that is already out there, but may project a category of audience that fits the ad. Thus ads can take us from conventional social categorizations (based on class, gender, or age) to more complex processes by which people identify themselves as part of a group. I will first review some of the terms in which advertisers target audiences, and then analyse in detail one case that shows how complex the targeting can be.

Defining audiences

Audiences, and categories of consumers, can be defined in many ways, and there is ongoing discussion in the advertising and marketing journals about which sets of categories are most relevant for each product (see, for instance, Lannon 1992, 1994). Advertising researchers and planners keep coming up with categories, partly because this is a way of presenting their strategies to the client as something new. Traditional categories and these new categories may overlap in complex ways, For instance, the target audience could be defined in terms of:

- *demographic categories based on employment* – These are the categories used in government surveys, such as A (executives and higher managers), or B (most professionals), or C1 (skilled employees), or C2 (most workers), or D (people with part-time, low-paid, or irregular work). One can't sell Jaguars to most shop clerks.

- *demographic categories of age and gender* – Most ads for fast-moving consumer goods (fmcgs) are targeted at women; most lager ads are targeted at men. Radio stations and magazines target audiences in fairly narrow age bands. An advertiser can try to create a niche by targeting ads in unconventional ways: ice cream for adults (see Chapter 5) or insurance for women in their 20s.
- *region* – Even where there are no political divisions such as states or provinces, regions can be treated as distinct audiences. So, for instance, the Granada ITV region is treated as a distinct entity not only for television ads, but for other media (see Chapter 7); for other purposes the Pacific north-west or the US south or Canadian Maritime Provinces or English Home Counties may be treated as having an identity (see Shields 1992).
- *lifestyle* – Marketing studies and planners' presentations refer to empty nesters (couples with grown children), green consumers, lads, clubbers, or gay people as consumers (see *Campaign* 20/1/98). In research for the Centre for the Study of Environmental Change, we have at various times recruited focus groups for categories we called (informally) Active Retireds, Risk Takers, Churchgoers, and Cyclists – all categories based on lifestyle rather than demographics (see McQuail (1997) for references).
- *product* – A social psychologist once said to me, 'when you know someone drinks lager, you know all you need to know about them'. (He was drinking bitter at the time.) Drinkers of bottled water can be treated as a social group, as can university applicants, or frequent flyers. But the correlations with other groups may not be as simple as one would think: most men's fragrances are bought by women, and baby clothes may be bought by grandparents as well as parents (see Chapter 2).
- *medium* – In the UK, Virgin Radio or Channel 4 or the *Sun* or *FHM* define specific audiences; in the US, there is a distinct audience for New Country radio stations, the Discovery Channel, the *National Enquirer*, or *Rolling Stone*. These audiences may cut across other categories (see Chapter 5).

This brief list suggests that advertisers' ideas of target audience are not simple; categories are defined practically and in various different ways for the task at hand. One important point that comes up in current marketing literature is that these audiences are becoming more and more fragmented and sharply defined. This is partly because the broad social categories of class and region are shuffled in a geographically and economically mobile population. The much discussed fragmentation of mass markets may also arise because marketers have much more information available to them (see Chapter 9), so they are more aware of differences that were earlier submerged in the broad brush treatment of class or region. (With the bar code scanner data now available, I await innovative studies on Thursday shoppers, or on vegetarians, or decaf coffee drinkers, as social categories).

Not all sellers target particular kinds of buyers this way. Clark and Pinch (1995) point out that the very successful market traders they interviewed refused to speculate on particular categories of consumers they might encounter. Their job was to get some action out of the people directly in front of them, and they had nothing but scorn for a pitcher who would blame his or her lack of success on regional unemployment, a preponderance of working-class over middle-class shoppers, or the gender or age composition of the crowd. The one relevant social distinction for them was whether someone was part of the crowd gathered at the stall for the pitch, or out of it. They address a general audience, but never a mass audience. Their remarks make me wonder whether some other retailers also set aside ideas of a target audience and aim for a general audience, but a general audience encountered in particular ways.

Though the definition of targets may change and narrow, there is still the assumption that advertising is a matter of one-way messages that may, or may not, hit the target, whether it is BC1 males, or 18–24 year old women who go night-clubbing, or the shoppers in Pontefract market on a rainy Wednesday. In contrast, current work in media and cultural studies, stressing the idea of an *active audience* (see AUDIENCE), suggests it may be more useful to think of ways audiences define themselves in relation to an ad, and the way an ad tries to encourage audiences to see themselves in it.

Drink driving ads

Every year, usually around Christmas, the UK government runs ads warning against the dangers of drinking and driving. Reviewing the most recent campaign, the creative director of BDDP CGT, Trevor Beattie, noted that the death of Diana, Princess of Wales, in a car driven by a drink driver, was the most reported event of the year in the UK, receiving perhaps the biggest media coverage of any event in history. 'Unfortunately, if an event of such global magnitude doesn't stop would-be drinkers in their tracks, what hope is there for a humble advertising campaign?' (*Campaign* 9/1/98). His remark points out some of the difficulties of the drink drive campaign – people know the message already, and there is a specific but hard to reach target audience.

Advertising against drink driving has several problems, even though everyone agrees with the message, or perhaps *because* everyone agrees with the message.

Identity. First, no one sees themselves as a 'drink driver', a terrible monster vilified in the press. They see themselves as normal people who had a normal night out and then had to drive to get somewhere.

Risk. Second, the risk of being hurt if one drives when drunk is tied up to the complex ways we deal with other huge dangers in the course of our daily lives: risks involved in eating, participating in sports, working. There is a possibility that people may simply dismiss the chance of death as a normal part of their activities, or toy with it as an extra excitement.

Scene. Drink-driving ads pop into our experience on late night TV or on posters, but not while drinking. That moment of having another drink is part of its own complex social ritual.

The problem, as highway safety officials see it, is getting around these well-constructed defences. The ads try ways of getting the viewer to identify himself (and they are almost always aimed at males, since males account for the great majority of offenders) as a possible drink driver, by loading each ad with ordinariness. They try to get the viewer to see the risk as a risk for him, by stressing the permanent consequences of damage to others or non-fatal damage to oneself. We can see how these strategies work in specific ads.

An anti-drink-driving campaign may seem a very odd example of targeting, because it is not paid for by a corporate sponsor, and does not promote a commodity – if anything, it could be said to convince people to consume less of a commodity. But it shows ways of thinking about target audiences that we can also see in ads for products:

- the assumption of a knowing, 'literate' audience
- the avoidance of claims based on trust
- the disruption of address
- the reflexivity about the medium (see REFLEXIVITY).

I chose these particular ads for analysis because they are shocking, and a shock may be a good place to begin to examine our own responses to ads.

Dave

This 30-second ad run just before Christmas 1995 is called 'Dave' for reasons you will see. It is very upsetting. It was also much admired, winning a Gold Award for Public Service Advertising in the British Television Advertising Awards.

secs	words	images and sound
00	A: What you drinking. Same again?	tracking forward down a hall, with a wreath on the left and Christmas decorations over a door frame, towards a woman in an apron at a blender
02	B: Yeah.	CU of a blender (FX: blender noise)
	D: Not for me	continues track down hall
	A: What?	
	D: I'm driving.	

05	A: You won't get pulled, not on Sunday	CU of blended green gloop
	D: Ah, give me half.	
	B: Half is what girls drink.	woman picks up tray
10	A: What's the problem here?	dissolve to MS of the woman seated by a paralyzed man, in a living room with photos, trophies, and Christmas cards
	D: I've got to go down to my mum's for dinner.	
13	C: Ah, your mum's for dinner.	ECU of slack lips encrusted with food
	B: Mummy's boy.	
18	A: Come on, Dave, just one more?	ECU of spoon, food oozing from mouth
	D: All right then, give me a pint.	
20		CU of woman's face (FX: his heavy breathing)
25	Mother: Come on Dave, just one more?	ECU of his unfocused eyes
27	text: Drinking and driving wrecks lives.	

Client: Central Office of Information
Agency: DMB&B
Writer: Steve Boswell
Art Director: Steve Drysdale
Director: Trevor Melvin

Visuals

The scene is a home at Christmas (we can see the decorations). There is a long tracking shot down a hall towards what seems to be some sort of kitchen preparation, then a dissolve to a scene in the living room, as a woman feeds the food prepared to an adult who is paralyzed, unable to communicate, and scarred on his neck with the mark of a tracheotomy. The editing establishes a rhythm between the medium shots of preparation and feeding, and the close-ups of the blender, the bowl, and the face, with extreme close-ups of his mouth and eyes. The colours are pale, greenish grey, in contrast to the heightened colouring of other Christmas advertising. Remarkably, it manages to suggest dreariness, slowness, and complete passivity in just 30 seconds, partly, I think because of this contrast of pace with the ads around it.

Sound

At first the soundtrack seems to come entirely from some other scene, a discussion marked from its first turn ('Same again?') as being in a pub. We hear someone, later addressed as Dave, being persuaded by his friends to have another drink. He tries to turn down a drink, and then just to have half; they insist that he is unlikely to be caught, and that drinking half pints is not masculine. When he finally gives in, it is in a louder and faster voice, a capitulation. This track is interrupted once, by the whirr of the blender that forces us to think how the two scenes are related. That is the only sound from the scene we are seeing until two-thirds of the way through the ad, when we suddenly cut from his loud voice (in the past) to the sound of his breathing (now). Then the mother repeats the words used to persuade him ('Just one more'), but now in the different context of carer to disabled person. On the second or third viewing, the words spoken in the pub ('mummy's boy') take on a different meaning. The friends' persuasion depended on questioning his independence and toughness, while now we see him as dependent, soft, passive. Most of all, he is now seen as permanently isolated in this quiet world, permanently out of the warm noisy companionship of the pub.

Effects

Why is this so upsetting? I know that when I have shown it, people are genuinely disturbed, especially if they've been out of the country and haven't seen it many times before. Apparently it worked well; the close-up pictures of Dave being fed were repeated in posters in a summer campaign, with punning texts like 'How hard can it be to say no to a drink?' and 'Do nothing for the rest of your life'. The key device in reaching the target audience is the superimposition of one time on another. On the sound-track, there is the time of the pub – noisy, happy, sociable. In this world Dave has a choice. On screen, there is the world of his mother's house – silent, isolated, slow. In this world, he has no choices, not even about eating a spoonful of soup. The effect is to heighten that everyday moment that is, unknown to him, the moment of choice. The ad is seen late night on television, in the living room, a place much like where Dave is sitting now. It works like beer ads in projecting a wonderful sociable world associated with consumption of their product. But then it reflects that back to where the viewer is sitting, and asks him to imagine himself confined there. That is one way of dealing with the problem of separate times, of trying to intervene at the moment of choice. It also draws in the other people in the pub as accessories to the crime. The idea seems to be that they will catch themselves, on some future night out, when they hear in their own sociable pleading the echo of these voices.

The campaign also had some unintended effects on non-target audiences. It received complaints from groups campaigning for the disabled, pointing out that it presents having a disability – or caring for someone with a disability – as literally a fate worse than death. So, for instance, there is no suggestion that Dave can communicate, or have any purpose in life. It must be a terrible thing to see if one has a relative or friend in the hospital or paralyzed. Here that paralysis is being shown as a punishment. There are similar unintended effects in other ads that use disability as a symbol for something else. For instance, a poster for the *Guardian* showed Britannia in a wheelchair to symbolize Britain's weakness as a world power. A postcard shows this poster with a demonstration of women in wheelchairs holding up the message, 'WOMEN IN WHEELCHAIRS ARE POWERFUL. THE GUARDIAN IS WRONG.'

Mirror

Let's compare the 'Dave' ad to the ad from the same agency used before the next Christmas. It continues the same strategy; the assumption is that drink drivers can not be convinced to suffer inconvenience to avoid killing themselves. Threats merely increase the sense of risk, and therefore, for some audiences, the attractiveness, not so much of drink driving as of the wildness with which it can be associated. The approach of the Central Office of Information and DMB&B is to stop threatening death, and to threaten something much worse. Both ads start, not with the person representing the target audience, but with someone else affected by his actions. This has become a common approach in public service ads – don't show the actor, but the victims: the bereaved child, or shocked parents, or here, the girlfriend.

secs	visuals	words
00	MCU over shoulder to mirror (scar becomes visible)	Nick, that's my boyfriend, still feels bad about it
05	gradual zoom throughout ad (glances at us in mirror)	It's as much my fault I guess. I got in the car with him. Not that he was drunk. I wouldn't have then. But he'd only had a couple.
10	CU	Anyway, we're still together.
		Although sometime I think he's only with me because he feels guilty.
17	ECU on scarred eye (she glances at us and away)	Then again, I wonder if I'm only with him because I'm scared I couldn't get anyone else.
25	text, white on black screen, with logo	If you're out for a drink, leave the car at home

Visuals

Here we see a shift from an ad in which the characters talk to each other, to one in which a single character talks to us. The ad starts with a shot over the woman's shoulder, from several feet back, and the camera continues to zoom in throughout the ad. The woman (who is unnamed) seats herself at the mirror at the beginning. Mirrors have a powerful effect in films; they are often used to suggest doubleness, dishonesty, fragmentation, tension – the idea of an inner self and an outer self. Because of the lighting, we don't see the scar on her face for the first few seconds, until she refers to 'it'. Here she glances at us – she is talking to us in the mirror, but also looking back to what she is doing, putting cream on her scar. As the camera zooms in, our relationship to her shifts. We no longer see the frame of the mirror; she is talking to us and we are staring awkwardly at her scar. At her last, bitter words she glances at us, and then looks away to the scar, and that glance carries a sense of shame.

I have stressed the mirror. The advertisement is also about a face. The face is how we see other people, how we recognize them as an individual person. The disfigurement is something terrible, because it not only makes them look different, as would, say, the loss of hair or a limb, but it can seem to change the relationship between two people; facial disfigurement is used to signal character in fairy tales and movies. Here this change is treated as a change in the relationship between her and her boyfriend, but it is also a change in the relationship between her and the viewer, over the course of the ad.

Sound

The whole effect of the ad is carried by her monologue. But it is, from the beginning, like a dialogue – she includes us by introducing Nick as her boyfriend. Every new addition is introduced by linking words, to make them seem to follow. Her monologue starts with his feeling of guilt, then her guilt, the guilt of those around the drinker, as in 'Dave'. Here, as in 'Dave', they are careful to emphasize that he didn't have that much ('Not that he was drunk'). What she is doing here is called 'troubles talk'. It has been well studied, and analysts have talked about how people get out of it and back to the conversation (Jefferson 1984). One way they do it is by this kind of summing up statement, they're still together. But here there is a sting, gradually revealed. They are only together because of the guilt and shame following from the accident. They are now tied to each other permanently, like Dave and his mum.

Effect

The explicit message is like that of 'Dave' – if you aren't afraid of dying from drink driving, there are worse fates. In both ads the threat linked to real aspects of the experience of young people, things they have reason to fear. In 'Dave', the threat is being stuck as a child in your parent's house for the rest of your life. In 'Mirror', the threat to the man is being stuck in a relationship you could never be sure was love, tied to the person whose face reminds you of your shame. And yet Nick is introduced as a good guy, an ordinary guy, not the monster we imagine as a drink driver. Again, as with 'Dave', I know this ad was terribly moving. It was also terribly offensive to some people, for the same reason; people whose faces were disfigured, for any reason, found their particular condition being held up as a terribly meaningful punishment.

The larger strategy, as with Dave, depends on telescoping different periods of time. Here the two times are the moment she got into the car with him, and the long time she spends in front of the mirror, preparing to go out. Again this long, bleak time stretching into the future is identified with the moment we are watching television, for we are watching her in the mirror ourselves, and going through our own uneasiness. Again the intended effect may be, not so much on the drinker, as on the people around him. It is not to change the practice of drinking, but to change the social attitudes around it so that it is acceptable to get out of the driver's seat or call a cab.

Targets and other audiences

Some practical lessons for analysing target audiences will stand out if we compare the drink driving campaign to some of the ads discussed earlier in the book.

Texts are usually (but not always) aimed at particular groups, not at the public in general. Anyone can drink 'Coke', but the 'Coke' ad I discussed in Chapter 1 was targeted at mothers shopping in supermarkets – even though the mother does not appear. Levi's ads can afford to be incomprehensible to people over 30 (but ads for Dockers, a brand from the same company, cannot). The Co-operative Bank ad is aimed, not at the deep green and ethical consumers who are already its customers, but at a wider range of people who had not yet thought of banks in this way.

The target audience is not always identifiable with the characters represented. In the drink-driving campaign, it may be intended that the target audience see themselves as Dave, but they do not necessarily see themselves as the woman in 'Nick'. Levi's may want the target audience to see their ideal selves in the slim women and muscular men of its ads, and Peugeot may want every businessman to see themselves in this particular businessman, and Häagen-Dazs may want us to see our ideal erotic selves in the couple licking ice-cream. But we do not necessarily identify with the Co-operative Bank voices, or the 'real people' in the Daz ad.

The audience is situated in a real place and time – in the sitting room, or on the street looking at a poster, or on a bus reading a magazine. The drink-driving ads both contrast a private setting with the public setting of the drinking. A surprising number of television ads address the audience in a private but social space. So, for instance, the Daz ads play on an intrusion into this space, while the Häagen-Dazs ads allow ironic distance so that they can be seen in a group without embarrassment. And as we saw, posters often play on the use of public space.

Responses are based on active engagement with the ad, changing through the ad, taking on visual, verbal, aural, and other signals, not on some simple message that is delivered. The drink-driving ads reveal their aim only gradually, and part of their effect is in the way we try to interpret them, making sense of the soundtrack of 'Dave' and the glances in 'Mirror'. Most of the other ads we have considered – the boys at the refrigerator in the ad for 'Coke', the swimmer in Levi's, the jarring juxtaposition of images in the Co-operative Bank and Peugeot 406, the colours of Häagen-Dazs – only make sense in the last seconds. The exception is the ad for Daz, which signals its message at the outset and proceeds to deliver it.

Effects on other groups may be as important as those on the apparent target audience. We have seen how people with disabilities or facial disfigurements could be unintended audiences for the drink-driving ads, and we have seen peripheral (but perhaps intended) effects on people besides the potential drink driver, making the drinker's friends ask about their own responsibility. The Levi's ads define a kind of youthful Americanness, and ideas of bodily perfection, whether one is in the target audience or not. This gap between intended and real audiences can also lead to ironic and playful responses, for instance teenagers sending up the Daz ads, or kids chanting the line from the 'Coke' ad in Chapter 1.

Advertisers often find, as with the drink-driving ad, that the most accessible or most influential audiences may not coincide with the more conventional market segments. Consider, for instance, ads for UK university courses (see Chapter 5). These might be directed to 18-year-old A-level students, but they may also need to reach careers advisors, parents, and working people who might be thinking of returning to study. The automotive industry, which based its earlier branding on social class, realized rather late that there was a niche for selling cars to young women. The Co-operative Bank targets a self-defined identity as socially concerned, not just the ABC1 social classes. Condom makers have tried to reach out to groups that do not see themselves as being at risk of Aids, but find a variety of different sexual practices and attitudes towards sexual pleasure, not simple divisions of straight and gay (Jobling 1997). In each case, rethinking the product means rethinking the categorization of target audiences.

Audiences and groups

Social categories, whether drink drivers, C1s, preppies, lads, nerds, empty-nesters, or deep greens, are socially constructed. They are not just out there, to be discovered by sufficiently refined market research; they are made, by a process of identification (by texts) and self-identification (by readers and viewers). Roberta Astroff (1997) describes how both academic ethnographies and market research construct 'a target market labelled "US Latino" '. The diverse groups in the US with Hispanic heritages are treated as one market, about which generalizations can be made, obliterating the differences between people of Cuban, Mexican, or Salvadoran ancestry, between recent and earlier immigrants (and those who were there before the Anglos arrived), between urban and rural. The group, once constructed, needs experts, consultants who can tell what this group is like. Astroff points out some of the absurdities, for instance a consultant telling a beer company that Latinos won't respond to their ads because they have no experience of mountains. The result is not just mistargeted ads; the various attempts to target this audience define a social group.

Often the purpose of an ad is to intervene in this process of self-identification, not just reaching the target audience but allowing the viewers or readers to pick themselves out as the target. In a series of ads for the Special Constables, each ad starts with apparently documentary footage, with some figures circled, and a text such as: 'These boys are the only actors in this scene'. In one ad, two boys in a shopping mall beat up a little boy as dozens of people pass by. It is seen on something like a closed circuit TV image, and must evoke memories of James Bulger, the murdered boy last seen in such a hauntingly indistinct image. The voice-over is of a woman commenting on what the scene looked like to her. We assume that she is the one whom we see step in at the end. The end-line says this is the sort of person they want for Special Constables. The ad is about the process of selecting oneself out, in the test case of the staged beating and the Good Samaritan, but also in the audience for the ad. We in the audience are identified with all the people who just watched and passed by, unless we too identify ourselves and do something. This group of people does not coincide with any demographic, regional, or lifestyle group; it is a moral category that can include all sorts of people not in the target audience for the advertiser.

Summary

I have stressed that ads are usually aimed, not at some general public, but at a target audience. But I have also shown how complex this targeting can be. Advertisers have their own sets of overlapping categories that they can use to talk about potential audiences, drawing on both demographic categories such as age, gender, or class, or lifestyle categories. The example of the drink-driving ads shows how ads can use the actual situation in which they are likely to be seen, how they can map one place on another, and one time on another. The ads get around an audience's sense that the drink driver isn't them, that it won't happen to them, and that the problem is somewhere else. The campaign also shows how ads have taken on conceptions of an active audience, whose members can put together a complex message out of bits, according to the relevance it has for them. It is now common to hear about active audiences both from academics and from advertising professionals. But, as we will see in Chapter 11, the older conception of a passive audience survives in the field of advertising regulation.

Suggested reading: target audiences

For general readings see AUDIENCE. There are particularly good treatments of target audiences for ads in Kathy Myers (1986: Chapter 3), Allison Clarke (1998), and in several chapters of a recent book edited by Mica Nava, Andrew Blake, Iain MacRury, and Barry Richards (1997): Paul Jobling on condoms, Andrew Wernick on nostalgic middle-aged Canadians, Stephanie O'Donohue on youth, and Reina Lewis and Catrina Rolley on lesbians. For the wider literature on active audiences and consumption, see Mica Nava (1992), Angela McRobbie (1994), and Celia Lury (1996). A classic study of drink drivers as a socially constructed category is Gusfield (1976). The postcard referred to, showing the demonstration of wheelchair users, is from The British Council of Organisations of Disabled People, Unit 4, De Bradley House, Chapel Street, Belper, Derbyshire, UK.

Woodpecker

11

Protecting the audience: complaints and regulation

Here's a television advertisement I've never seen. Two *Pulp Fiction*-style gangsters in business suits go through a hospital in a developing country, joking and grabbing a blanket from a baby, making wisecracks as they go: 'He owes us $250. The people we work for lend money to make money. You borrow, you pay it back'. The ad says that this is what banks are doing to developing countries when they force repayment of crushing debts, and ends, 'Cancel this madness'. I never saw it on TV, because the Broadcast Advertising Clearance Committee would not allow it to be shown in the UK, on the grounds that political ads are prohibited by the Independent Television Commission Code. The advertisers, Christian Aid, pointed out that ads showing the banks as helping developing countries were not seen as political, but commercial; Christian Aid were just presenting the other side of the story.

This case, one of scores that arise with the regulation of ads on television and other media in the UK each month, reminds us that advertisers are constrained in what they can say and how they can say it. Legal, voluntary, and conventional constraints have an effect even when a particular ad does not fall foul of any of them, because advertisers learn how to work within them, or, as we will see, how to break them to the advertiser's advantage. Just as advertising research constructs various kinds of audiences, regulators make assumptions about the audiences they are protecting. They assume:

- the literal reading of ads (with an important exception I will discuss later);
- the vulnerability of the audience to emotional responses;
- shared standards of decency;
- normal practices of purchasing, such as comparing brands and examining claims.

There are clearly tensions between seeing the audience as sceptical and rational on the one hand, and as vulnerable on the other. There is also a tendency to generalize, to create a homogeneous 'public' that underlies the regulatory demands for honesty and decency.

To understand how the complex and contradictory systems of regulation evolved, we need to consider the history of regulation in the UK and US. I will then look at some specific passages from codes, to discuss the way their wording focuses on explicit, literal meanings. Then I will review a range of regulatory issues – complaints procedures, issues of deception, interpretation of disclaimers, definitions of indecency, and uses of ownership – with some examples of specific ads that have been challenged. Then I'll return to the issue of the political and the commercial raised by the Christian Aid ad. Finally I will step back to look at ways advertisers use and subvert the system, and at what the system may tell us about audiences.

History

The tensions within advertising regulation arise because different kinds of rules were set up as the results of different movements, with different purposes: protecting health, preserving competition, preserving public service television, defending investments in trademarks and brands, and resisting what was seen as a potentially excessive influence on the consumer (see REGULATION). Some of the earliest laws in both the UK and US, providing a pattern for later developments, concerned potentially useless or dangerous products such as patent medicines. These were products that promised remedies for a huge range of ills, many of them problems directly related to living conditions in industrial society. Most of them were composed of more or less the same ingredients – alcohol, glycerine, and various cocktails of stimulants and depressants. Most of the stuff was harmless, some potentially had powerful effects, and some of it was downright dangerous. The makers would protect their formulae by applying for patents, thus the name. Very few of the products were successful; those that were, spent a larger proportion of their income on advertising. You can see the result by looking at any nineteenth-century newspaper, or a photograph of a street scene, and noting just how many of the ads are for patent medicines. The medicines, and also their ubiquitous ads, were a major part of Victorian culture (Richards 1990; Lears 1995).

In response, there were repeated attempts at regulation to control the quacks – nine bills in the UK in the 60 years before the First World War, and a range of Pure Food and Drug legislation in the US in the first decade after 1900. The laws can be seen as part of the professionalization of both medicine and advertising. The main attacks on patent medicines came from medical associations, seeing off the rivals of doctors in defining health care. But advertisers were also involved in this movement; they felt the quack origins of advertising gave the whole industry a bad name, and the public rejection of such ads demonstrated the new respectability of advertising as a profession.

The same wave of Progressive Era legislation in the US that established the Pure Food and Drug laws also established the Federal Trade Commission, in 1914. The FTC, which is now one of the main regulators of advertising, did not originally consider claims of deception; its remit was to promote fair competition, and it would only intervene where it could be shown that the deceptive advertising gave one company a monopolistic advantage. But its powers were extended in the 1930s, and by later legislation; the rulings of the FTC are now a regular feature of the business news. In the UK, a similar role is played by the Trade Descriptions Acts of 1968 and 1972, which, among other provisions, require advertisers not to lie about the size, composition, usefulness, or availability of products. In the UK, these provisions are enforced by local trading standards officers, not by a national agency. There are also a number of other acts, in both the UK and the US, governing specific practices in consumer credit, mail order, labelling of tobacco products, and product safety. A list of UK laws (See the Advertising Standards Authority web site) goes from the expected restrictions on tobacco and pharmaceuticals to 'The Tattooing of Minors Act 1969'. The terms of contests are covered by the Lotteries Act; as you may have noticed, contests have to have some element of skill, even if the skill involved is very little indeed ('name all five Spice Girls'). The list of acts is so long and bizarre because each law was enacted to curb a specific kind of abuse; there were no laws addressing public worries about advertising in general or the indirect associations that we have seen used in other chapters of this book.

The current controversies over tobacco advertising must be seen in the context of long slow changes in marketing and advertising, starting with the first government medical reports in both the US and the UK, in the mid 1960s, linking smoking to cancer and other diseases. Before tobacco advertising was regulated, the ads made claims that now seem nothing short of shocking, such as an ad in a 1945 *Life* magazine that says, 'More Doctors Smoke _____'. (I'll leave the brand name out to avoid litigious tobacco companies). The successive waves of regulation cut out many of the traditional appeals to sex, social status, or testimonials in tobacco ads. In response, British advertisers, following Benson and Hedges and Silk Cut, developed enigmatic puzzles that seemed to say nothing at all about the product except the colour of the pack (Pateman 1983; Myers 1994). One joke on this tendency got as far as the planning stage (see Knobil and O'Dwyer 1993); it shows a man with a six-foot-tall rooster and says, 'We're not allowed to tell you anything about _____ cigarettes, so here's a man with an enormous cock' (I think I can see why the client had second thoughts about this one).

In the early years of the twentieth century, the critics of advertising shifted ground, from commenting on a few flagrant cases of misrepresentation, such as those around patent medicines or mail order, to questioning the function and power of the emerging industry of advertising, which was coming to play a key role in selling most products. Critics argued that advertising added to the cost of products, or misled consumers, or promoted unnecessary, vulgar, illusive, or anti-social desires. The response of both UK and US professionals was to establish bodies for self-regulation, to forestall legislative regulation. UK advertisers set up a (very weak) Advertising Code in 1924, after a wave of criticism of advertising as unproductive. Calls for legislation have arisen periodically since then, and with them efforts within the industry to tighten self-regulation. The Advertising Standards Association began in 1962; it is still the main organization for complaints about print ads. The various regulatory boards involve members of 'the public' (usually business leaders and aristocrats), but are dominated by advertising and media interests. In the US there were similar defensive efforts, also presented as protection of the consumer, in the Better Business Bureau.

Another line of regulation concerns the media through which the ads are presented. In the US, broadcasting, which was entirely in the hands of commercial organizations, was largely unregulated until the 1950s. The Federal Communications Commission (FCC) regulates the amount of advertising allowed; they also regulate some aspects of the ads themselves, such as ads directed at children (these regulations were much relaxed in the 1980s). In the UK, commercial television arrived only in the 1950s, after extended controversy about its effects (see Williams 1998). As part of the planned safeguards for the public, the Independent Television Commission established a Broadcast Advertising Clearance Committee (BACC) that checks scripts before they are broadcast, following the Code of Advertising Standards and Practices. Some of the rules concerning alcohol, drugs, or advertising to children are similar to those in other media and other countries. But there were also rules concerning the relation of sponsors to programmes and the strict separation of commercials from programming (see Chapter 7); these were enacted specifically to avoid the blurring of the boundaries of commercials and programming that was common, and is still common, in US television. For commercial radio, which came later in the UK, a similar function is played by the Radio Authority.

It is the BACC that rejected the Christian Aid ad on Third World debt mentioned at the beginning of the chapter, as offending against section 10 of the ITC Code:

> No advertisement may be inserted by or on behalf of any body whose objects are wholly or mainly of a political nature, and no advertisement may be directed towards any political end. No advertisement may have any relation to any industrial dispute. No advertisement may show partiality as respects matters of political or industrial controversy or relating to current public policy.

And it adds as a note:

The term 'political' here is used in a wider sense than 'party political'. The prohibition precludes, for example, issue campaigning for the purposes of influencing legislation or executive action by central or local government ....

The BACC can reject scripts or ask for alterations. There is then a lot of room for 'tweaking' the ad in production; sometimes the ITC bans an ad on broadcast that was earlier cleared as a script. Thus UK advertisers have to deal with several different regulatory authorities, the ASA handling complaints about ads in print, outdoor, direct mail, or cinema, and the ITC handling terrestrial television.

Examples of codes

Both the ASA and the ITC Codes that have at their heart this statement: 'advertising should be legal, decent, honest and truthful.' The codes are constantly revised, both in their texts, and by treatment of the cases submitted to the bodies. The Table of Contents of the ITC Code (Table 11.1) gives an idea how it ranges from broad issues of Privacy and legitimate persuasion to quite specific sales practices (subliminal advertising or use of the word 'free') and products (lotteries or instructional courses).

Here is part of one section of the code, as a sample of the wording:

Section 40 – Alcoholic Drink
subsection (b) No advertisement for alcoholic drinks may feature any personality whose example people under 18 are likely to follow or who have a particular appeal to people under 18.
(g) Advertisements must neither claim nor suggest that any drink can contribute towards sexual success or that drinking can enhance sexual attractiveness.
(h) Advertisement must not suggest that regular solitary drinking is acceptable or that drinking is a means of resolving personal problems.
(j) No advertisement may suggest that drinking is an essential attribute of masculinity. Treatments featuring daring, toughness or bravado in association with drinking must not be used, and alcoholic drinks must not be advertised in a context of aggressive or antisocial behaviour.
(m) ... references to buying rounds of drinks are not acceptable.
(n) Advertisements may employ humour but not so as to circumvent the intention of these rules.

These rules are so complicated because they are trying to find a way of resolving the tension between the promotion of an allowable product, alcoholic drinks, and the suppression of an unacceptable behaviour, drunkenness. They are trying to imagine every possible appeal that could be linked to alcoholism, and forbid it, without restricting all the associations that

Table 11.1 The ITC Code – contents

1–4 – General Principles
5 – Separation of Advertisements and Programmes
6 – Programme Performers
7 – 'Subliminal' Advertising
8 – Captions and Superimposed Text
9 – Noise and Stridency
10 – Politics, Industrial and Public Controversy
11 – Religion (see also Appendix 5)
12 – Charities (see also Appendix 4)
13 – Taste and Offence
14 – Discrimination
15 – Protection of Privacy and Exploitation of the Individual
16 – Appeals to Fear
17 – Superstition
18 – Unacceptable Products or Services
19 – Lotteries and Pools
20 – Health and Safety
21 – Motor Cars and Driving
22 – Protection of the Environment
23 – Animals
24 – Misleadingness
25 – Price Claims
26 – Comparisons
27 – Denigration
28 – Reproduction Techniques
29 – Testimonials
30 – Guarantees
31 – Inertia Selling
32 – Use of the Word 'Free'
33 – Competitions
34 – Homework Schemes
35 – Instructional Courses
36 – Mail Order and Direct Response Advertising
37 – Home Shopping Features
38 – Premium Rate Telephone Services
39 – Matrimonial and Introduction Agencies
40 – Alcoholic Drink
41 – Advertising and Children (see also Appendix 1)
42 – Financial Advertising (see also Appendix 2)
43 – Medicines, Treatments, Health Claims, Nutrition and Dietary Supplements
(see also Appendix 3)
44 – Advertising on Ancillary Services
45 – Pan-European or Non-UK Advertising

Appendices
Appendix 1 – Advertising and Children
Appendix 2 – Financial Advertising
Appendix 3 – Medicines, Treatments, Health Claims, Nutrition and Dietary
Supplements
Appendix 4 – Charity Advertising
Appendix 5 – Religious Advertising
Appendix 6 – Statutes Affecting Television Advertising

advertisers of alcohol would want to use. But you can already see how hard some of these rules are to enforce. Is it really the case that no approved beer ads suggest that 'drinking is an essential attribute of masculinity'?

Table 11.1 shows that medicines and health claims have so many regulations governing them that they require a separate appendix in the code. The rules there forbid any ads for non-registered products, any claims for some processes, such as cures for baldness, any use of doctors, dentists, etc., any use of celebrities, use of the word 'cure', use of the word 'tonic', generalized claims for 'goodness', or refunds of money. These rules help explain many of the odd phrases in drug ads. For instance the appendix says:

> (22) A 'tension headache' is a recognized medical condition and analgesics may be advertised for the relief of pain associated with this condition. However, no simple or compound analgesic may be advertised for direct relief of tension. In such advertisements there must be no reference to depression.

They seem to be worried here that drugs like aspirin could be presented as mood drugs, like the old tonics, and thus abused. Clearly these highly explicit rules are the result of more than a century of wrangles over patent medicine before television and the ITC came along. But the rules are also oddly ineffective, because they are still fighting the battles of the patent medicine wars about absurd explicit claims. The actual claims in most ads today hardly matter, it is the associations with them, and what viewers do with them. And the ITC has a hard time controlling such associations and practices.

Besides UK laws, there are further European regulations. For instance, there are strict laws on political advertising, here and in other European countries. Each European country restricts tobacco ads (I know of none that allows broadcast ads), but the regulations differ in complex ways, as you can see from posters on your European travels. European countries forbid advertising aimed at children, but advertising on UK-based children's satellite channels still reaches them. As new international media develop, they can get around the national regulations on advertising.

All these attempts at legislation leave their legacy. Pharmaceuticals are still the most heavily regulated sector of advertising in the US and most developed countries. (They are less regulated in some developing countries, and drug companies have been accused of dumping their less successful efforts where there is no regulatory system to counter their claims.) Alcohol ads are widely restricted as another form of protection for the public. Mail order and financial services are covered by a number of regulations, on the grounds that the buyers cannot reasonably judge the product for themselves, but must rely on what they are told about it. Tobacco ads have been subject to growing restrictions, and may finally be banned in the UK. Advertising to children is restricted by complex regulations on the grounds that they have not yet developed the scepticism and perspective that is assumed in adult consumers. As a new Labour government begins in the UK, and tobacco companies contest suits in the US courts, the pattern continues: calls for legislation are followed by widely publicized attempts at self-regulation within the industry.

Examples of regulatory issues

This complex history of regulation, self-regulation, and response has led to three kinds of constraints. First, there are *laws*, both specific legislation applying to various products (such as drugs), and commercial law dealing with such issues as trademark ownership. If an advertiser breaks these they can be fined or jailed, as they could with any other law; the FTC can also require corrective advertising to try to remove any false impression created in the minds of the public. Then there is *voluntary self-regulation*, policed by industry organizations like the ASA and the BBB. The penalty here is usually that the ad is withdrawn; it is felt that the public attack on it is enough of a deterrent. Many of the common constraints are just matters of *conventions* within the industry. For instance, both UK and US law now allow comparative advertising, if it makes claims that can be shown to be true and not defamatory, but advertisers (especially in the UK) are still very cautious with it, because it can backfire and provide publicity for a competitor. Similarly, spirits manufacturers in the US have voluntarily foregone TV advertising, wary that any insistent ads might provoke calls for restrictive regulation of all alcohol advertising. A similar conventional restraint applied in the UK until recently, until it was broken by one company and others immediately rushed in.

Regulations and their enforcement differ in the US and UK, and change constantly and subtly with new cases and challenges; I will leave the specifics to the experts (see Suggested Reading for references and web links). But we can see some of the general issues raised by regulation in some of the current cases.

Complaints

The British newspapers have monthly reports on complaints against advertisements in the press and on television; indeed these reports account for the bulk of news stories on advertising. But it may help to put these complaints in perspective by listing some of the most complained-about television ads from one year (1994), and recalling the problems with them (see Table 11.2). Note first how few the complaints are. Admittedly, this is just the tip of the iceberg, since many people who were offended won't have complained, or known how to complain. But it means that if the students in one good-sized university lecture all decided to knock one ad, even something

Table 11.2   UK complaints about TV ads, 1994

Advertiser	Complaints	Issues
Tango	253	Character slapping on the side of the head led to imitation on play-grounds
Neutralia	199	Nipple showing in soap ad
AA Recruitment	94	Induces fear in women
Andrex	75	Boy on a toilet
Tango Still	69	
BSkyB	45	
Orbis Publishing	44	
HEA measles immunisation	42	Induces fear in parents
COI speed campaign	41	Refers to deaths of children
Lilt	41	Sanitary protection

(Source: *Campaign*)

unremarkable for soap powder or packet soup, it would, with them alone, have more complaints than any other ad all year. In the case of this sample, the most-complained about ads were the focus of newspaper articles suggesting people complain. The two ads most complained about in 1997 were both part of a campaign for tighter controls on guns; the complaints received by the ASA were largely the result of an organized campaign by gun organizations.

Falsehood and deception

I have noted that the Federal Trade Commission in the US and the Trade Description Act in the UK prohibit false and deceptive claims in ads. Since you see many ads that are not literally true, you may wonder how some ads get by these laws. This is the exception to the literalness that characterizes so much of advertising regulation; the interpretation of falsehood and deception turns on some assumptions about how people interpret ads, not just on what the ads literally state. The issues in US law are covered fully by Ivan Preston (1994; 1996); one starting point is to note that US and UK law as currently interpreted forbid deception, but not falsehood. That is, one can say things that are false, if they were not intended to deceive. Otherwise, a Benson and Hedges poster showing a cigarette in someone's hand, in the foreground, and a freight train in the far background, and saying 'Longer than a train', would be illegal. The ad is legal because it is assumed that anyone can see that the picture is a trick, so it is not deceptive.

Two cases, one in the US and one in the UK, illustrate the ways that the apparently simple commitment to truthfulness is a matter of interpretation. In 1990, Volvo ran an ad in the US in which a huge truck drives over a row of cars, crushing them all except a Volvo. The Texas Attorney General filed a lawsuit charging deception, because some extras had said that, to get this demonstration to work, the director of the commercial had to weaken the frames of all the other cars, and put extra steel beams inside the Volvo. Volvo defended the ad on the grounds that Volvos had passed a similar test before; the deception was just making this test look right, like using mashed potatoes instead of whipped cream for food shots. But after a flurry of bad publicity, Volvo withdrew the ad and fired the agency (Savan 1994; Preston 1994). In the UK, Nissan ran an ad with a Terrano on top of a steep pile of sand. It turns out they got it there with a crane. The agency claimed that no one would think the car had driven up it, just as no one thinks that a Ford got to the narrow top of a rock out at sea by itself (or that Benson and Hedges cigarettes are longer than freight trains). The ASA rejected this, saying that viewers would reasonably believe it was driven there, and the ad was a demonstration. The more complex and subtle charges of deception are usually brought by competitors. In a famous case in the US in the 1960s, Campbell's was ordered not to use marbles in soup bowls to push the vegetables to the surface of the soup. As one might expect, the complaint came from their rival Heinz, not from some sharp-eyed pea-counting consumer.

Preston (1994; 1996) deals with a category of advertising known in US law as 'puffery'. These are terms that 'praise the product using subjective terms, stating no fact explicitly, and thus representing no factual content to consumers and so creating no basis for them to believe anything about the product that would affect their purchasing decision' (Preston 1996: 12). This is a legal recognition of what Leech (1964) pointed out as the vagueness of advertising; Preston gives a spectacularly long list of meaningless claims: 'Great', 'Best', 'Favorite', 'Wonderful', 'Terrific'. The long-standing argument that these claims are not a problem is based on the assumption that consumers discount such vague claims. Preston's argument that they are a problem is based on evidence that such deception is so general that it obscures genuine consumer information.

Consumer information

The disclaimers that appear in many ads are one familiar result of regulation. The phrase, 'Batteries not included ...' in ads for toys in the US became well-enough known to be used as the title of a children's film. Other disclaimers include:

- Your home may be at risk ...
- The value of stocks can go down as well as up ...
- Serving suggestion ...
- Read the label. (UK)
- Use only as directed. (US)
- Full offer is made only in the brochure.

These constraints interest me because they have a large, though not often discussed, effect on copy. It is particularly interesting in radio ads to hear how they try to work these disclaimers into the spoken words.

Where do all these bits of small print come from? One example that was discussed in the news a couple years ago, after complaints to the ITC and hearings in a Parliamentary Committee, concerned the contracts for package holidays. One of the complaints is that to get cheap holidays, you have to buy the company's travel insurance. Some people want to insist that the ads add a spoken disclaimer, something like:

> Price subject to purchase of insurance which may significantly increase the advertised price.

The advertisers say this would make a mess of their TV commercials – you can imagine the voice droning this message at the end of a lively 30-second montage of pools, sun, and seafood dinners, and then again in the 10-second reprise later in the break. Advertisers also say that the regulators underestimate the intelligence of the consumers – they are smart enough to know that if a company charges less in one area, it will have to make some money in another area. Proponents of the change say that there are disclaimers like this on many other expensive purchases – such as mortgages and financial services – and making this sales strategy explicit would encourage fairer competition, by pointing out the need for close comparison of contracts as well as prices. It is a typical debate, and there are others like it going on all the time as advertisers and regulators test the limits of constraints.

I've looked at about 20 TV ads (Channel 4 in 1995; see Chapter 7) and noted some of the 'small print' that seems to me to arise because of these various regulations (see Table 11.3). In the case of the Going Places ad, dealing with issues of vacation terms similar to those I've just discussed, it is literally small print – so small I could hardly read it. Others are more subtle. For instance, in the gum ad, they don't say that dentists recommend the gum (which would violate ITC regulations). They say that a dentist would say that damage to the enamel increases risk of cavities – for that they could provide plenty of evidence. This ad also has the small print, as required, saying that it must be part of a larger dental treatment, just as diet ads say that they only contribute to weight loss if they are part of a calorie-controlled diet.

The assumption behind such disclaimers is that the interpretation of advertising is entirely a matter of absorbing information. The small print is supposed to balance out any impression left by the ad, and enable us to be rational consumers. The same assumption underlies corrective advertising in the US, when a company is required to spend part of its money on advertising to reverse an impression given by previous ads. Perhaps because it is lawyers, not advertisers, who devise such tasks, they focus on the explicit statement of an ad in a way that seems naive, given what we have seen in other chapters about the complex effects of ads.

Table 11.3   Small print in TV ads

Advertiser	Small print	Other copy
Norwich Union	Registered with the Personal Investment Authority	
Going Places (long and short versions)	Full offer is made by the brochure. Provided our insurance is purchased. Limited period only	
Steradent		Helps keep gums happy
Persil	economy brand [no brand name given for comparison]	
Philips CDI	[copyright lines on film clips]	Available from £299.99
Paul Eyre Carpets		When you buy underlay …
Tell Me a Story	Complete in 24 fortnightly parts	
Orbit gum	Chew as part of your dental care	These acid attacks can weaken the enamel, which as your dentist will tell you, can increase the risk of cavities
Liverpool Direct Holidays	For full details of the promise see brochure	
B&Q	Offers subject to availability	[previous prices crossed off]
Norweb	On a range of products. Offers subject to availability.	
Olbas	Always read the label	
Orange	Excludes calls to mobile phones	
Rover	*Excludes Number Plates, Road Tax, and Delivery.	From just £11,635*. How do they do it?
Head and Shoulders	Use regularly	

Decency

We saw in Table 11.2 that most of the complaints from the public have to do, not with advertisers' claims, but with offences to taste: nudity, jokes, references to taboos. Legal, Honest, and Truthful don't get much attention, but Decent does. The poster for the movie 'Disclosure', showing a woman (with her back to us) with her dress up and her legs wrapped around a man, was discussed in Chapter 6. Another recent complaint concerned a TV commercial for Accurist. The first commercial in the break showed a man and woman making love. At the end, the woman's head turned to reveal the face of what was said to be an 'ugly hag'. The text said 'He who does not give Accurist for Christmas deserves what he gets.' Then the last ad in the break had a 'beautiful woman' and the text, 'He who does give Accurist for Christmas gets what he deserves.' This offended people on grounds of both decency and sexism, and the complaint was upheld.

Issues of decency depend on the target audience. Inter-Rail had a poster promoting a European rail card for young people, with 12 yellow condoms in a circle against a blue background. There were two complaints, that it encouraged promiscuous sex, and that it desecrated the flag of the European Union. Both were upheld, though the advertising agency pointed out that young people didn't need any official encouragement to have sex on their travels; the ad was just encouraging them to have safer sex. In a recent decision, French Connection UK was allowed to use its previously banned poster, saying 'fcuk advertising' if it inserted full stops after the first four letters to show it was an acronym (get it?). The ASA also said that they allowed more latitude for the ad in fashion magazines, where the audience was less likely to be offended by the word referred to than they would be facing a poster on the street.

An example of the kind of logic in applications of the codes is shown in the decision on a cider ad from H. P. Bulmer, which had some words in very large type, and gave a literally true message undercutting it in the smaller type. (Another ad from the same series is reproduced at the beginning of the chapter to show how it works. Underneath the big type, the small print recommends liberal applications of fertilizer to your chestnut tree.) I will give the decision in full, if only so that you will now feel you have official permission to use the word 'orgasm' in public.

H P Bulmer Ltd
The Cider Mills
Plough Lane Hereford HR4 0LE
Media: National press
Agency: Mellors Reay & Partners
Sector: Alcohol
Complaints from: Nationwide (25)
Complaint: Objections to an advertisement for a bottled cider in The People and the Daily Mirror. It was headlined 'BETTER THAN AN ORGASM' and claimed 'Woodpecker Red. It tastes rapturous but is of course nowhere near as pleasurable as carnal relations.' The complainants objected that the advertisement was offensive and in very bad taste.

Adjudication: Complaints not upheld. The advertisers said the advertisement was one in a series and was designed to be humorous. They pointed out that they had checked the campaign with the Copy Advice team. The publishers said they believed the advertisement was humorous and unlikely to offend their readers. Although noting that the advertisement had caused offence, the Authority considered that neither the word 'orgasm' nor the reference to 'carnal relations' would cause serious or widespread offence. (ASA, March 1997)

Regulation of decency in ads has all the problems of censorship of other kinds of texts. As with other texts, the possible offence is judged in relation to a likely target audience; the two newspapers where it appeared have pictures of topless women on page 3. (A cheeky reviewer in *Campaign*'s 'Private View' said the brand name 'Woodpecker' by itself violated the ITC Code – see Section 40(g) quoted above.) Ads push at the edge of any boundaries drawn, because their goals are both to attract attention and to define their brand as different from others.

Ownership and legal challenges

Not all the disputes about ads have to do with regulatory issues; conflicts may arise in other aspects of law dealing with contracts, ownership, defamation and libel. Issues of intellectual property rights in advertisements are very complicated. British Telecom was recently threatened with legal action by the BBC for using actors who played characters from the soap *EastEnders* – the actors can do what they want, but the BBC owns the characters. When Tom Waits successfully sued Levi's and their agency Bartle Bogle Hegarty for using his song 'Heart Attack and Vine' in an ad, the issue was one of copyright law, not some regulation special to ads. The pink toy bunny banging a drum was originally used in ads for Duracell; in the US it then appeared in parody ads from the rival brand Energizer (Fowles 1996). In a bizarre legal agreement, he now belongs to Energizer in the US and Duracell in Europe (*Campaign* 16/1/98). Members of the public may feel that such complex and technical issues can be left to the lawyers. But advertisers can use their ownership rights to suppress public discussion, as any author knows who has tried to get permission to reproduce controversial ads, or even just quote the slogans from them (see BRANDS).

Political issues

US readers may wonder, reading about all these carefully devised regulations, why they don't cover the outrageous and absurd claims and implications made in US political spots for both parties. In the US, advertising regulations about deception do not apply to political ads, which are fully protected by constitutional guarantees of free speech while commercial messages only have more limited protection. (I like to imagine what the 30-second spots for political candidates would sound like if they had to provide the sorts of support for factual claims required of commercial advertisers – with appropriate printed disclaimers as to the suitability for use: 'for full details of the promise see brochure' or 'use only as part of a democratically controlled government'.)

In the UK, which has no constitutionally protected freedom of speech, there is currently controversy over whether political ads should be covered under the ASA Code, and if so, what provisions for enforcement would apply. In 1996, the ASA and another body representing the advertising industry, the Institute of Practitioners in Advertising, clashed over the Conservative Party's poster showing Tony Blair with 'demon eyes', red devilish eyes superimposed on a photograph. The ASA banned it on grounds of defamation and Blair's ownership of his image; he had not, obviously, given permission for it to be used in this way. The IPA said that such a decision could be interpreted as showing political bias, and thus compromising the independence of the ASA.

The UK does not allow the broadcasting of paid political advertising, but does accord each major party regular slots for Party Election Broadcasts, with single slots for each of the smaller parties. In the 1997 British elections, the far-right-wing British National Party produced a Party Election Broadcast showing West Indian and Asian people on the street, with a voice-over about the invasion of Britain by immigrants. Note that this broadcast could easily have obtained approval based on the script; it was the juxtaposition of words and images, not the words themselves, that was particularly offensive. The BBC ran it, so as not to give the BNP grounds to claim establishment bias. But of course the BBC, which has no advertising, is not bound by the ITC Code. Channel 4, a commercial channel, said that the Party Election Broadcast would need to be edited to conform to the ITC Code, and in the end they did not run it. But ITV, following the same code, did. One advertiser saw a way of taking advantage of this decision to make their own, very different point. The media buyers for Nike got time in the commercial break before the BNP broadcast for their ad featuring Tiger Woods, the brilliant American golfer whose parentage is African American, Thai, and Chinese; they thus made their own comment, by juxtaposition, on the kind of racial purity promoted by the BNP.

The ads of campaigning organizations like Greenpeace or Friends of the Earth are regularly challenged by their opponents and withdrawn; BP challenges a Greenpeace ad, and a meat industry organization challenges claims of the Vegetarian Society. In a Friends of the Earth cinema ad, a mahogany toilet seat is covered with overflowing blood, while an announcer says that in Brazil, Indians are murdered if they won't give over their land to loggers. The Brazilian Embassy and the Timber Trade Association lodged a formal complaint with the ASA (*Campaign* 28/4/95), charging that it is selective, because other countries produce mahogany too, and misleading in implying that all the mahogany came from Indian lands. The Brazilian ambassador also charged the ad was meant to shock. The ASA found for the complainant, accepting their literal-minded arguments. FOE then put the ad on its web site, so that people could download it. (Christian Aid did the same with their banned ad 2 years later, providing it on their web site and suggesting viewers writer to their MP.)

In these cases of Friends of the Earth and Christian Aid, the controversy gives more publicity to the organization than they could ever buy with their limited budgets. The International Fund for Animal Welfare regularly has its ads banned. One example features 'the medical photograph of John Bobbitt's penis' with the headline: 'When it happened to John Wayne Bobbitt it got worldwide exposure. When it happens to 10 000 seals it gets slightly less coverage'. The ad then urges a boycott of Canadian fish products, and it was the Canadian government that complained to the ASA. The ad was much admired by other advertising professionals, and won an award for press advertising, but was disqualified because of the ASA ban.

Using and subverting the system

As one might expect from these examples, there are complaints about the UK system of self-regulation of advertising, both from members of the public who see it as ineffective, and from advertisers who see it as absurdly literal-minded. I have noted how advertisers, especially those with small budgets, may flout the regulations and enjoy the publicity generated by complaints and regulatory action. This has raised the question of whether self-regulation as practiced in the UK has backfired. Club 18–30 can spend a tiny amount on posters, and get millions of pounds worth of free advertising as they are reproduced in press articles (see Chapter 10). Similarly TBWA boasted that their posters for Wonderbra showing the model Eva Herzigova with suggestive headlines such as 'Hello Boys' (see Chapter 4) got millions of pounds worth of coverage (each disapproving newspaper article going to the trouble to reproduce the offending picture). Benetton has made the attacks on their ads a part of their brand building. The outrage of newspapers, regulators, and talk show guests at such images as the newborn baby or the arm tattooed with 'HIV' has confirmed for at least some audiences that Benetton can claim to be a different sort of retailer, challenging the usual constraints.

One of the most outrageous cases of flouting the regulations was that of Live TV, a cable provider trying to develop a brand based on irreverence and unpredictability, with features such as topless darts and a news chicken. One of their ads (before the death of Diana, Princess of Wales) had the wedding picture of Diana and Prince Charles kissing, but altered so that the footballer Paul Gascoigne replaced Charles. The text said 'Who knows what the future holds?' The Lord Chancellor's office complained about a use of

Diana in an ad for Live TV because the law says that images of members of the Royal Family (she was one then) cannot be used in ads without permission. Live TV finally amended the ad in a way that did not make it at all more suitable – she was shown kissing Will Carling (a rugby player who was a friend of the Princess) rather than Paul Gascoigne. These strategies can work because the regulation of posters and press ads comes after the fact; by the time the decision comes down, the posters have been up a month or so, and the reports will only revive interest.

While these examples make the system of self-regulation seem lax, enforcement of any advertising code will lead to some examples of literalism pushed to the absurd. One recent example in the UK system is the ITC ban on a lovely ad for Ford Fiesta, showing the face of a baby, altering to that of an old man in ten seconds. The strap-line said, 'The Fiesta 1.4 does 0–60 in 10.8 seconds.' The ITC held that this contravened the code, which says,

> References to power or acceleration in advertisements for motor cars or automotive products must not imply that speed limits may be exceeded and there must be no accompanying suggestion of excitement or aggression.

Presumably the reason this imaginative ad contravenes the code, and the dozens of ordinary ads showing cars careering along mountain roads or streaking across empty deserts do not, is that this one refers to the acceleration in the strap-line, even though the acceleration is only shown metaphorically. Leon Jaume, the Ogilvy and Mather creative director on the Ford account, told *Campaign*,

> It's sanctimonious bollocks. The Fiesta ad was researched, pre-vetted by the BACC and received no complaints from viewers. We don't feel that we have contravened the wording of the ITC code. (8/8/97)

The sort of literal-mindedness shown in the Ford Fiesta decision enables the regulators to justify their decisions, which can have huge financial consequences, and to distinguish between cases. But it has no relation to the way people see or are affected by ads.

Summary

I have been arguing that regulations have shaped the content of ads, particularly the copy. This is less to do with legislation, or even direct regulation, than with advertisers' anticipation of potential trouble. To understand regulation of ads we have to put it in the context of politics, courts, media, and the odd set of beliefs about ourselves that we call Decency, Honesty, and Truth. We also have to consider the various historical struggles from which the various forms of regulation emerged.

One interesting effect is that regulations tend to shape the copy of an ad, but they can have very little effect on imagery, story, music, associations – the things that really make ads work. The things that really offend people, such as the patronizing tone, or the assumptions about women or men or children, or the ruthless appeals to one's role as a parent and love of one's family, aren't covered by regulation. Instead the regulations focus on various claims and the details of how they are presented, as if all that ads did was to provide information to consumers. They tend to miss the big picture and concentrate doggedly on the small print.

Just as advertising research constructs an imaginary set of audience categories, and ads project a target audience, the regulation of advertising assumes a kind of audience it can protect. The members of this imaginary audience are blank slates formed only by advertising: vulnerable (acting on any suggestion), gullible (the car on a sand hill in a demonstration), easily offended (the nipple in Neutralia), and relentlessly literal-minded (Ford Fiesta). As we will see in Chapter 12, this is not the view of the audience taken either by the people who make up audiences, or by advertisers themselves.

Suggested reading: regulation

For US law, I have relied on Preston (1994; 1996) and Batra, Myers, and Aaker (1996), both of which give extensive legal references; Savan (1994) has witty discussions of cases. Brierley (1995) gives a good, if disjointed, listing of relevant features of UK regulation; Jefkins (1994) lists relevant laws without discussion. The account of Turner and Pearson (1965) is now of course very dated, but gives good details on the origins of the regulatory system. Some examples of banned ads, as well as ads that were rejected by clients for other reasons, can be seen in Knobil and O'Dwyer, *The Best Ads Never Seen* (1993). Decisions on well-known ads appear in daily newspapers, usually just following the press release; more detailed discussion of particular cases appears once a month in *Campaign* and in almost every issue of *Advertising Age*.

> Primary documents on codes and decisions are often available on the Web:
> www.asa.org.uk (the Advertising Standards Authority includes an excellent overview of relevant laws, and monthly reports of decisions in full);
> www.itc.co.uk (the Independent Television Commission);
> ourworld.compuserve.com/homepages/almad/itccode.htm (the ITC Code for downloading);
> www.bbb.org (the US Better Business Bureau, a self-regulatory trade body);
> www.ftc.org (the US Federal Trade Commission).

The ad mentioned at the beginning of the chapter can currently be seen at the Christian Aid site, which can be accessed (along with a great deal of other information about Third World debt) through www.oneworld.com.

Nissan

12

Advertising literacies: what do audiences know?

I am sitting in a front room in Thornton, a village in Lancashire, at a focus group with a research colleague and eight participants, watching TV. I am showing them four ads we have carefully chosen and analysed as part of our research project: Norwich Union (see Chapter 4), Red Cross Landmines Appeal (African victims longing to pursue normal lives), 'Coke' (Mum searches for children and finds hundreds of them when she gets the 'Coke' out of the fridge), and the Special Constabulary (only one passer-by tries to stop a man from jumping off a bridge). But these 'Active Retireds' don't seem to be watching. They *talk* during the ads. They talk about the son of a friend who joined the Special Constabulary, Diana and landmines, the mountain landscape in the 'Coke' ad, the uselessness of insurance, which ads they've seen before, other ads they like better, what programme they were watching last night. When I try to probe their responses, I don't get far: they say that all the ads are trying to get them to do something, and they either buy that thing because they want to, or ignore the ads.

I was frustrated at the time, but later, when I'd talked with my colleagues, I realized I was seeing how most people watch ads. I've watched these particular ads endless times, analysing every frame and sound, trying to reconstruct the strategies underlying them; clearly the response of ordinary people in ordinary TV watching is different from mine. On the one hand, they know much more about ads than I do (as do most of the people in most of the groups); they know past ads for the same brands, current ads, parodies, allusions to celebrities and programmes. On the other hand, they care much less about ads than I do; they treat the ads as not worth thinking about.

The knowingness and scepticism of advertising audiences are now taken for granted by advertising professionals and media studies analysts, and we have seen references to this knowledge many times in the book, in discussing branding (Chapter 2), or television flow (Chapter 7), or interaction on the Web (Chapter 8), or advertising research (Chapter 9), or regulation

(Chapter 11). The knowledge of the audience, and their indifference, pose problems both for the advertisers and for analysts of advertising. For the advertisers, the problem is getting around the scepticism, the knowingness, and the boredom, and still having an effect, or even using these responses for their own purposes. For the analysts, the scepticism and knowingness undermine simplistic critiques of advertising effects, in which people do what ads tell them, accept the roles offered in ads as representations of the world, and take up the positions offered by advertising texts. But if they know how advertising works, does this protect them against its effects? Or is their knowingness limited and ultimately deceptive? In the cartoon strip 'Calvin and Hobbes', Calvin recites the standard line of media studies researchers on audiences, and Hobbes says simply, 'I think I hear advertisers laughing.'

Advertisers and academics in marketing have written about 'advertising literacy' (Ritson and Elliot 1995; 1997). The implication of the phrase is that consumers have, or should have, a basic competence in interpreting ads, as they do, or should do, in reading or arithmetic. Consumers know a lot of ads, know about their forms and conventions, and what is more they know about advertising, the purposes of advertisers and the organization of media that convey the ads. Some of the same observations about the knowingness and scepticism of audiences have been made by critics of advertising writing about promotional culture (see PROMOTIONAL CULTURE). But they see this knowingness as no defence against the transformation of all sorts of institutions – party politics, religion, education, the arts – into competing organizations dependent on relentless promotion. Both advertisers and critics have noted that ads enter more areas of life, and are more indirect and reflexive. But for the proponents of advertising literacy, the knowing audience presents problems for advertisers, while for the critics of promotional culture, the strategies of advertisers present problems for consumers. In the view of the critics, the worst danger is that people will forget that they are not just consumers, they are also citizens, artists, students, creatures, and humans.

In this chapter I will consider some examples where we see advertising literacy at work – ads referring to other ads, parodies of ads, anti-ad ads, and boycotts – and then return to this issue of whether advertising literacy gives audiences control of their responses, or leaves them open to more subtle and far-reaching forms of manipulation.

Ads on ads

References by one ad to another ad are so common that it is hard to know where to start. As Iain MacRury says, 'spotting intertextual moments in contemporary advertising is a little too much like looking for hay in a haystack' (1997: 242). This poster will serve to make the point:

NISSAN. AGENCY: TBWA SIMONS PALMER

Concentrated

Vanette Cargo

(middle: block yellow letters edged in red, at an angle)

NEW

(upper left: white against red burst)

BETTER RESULTS from a COMPACT BOX

(bottom)

TACKLES EVEN THE HEAVIEST LOADS

(black in an arrow at right, pointing to the product)

980Kg

payload

(lower right)
illustration: red van with man in white coat holding a yellow box, gesturing to it
left: washing symbols
background: sun ray effect behind the van

What do people have to know to make sense of this poster, in the way intended by TBWA and Nissan, as they sit there stuck in traffic? They have to recognize words such as 'new' and 'better' as just the vocabulary of general puffery associated with ads (see Chapter 11), and yet still retain the possibility that this really *is* new and better. They have to see it is in the form of an ad for laundry detergent, with the visual style and lettering one would expect from a detergent box, with the usual place for the volume of a box being taken by the figure for the payload. Finally they have to pick up a set of parallels in which the laundry detergent terms work for the van: 'concentrated', 'compact box', 'heaviest loads'. The ad works by mocking old-fashioned detergent ads and packaging, but also conveys a claim about the product.
  References to other ads can work in several ways.

- One ad can incorporate another ad ironically. (In a US Jordache jeans ad a mother says 'I hate this commercial' and turns it off, while the daughter turns it back on (Savan 1994).)
- An ad can parody a whole genre of ads. (Paul Merton in an ad for Cusson's English Leather parodies demonstrations: the two women are not twins, but a young woman and an old one; the woman using Brand X is washing with a floor scrubber and industrial soap, and the vertical line dividing them is carted away by the crew.)

- An ad can refer to earlier ads in the same series. (In an ad for BT, the new announcer comments on how Bob Hoskins, as the announcer in earlier ads, could walk though scenes unobserved by the people on whom he was commenting. The new announcer finds this invisibility does not apply to him, however, when people comment on his odd behaviour.)
- An ad can parody the form or vocabulary of advertising. (In a US Ford ad, two kids in the back seat extol the virtues of the car in adspeak.)
- An ad can parody attacks on ads. (In the US, the Amstel Light home pages are devoted to 'Garrison Boyd's Homepage of Decency' saying 'Wake Up America: Avoid Amstel'; in the UK, an ad for Mazda is headed 'Another advertisement trying to sell a car using sex' – it shows nothing but the dramatically lit curves of the car.)
- Ads can parody other forms of broadcasting: soap operas (Gold Blend), game shows (Iceland), chat shows (Worthington's Bitter; Miller), detective programmes (Inspector Morse in electricity privatization), sports commentaries (Tango), news (Pot Noodles). These are all UK examples, but US advertisers have similar parodies.

In the examples in Chapter 7, Hyundai parodies *Jaws*, Victoria's Secret parodies testimonials. Toaster Pockets, drawing on a popular character from Harry Enfield's comedy programme, parodies the conventional form of ad in which whining children are pacified by smart mums bearing packaged convenience foods. When such ads work, they show the advertiser knows that we know about advertising, and show at the same time that the advertiser doesn't take themselves too seriously. Such ads are sometimes criticized by other advertisers as being self-indulgent, but they have a marketing logic to them, and can convey all the product claims, as in the Nissan Vanette poster. Clearly advertisers think that audiences know a lot about ads, enough to recognize, not only the verbal clichés, but the typefaces associated with a period or product, the different styles of illustration, the typical forms of editing and use of voice-over.

Parody and allusion

In a Christmas episode of the situation comedy *Friends*, Ross gives Rachel a present in an attempt at reparation. He opens it for her and says:

> It's a Slinky ... Remember? ...
> [sings] 'It walks down stairs, a load of repairs, everyone knows it's ... '
> [stops singing]
> just a big spring.

The decades-old jingle is meant to evoke something of the intended playfulness and affection of the gift. When it flops, he is left with the silliness of the product itself. So it is not just advertisers who draw on this remarkable shared knowledge of ads. There are now whole television shows and videos devoted to classic or comical ads, and slots on programmes such as *How Did They Do That?* to explain the special effects, and there is currently a game show on the BBC in which minor celebrities and major figures from advertising try to guess what an ad is for (its title parodies a beer slogan: *Probably the Best Game Show in the World*). There are dozens of pages on the Web, devised by members of the public as well as by businesses connected to advertising, devoted to loves and hates, collecting of old jingles, comparisons of suspiciously similar campaigns, and parodies (start with www.blipp.com/adland/debate.html). There are regular reviews of ads, not only in the specialist press, but on radio and in the *Independent* and the *Village Voice* (whose columnist, Leslie Savan, I have cited frequently). Pop songs make frequent reference to ads, and albums have appeared collecting the bits of classical music used in popular ads. One could fill books with the jokes that require a knowledge of ads for their punch lines. A novel like Douglas Coupland's *Microserfs* will require extensive footnotes if it is to be read in just a few years, because the characters keep alluding, nostalgically or satirically, to advertising slogans. For all these uses, advertisements are part of current popular culture, but even more widely shared than any one programme, song, or magazine.

And of course advertisements are ripe for parody, because the characters, the intonation, the typefaces, the visual design are already so excessive, and because the underlying intention of the message is always so obvious, the heightened claims so easily ironicized by juxtaposition with some drab reality. Some of these parodies are explicitly critical. *Mad* magazine in the US introduced a whole generation in the 1960s to mockery of commercial culture. A *Saturday Night Live* parody of an ad for the US Navy uses the jaunty music with shots of menial work such as toilet cleaning. ('The Navy. It's Not Just a Job, It's an Adventure' becomes 'The Navy. It's Not Just a Job, It's $92.78 a week'). *Adbusters* calendars (see www.adbusters.com) are meant to make us think about the domination of our lives by commercial images and consumption. But other parodies are oddly affectionate in their attention to the stylistic details of some trashy text. In this category I would put the famous *Saturday Night Live* ad parodying the day-time TV direct response commercials for kitchen products, commercials that follow very closely in the tradition of the British market traders discussed in Chapter 8.

Bass-o-Matic

[CU: Dan Ackroyd in loud patterned jacket against cheap wood panelling, holding a fish]

DA: How many times has this happened to you? *You* have a bass. You are trying to find an exciting *new* way to prepare it for dinner. You could scale the bass, remove the bass's tail, head, and bones, and serve the bass as you would any other fish dinner. But why bother, now that you can use Ralphco's new kitchen tool, the *Sup*er Bass-o-Matic '76.

[medium shot]

Yes fish eaters, the days of troublesome scaling, cutting and gutting are over. Because Super Bass-o-Matic '76 is the tool that lets you [points] use the *whole* bass, with no fish waste, without scaling, cutting, and gutting.

Here's how it works. Catch a bass, remove the hook, and drop the bass, that's the whole bass, into the Super Bass-o-Matic '76. Now adjust the controls, so that the bass is blended just the way you like it.

[tries to hold down top of blender as it leaps about, turning the fish to greyish sludge]

Yes, it's just that simple.

[cut to Laraine Newman, drinking greyish sludge from a glass]

LN: Wow, that's ter*rifi*c bass.

[cut back to Dan Ackroyd]

DA: We've got fish fast and easy and ready to pour. Super Bass-o-Matic '76 comes with 10 interchangeable rotors, a 9-month guarantee, and a booklet, '1001 Ways to Harness Bass'. Super Bass-o-Matic '76 works great on sunfish, perch, sole, and other aquatic creatures. Super Bass-o-Matic '76. It's clean, simple, and after 5 or 10 fish, it gets to be quite a rush. Super Bass-o-Matic '76 – you'll never have to scale cut, or gut again. Order now P.O. 25 Pier 25 New York New York. [card of address]

Reproduced by permission of the National Broadcasting Corporation, Inc.

This could serve as an index to the clichés of low-budget advertising: the relentless direct address, the repetition of the very long product name, and of phrases like 'scaling, cutting, and gutting', the selling words like 'new', 'now', 'simple', 'terrific', 'fast and easy', 'great', and the opening question with its presupposition that that you have this problem – dealing with an excess of this particular game fish. The parody is not undermining the claims of the real kitchen product ads, but is drawing on the pleasure of a shared memory of the unnecessariness of the products, their highly specialized uses, the fast-talking, exaggerated delivery, and the low production values compared to the slicker ads. *Saturday Night Live* has done so many parodies because ads (like names of characters in old sitcoms, or players on teams, or not-quite-hit tunes) are a quick signal of the popular culture of a particular time, and a particular time in each of our lives.

All these examples, from popular culture referring to ads, and ads referring to other ads, suggest that audiences have an astonishing knowledge of ads, and that when we tap into this knowledge we are not necessarily being critical of advertisers or advertising. But that does not show audiences understand advertising as an institution, any more than an encyclopaedic knowledge of batting averages makes one able to play baseball. We must look beyond slogans and styles, to what audiences know about what ads do.

Anti-ad ads

One indication of people's awareness of how advertising works is in the ads that tell us they are setting aside the hype of advertising. This kind of ad has been common ever since the 1920s. To take just recent examples of car ads:

- Volkswagen ads, stressing how cheap the ads are, show a toy car driving around a toilet seat, or against a holiday postcard.
- Subaru uses a flat, unemphatic voice-over to argue that one should buy a car on purely functional grounds (Rothenberg 1994).
- Isuzu has a character making wild product claims while sub-titles say 'He's lying' (Savan 1994; Fowles (1996) notes that the campaign was a disaster).
- An Audi ad with a picture of the car on a road has, on the facing page, a little packet of stick-on decals to include the lightning, rock-falls, smoke, traffic cones, and flying gravel characteristic of car ads.

In their different ways, these ads sell by saying that the product doesn't need a sell. They may be especially common with car ads, where the size of the purchase would make it particularly absurd for the purchaser to be persuaded only by advertisements. (I saw the last example in *Campaign*, where the readership is presumably particularly open to self-reflexive jokes about advertising.) The same sort of advertising by attacking advertising is often made jokingly in beer ads, such as the John Smith's bitter ads in which the comedian Jack Dee refuses to appear with any advertising gimmickry (but dancing penguins come in during post production), or the Dennis Leary ads for Holsten Pils, in which he mocks the choirs and outdoorsiness or the virtual reality tricks of other lager ads, reasserting the brand as genuine and without additives.

These anti-ad ads suggest that advertising literacy goes beyond a pool of shared allusions. But the literacy in these examples still seems rather thin; these ads reject one kind of sell to pursue another. Do people unpick the association between product and meanings that is at the heart of branding?

Boycotts

The advertisers' fondness for anti-ad ads can be dismissed as manipulative marketing; their responses to boycotts, though, suggest that they see their carefully built structures of products, brands, media, and distribution as vulnerable to sudden dismantling. A boycott is like an advertisement in

in our research design (research would be boring if groups conformed to the researchers' preconceived social categories). It certainly wasn't the audience projected in the ads we showed them. It wasn't the passive, vulnerable audience imagined in regulations, or the brainwashed consumers imagined by some critics of advertising. People use ads in different ways.

The examples in this chapter suggest ads are ubiquitous in our culture, but are not omnipotent or monolithic. The study of advertising can lead us through crucial areas of contemporary culture, to issues of consumption, media, and social identities. We have seen this in earlier chapters, as ads led us to issues of human rights (Chapter 3), cross-cultural interactions (Chapter 4), public space (Chapter 6), constructions of time (Chapter 7), conceptions of interaction and presence (Chapter 8), and ideas of risk and responsibility (Chapter 10). There are many ad worlds. But the study of advertising should also tell us, even as we see the huge output of posters, magazines, commercials, and junk mail, that ad worlds are not the whole world.

Suggested readings: advertising literacy

I have taken the term 'advertising literacy' from Mark Ritson and Richard Elliott (1995; 1997). Debates about the place of advertising in culture are found in many of the books listed in previous chapters. Critics of advertising and consumption as colonizing other areas of life include Ewen (1976), Vestergaard and Schrøder (1985), Wernick (1991), Goldman (1992), Lears (1994), Goldman and Papson (1996), McAllister (1996), and the ongoing work of Adbusters (www.adbusters.com). Despite my rejection of some of their criticisms, I find valuable analyses in each of them. Responses to critics can be found in the 'Afterword' to Schudson (1993), Davidson (1992), Fowles (1996), and Nava *et al.* (1997). More general studies of consumption and culture can be found in Nava (1992), Richards (1990), Lury (1996), and Keat, Whiteley, and Abercrombie (1994). Good selections of readings on these debates are found in collections edited by Curran, Morley, and Walkerdine (1996), Marris and Thornham (1996), Miller (ed.) (1998), and Mackay (1997).

Glossary of keywords

address – Some media theorists use this word to refer to the way a text sets up a relationship between the voice and image in the text and the person who is projected as the audience. It can involve the use of pronouns ('we', 'you'), the naming of the group addressed ('Hey Kids!'), deictic references (pointing words like 'here', 'there', or by extension, 'now'), the gaze of the people on screen, voices, and represented point of view (Myers 1994: Chapter 6). John Corner (1995) treats the term as combining this idea of address as someone talking to others, and the idea of address as in addressing a issue, presenting a stance.

This wider sense of address has been a useful term in bridging a gap that had opened up in media studies. Key texts of the 1970s and 1980s (for instance Williamson (1978) on advertising) showed how texts positioned readers and viewers by interpellation; the reader responding to the text was like a person on the street responding to a police officer saying 'Hey you!' To respond to such interpellation was to construct oneself as a subject and as subject to that text and the social structures it embodied. This approach explained how texts could have social effects far beyond what they actually said or claimed to do. But it left readers and viewers in a passive position. And it focused researchers' attention solely on the structure of the text, as determining the structure of response.

Partly in response to the limitations of analysis based on interpellation, audience research in the 1980s tried to show how readers and viewers actively constructed texts, so that the same television programme or book could have quite different readings in different settings and for different groups (see AUDIENCE). But this approach focused on what people said and did around the text, and tended to have little to say about the text itself.

Focusing on address means looking again at the text, and just what is going on within it. Examples would be John Corner's (1995) analysis of a Levi's advertisement, Andrew Tolson's (1996) chapter on changing address in advertisements, and Paddy Scannell's (1996) historical study of talk on radio and television.

advertisement – The first sense of this word recorded in the *Oxford English Dictionary*, dating from a written citation of 1582, is as 'a paid announcement in a newspaper'. Of course the word has now taken on a much wider meaning, but this early use already contains the idea that the announcement is paid for, and is to be read accordingly. Current usage is closer to the definition in the *Concise Collins Dictionary* quoted by Guy Cook (1992): 'the promotion of goods or services for sale through impersonal media'. This tells us that the purpose is (usually) to sell, and it draws a distinction between the personal medium of the salesperson in a shop or on the doorstep, and the impersonal media of print and broadcasting. It reminds us that there are other forms of promotion, for instance through public relations, contests, premiums, or price reductions (see AGENCIES). But it still focuses on the information in the message put across by advertisers. In this book, I have drawn on the ideas from cultural studies (Davidson 1992; Lears 1995) and from advertisers themselves (Mayer 1991; Lury 1994) to argue that advertisements add value by associating meanings with brands. The usefulness of this definition of what ads do is that it places them within marketing and within wider systems of meaning; it leads us to the issues of 'ad worlds' that are the concern of this book (see DISCOURSE, GENRE).

agencies – Advertising agencies arose in the United States in the late nineteenth century to sell advertising space in magazines and newspapers (for a history, see Fox 1990). They took on their present role only when they stopped getting their commissions from the publishers, and started getting it from the advertisers. By the turn of the century they had begun writing and designing the ads as well as placing them, and by the 1920s the modern structure of an agency was in place, with account executives dealing with the clients, creative teams doing the ads, and media buyers placing them. British agencies in the 1970s added planners who would co-ordinate these separate teams and keep them to the brief.

Agencies have traditionally earned their income through a 15 per cent commission on the total cost of the advertising (though there have been moves to replace this with payments of fees for services). The commission is paid only for ads in the traditional media (see MEDIA), what are called 'above-the-line' services. Direct mail, trade fairs, promotion, and other services are paid for by fees, and are referred to as 'below-the-line'. Agencies claiming to do both say they offer 'through-the-line' services (see INTEGRATION). Below-the-line expenditures are growing, but the prestige and public attention still goes to above-the-line advertising.

The largest US firms have been international since the 1920s. In the 1960s, McCann-Erickson, with its Interpublic Group, developed a network of agencies that would, they said, be able to offer a full range of services to large clients. Most of the larger agencies are now members of such networks, and the networks are owned by even larger holding companies like WPP, which owns both J. Walter Thompson and Ogilvy & Mather, Cordiant, which until recently owned both Ted Bates and Saatchi & Saatchi, and Omnicom, which now owns the BBDO, DDB Needham, and TBWA networks. One difficulty in the merger and de-merger of agencies is that agencies must avoid conflicting clients; one agency cannot advertise two brands of cars or soft drinks or soaps. (For a fascinating comment on how these corporate changes relate to styles of dress, see Nixon 1997.)

audience – The original senses of the word have to do with the act of hearing, and being present to hear, as in 'being granted an audience with the king'. *Webster's Third New International Dictionary* has definitions that show how the meaning slips to include a wider range of consumers of a performance or text: '3a: a group or assembly of listeners ... 3b: a group or assembly of spectators ... 3c: those attending a stage or film production or viewing a televised program ... 3d: the public reached by books, newspapers, magazines, or other similar media.' Leo Bogart (1990) points out the importance of this etymological slippage in understanding why audience research is so complex. Performers of drama or music in front of an audience have a powerful, immediate sense of how they are responding, and even the audiences for movies, separated from the movie-makers, have a strong sense of each other, responding as a group, but the audiences of broadcasting and the press are at a distance from the producer, and isolated from each other. Audience research tries to rebuild some of the links between producer and consumer, but it also assumes, in its use of the word 'audience', that there is such a coherent collective out there.

In advertising, audience research can mean just the determination of the numbers of people who encounter a performance or text, and the social composition of this group. Bogart deals with the responses of these people to ads in a separate chapter, as 'effects' (see EFFECTS). In cultural studies, audience studies arose in the 1980s in reaction to the heavy emphasis on the text itself in structuralist approaches to media in the 1970s. One can see the shift in the literature on advertising between Williamson (1978), in which the reader is just a position in relation to the text, and Nava (1992), with its discussions with young people about their complex responses to ads as texts. These new studies of audiences distinguish between audiences as the generalized, abstract, coherent body of receivers projected by broadcasters, and audiences as the specific people who actually watch, listen to, or read the text, often with quite diverse motives and responses. There is a concise outline of the issues, with references, in Watson and Hill (1997: 10–12), and a good introduction with readings in Moores (1997). For reviews, see Ien Ang (1991), David Morley (1992), James Ettema and Charles Whitney (1994), and for an overview with extensive references, Denis McQuail (1997).

brand – The *Oxford English Dictionary* dates the commercial sense of the word, as a class of goods identified as being the product of a single firm or manufacturer, from 1827. *Webster's Third International Dictionary* cites an earlier, more general meaning as 'a mark of a simple, easily recognized pattern ... to attest manufacture or quality'. The original idea, then, is of products that are bought and sold on the basis of a mark that guarantees their uniformity. Brands were unnecessary as long as most purchases were made direct from a producer or a merchant who could be held accountable. But with the rise of mass production, and the social dislocations of migration to the cities, some common commodities such as soap, matches, and patent foods began to be marketed as brands. Ads don't sell things – they sell brands (see Bogart 1990, Davidson 1992). It isn't usually worth paying for an ad to say BUY SOAP, but experience showed that it was worth paying for an ad to say BUY SUNLIGHT SOAP.

Brands were once associated mainly with certain kinds of consumer goods, such as medicines, tobacco, cars, and processed foods. Under competitive or political pressures, branding was taken up in other sectors, carriers such as British Rail, business suppliers such as Intel, financial services such as Prudential, health plans such as BUPA, and arts institutions such as the Victoria and Albert Museum. For political parties, branding is often achieved by negative ads on other brands, as in the Tory's 'Labour Isn't Working' (see Kline 1997). Now it is hard to imagine any sector of society in which branding and market decisions are not relevant. One could take as an example the way Wensleydale cheese is sold – until very recently, one bought it off a block in the market. Now the Hawes creamery markets its cheese with a brand with Wallace and Gromit on it. Or, closer to home, the discussion of a new degree in academic committees will consider a department's 'niche', 'branding' of the degree with a clear identity, a logo, and ways of conveying 'unique selling points' through advertising and public relations (see Chapter 5).

The trademark indicating a popular brand can be the most valuable asset of a large company. The care they take to keep the trademark standardized and distinctive can be seen in this book, where I have followed advertisers' requirements in the use of trademarks, for instance putting them in quotation marks, or using them as adjectives rather than nouns.

consumption – The dictionary definitions focus on the idea of using something up, or wasting something, or decline (it was the popular name for the disease tuberculosis), and the word keeps some negative associations. But current cultural studies sees it as creative, a part of the individual's and group's construction of identities (Mackay 1997). A key issue in evaluation of consumption is deciding just what counts as a need and what as an artificially induced desire. One traditional line of criticism of advertising is that it creates new desires, instead of addressing genuine needs. This criticism was put eloquently by Raymond Williams in 'Advertising: The Magic System':

> It is impossible to look at modern advertising without realising that the material object being sold is never enough; this is indeed the crucial cultural quality of its modern forms. If we were sensibly materialist, in that part of our living in which we use things, we should find most advertising to be of an insane irrelevance. Beer would be enough for us, without the additional promise that in drinking it we show ourselves to be manly, young in heart, or neighbourly. A washing machine would be a useful machine to wash clothes, rather than an indication that we are forward-looking or an object of envy to our neighbours'. (Williams 1961)

Later critics have seen consumption as a more complex process than just fulfilling material needs. Kathy Myers argues,

> It is not so easy ... to decide what is a socially necessary commodity. At its simplest there are clothes, heat, food, and shelter; but in an advanced technological society most of these needs should be at least met. The problem becomes more complicated when discriminating between different cuts of coat, different styles of housing or different kinds of food. At what point does a decision based on a principle of style, taste, or fashion move from the necessary to the excessive? Is the 'aesthetic' arguably as important a consideration as the 'function'? (Myers 1986: 129–30)

Surely clothing is a necessity, but what about expensive athletic shoes? What about the status that goes with wearing a pair of the latest Nike trainers on the street; is that status something unnecessary, and the padded foot covering the only real need? What about eye make-up, food processors, Internet connections, concert tickets, satellite or cable access to sporting events? All of these are easily seen by some groups as unnecessary, but seen by at least some people as essential parts of life. (Mine is the food processor.)

This academic insistence on the importance of cultural meanings in consumption sounds like the argument of the advertisers that they add value to brands. But it goes further, because it is not just advertisers who add value, but consumers, transforming brands with unforeseen uses and meanings (as in Doc Marten boots as footwear for clubs, or mountain bikes as urban transportation). This approach has become the orthodoxy of cultural studies on consumption, but it is challenged by critics such as Don Slater (1997), who argues that there are indeed rational grounds for discussing needs and preferring some values to others, 'principled grounds on which one can *judge* consumer culture' (61).

culture – Raymond Williams (1974), in a classic short essay, based on an entry in the *Oxford English Dictionary*, comments on the changing meanings of the word. He traces it from its origins in a sense of growing things (as in 'agriculture'), to its different uses in criticism referring to high culture (such as classical music and painting), and to its uses in anthropology referring to the whole system of beliefs of a people. In contemporary cultural studies (in which Williams is a key figure) it is extended to refer to popular music, fashion, magazines, best-sellers – and advertising.

'Culture' is sometimes used to refer to the beliefs, identities, and material objects of other peoples. William O'Barr uses it that way in *Culture and the Ad: Exploring Otherness in the World of Advertising* (1994), which is a series of studies of how US mainstream advertising represents blacks, native Americans, and foreigners. In contrast, Howard Becker is one of the scholars who would present culture as integral to all our activities; it is 'doing things together', exemplified by the ability of a pick-up jazz group to play together without rehearsing, given only the name of a standard tune, the tempo, and the key (Becker 1986). This sense of the word is close to that used by advertisers themselves when they distinguish the 'agency culture' of Abbott Mead Vickers from that of St. Lukes, or J. Walter Thompson from Wieden and Kennedy. The agencies claim they build up ways of doing things together that all employees take for granted, and they market this culture as the essential attribute of the agency, something apart from its individual stars, who might come and go.

The term 'culture' is used in this book to refer to shared, taken for granted, learned beliefs and practices, embodied in symbol systems (this definition is based on that in Abercrombie, Hill, and Turner (1988)). This may seem to include everything, but sociologists often contrast cultural systems with the socio-economic systems, so they might, for instance, discuss advertising as a set of symbols and meanings separately from advertising as a part of the production and distribution of goods. Some sociologists would insist that not everything is cultural (there's money and law and power), while cultural studies researchers might argue that everything is (even money and law and power would be seen in cultural terms).

It is perhaps best to remember that the term is always a point of contention, between different academic disciplines, and sometimes between different approaches within a discipline; to use it as it is used in cultural studies is to assert the importance of popular practices (such as music, dancing, fashion), not just to draw on a definition everyone shares.

discourse – Social scientists use this term with a number of meanings, but it is worth distinguishing between several common uses (compare GENRE). Linguists may use it to refer to a level of analysis beyond the sentence, studies of how texts hold together and make sense as a whole (for instance, Georgakopoulou and Goutsos (1997) analyse advertisements as part of a more general introduction). So in this sense, when one analyses ads as discourse, one analyses their construction and meaning, as in Cook (1992). Linguists also use the term to refer to specific discourses, uses of language tied to social activities, such as the discourse of sports, or of science, or of politics, so a specific ad may draw on the discourse of feminism (Talbot forthcoming) or of the environment (Myers 1994, Goldman and Papson 1996).

But the term is now widely used to mean 'language as social practice' (Fairclough 1992; 1994: p. 16), the whole structure of knowledge, action, and material culture such as buildings and commodities that makes it possible to talk or think about something. For instance, the way we talk about body shape, and show it in ads, and treat it in medical and educational institutions, could be taken to constitute a discourse. In this sense, which is that most used by social scientists, advertising is one of the institutions within which discourses are constituted. As Alistair Pennycook puts it (1995), in one sense discourse is a part of language, and in the other sense language is a part of discourse.

effects – When non-advertisers think of advertising effects, they are likely to think only of the most immediate effects on sales. But this is not the only goal of advertising. Almost every textbook on advertising research includes a reference to DAGMAR (Colley 1961), an acronym for the title of a report, *Defining Advertising Goals for Measured Advertising Results*. It lists a variety of possible goals, including 'near-term' and 'long range' sales, positioning against rivals, providing a background for sales, or building goodwill and corporate reputation, and suggests the results must be measured against the specific goals of that campaign. That is one reason that the advertising business finds it difficult to agree on awards for 'effectiveness'. For instance, in 1996 the BT campaign, 'It's good to talk', won an Advertising Effectiveness Award in the annual competition sponsored by the Institute of Practitioners in Advertising. Response was mixed, between those advertisers who said it was an example of a creative response to a brief, and those who said it was an annoying campaign that had its effects due mainly to huge spending.

Of course effects go beyond those concerned with the product; ads affect our sense of the social world, our roles, our bodies (Davidson 1992; Goldman and Papson 1996). Academic study of advertising is often concerned with these other effects, for instance the reflection or reproduction of gender (Goffman 1979, Goldman 1992, Lazar 1993, Thornbarrow 1994, Talbot forthcoming). Even the use of the term 'effects' suggests already a conception of media texts as causing some action or response. This conception would be challenged by analysts who see readers as constructing texts or using them, not just responding to them (see AUDIENCE).

genre – The term has different uses in film theory, the study of academic writing, and some approaches to grammar (see Swales 1990 for references). In its most general sense, genre is a textual form corresponding to a stereotypical social action, recognized and given a name by participants (Miller 1984). This definition is useful in the study of advertising, because ads are instantly recognizable by audiences as a particular form, serving a particular purpose. Ads can imitate other forms of popular culture (sports commentary, or game show, or mystery, or soap, or pop video), but they are still interpreted, in the end, as ads imitating these forms. Within advertising, there are various genres recognized by advertising practitioners, such as demonstration ads, testimonials, slice-of-life ads. Again, we know that audiences are aware of these categories, because they are amused (usually) when the expected boundaries are broken, for instance when a comedian sends up the conventions of a demonstration. Vijay Bhatia (1993) places ads as part of a larger genre of promotion, which would include, for instance, job applications and sales promotion letters.

globalization – The term is used to draw attention to processes in which flows of money, images, products, and people disrupt and supersede national and regional social structures (such as national markets, regulations, and political representation) and local cultural norms (such as language, music, and sometimes religion). For surveys, see Appadurai (1990), Giddens (1990) and Lash and Urry (1994), and Thrift (1997). Key readings relevant to advertising are collected in Sreberny-Mohammadi *et al.* (1997). Almost as soon as the idea was put forward, social scientists began to stress that these processes went with other processes of increased local identities, or 'glocalization' (Robertson 1995). Critiques of the idea that national cultures are weakening are offered in Michael Billig (1995) and Morley and Robins (1995).

The awful word 'globalization' didn't start with sociologists or theorists, though it has had broad effects in social theory. It started with Theodore Levitt, an influential Harvard Business School marketing professor who was giving advice to corporation heads. His thesis (Levitt 1983) was that there would be a competitive advantage in some sectors in marketing the same product in the same way around the world, gaining what might be called symbolic economies by focusing all one's marketing on one brand presented as the best. The way forward, he said, was to make a good product, and make people adapt to it. Too expensive? They'll find the money. Too high-tech? They'll learn. Too British (or Japanese or German or American)? It will be seen as an advantage.

But is this really the future of marketing? Martin Mayer (1991) points out that very few products are really the same in all countries. And very few products dominate the market in all countries. If you walk past the shelves of a US or French supermarket, you'll be surprised by the number of familiar names, and even more, of familiar corporations – but you will also find some striking differences. US breakfast cereals still don't dominate European markets. Or try loo paper, insurance, or lorries. There is still a need to adapt to local markets. If globalization of products were irresistible, marketing would be much easier than it is. There are also critics in cultural studies who argue that the same product does take on different meanings in different cultures (Miller 1998). But it is useful to take Levitt's simplified statement as a starting point.

integration – One of the keywords in advertising jargon these days is *integration*, the way messages work together in different media, and in particular, the way above-the-line campaigns in traditional media work with below-the-line campaigns using direct mail, public relations, sponsorship, and other forms of promotion (see Batra, Myers, and Aaker 1996: Chapter 3). Every 'full service' ad agency claims to be particularly good at integration, and *Campaign* has a regular section devoted to it. Integration might be shown in:

- posters as teasers for or reminders of television ads;
- press ads that link to a direct mail campaign (so the recipients are more likely to open the letters);
- point of sale ads that link to a television campaign (so purchasers make the connection to an endorser 'as seen on TV');
- national ads that link to local dealers (perhaps with a slot for their address and local events);
- product design and packaging in relation to advertising (for instance, incorporating an endorsement or slogan);
- advertising targeted to work with press reports (as in major promotions such as those for the launch of Corsa, Windows 95, or the blue packaging of Pepsi).

There is a competitive reason for agencies wanting to claim integration. Their largest clients may want to do much of this work, especially below the line, in-house. Or they may farm out different projects to various agencies on a roster. Each agency wants to show itself capable of taking on the whole task, and imposing coherence that will mean the advertising money is spent more effectively (and spent through them).

interaction – Advertisers use the words 'interactive media' with several related but not always compatible meanings. First, an interactive medium may be one in which the source of the message may get a 'response' from the audience, as when a TV commercial asks viewers to phone in, or the audience may get a response from the source, as in a multimedia CD-ROM. It can also mean a more complex 'participation' in which the audience may feel that they can shape the outcome of events, as with computer game or simulation, or a press ad with a quiz. It can also mean a simulated 'presence' in which technologies are used to capture or transmit for distant or later use the density of face-to-face experience, in what is imagined as virtual reality, with video and audio replacing one's own immediate senses, and one's sense of position in place and time.

Claude Hopkins pioneered a kind of interaction in *Scientific Advertising*, a book written in 1923. He argued that all print ads should be tested by running split runs of, say, the same ad with different headlines, or pictures of different sizes, or long and short copy, both ads making the same offer (see Chapter 9). The same sort of interaction is possible in broadcast ads with a toll-free telephone number. This is interaction as response: the advertiser puts out a message and at some time later the audience gives a message back. Note that in each of these cases, a different medium is used for the advertiser's message and the audience response – magazine and post, or television and telephone. The ad industry is fascinated with cable television because it offers the technological possibility of sending out a message and getting back a response in the same medium, instantly. But it is still just a response, and that is not all there is to interaction.

Another sense of interaction would be where the audience could have some say about what they got from the advertiser, and have a sense of participation, the way the crowd at the market participate in the performance of the trader. Again cable TV seems to offer possibilities. In one of the few areas of the UK with pilot versions of interactive cable, JWT has arranged an ad for Kellogg's Frosties that allows viewers with special controls to respond as the ad goes on, choosing different further developments. Pushing the red button and not the blue, getting a surfing Tony the Tiger rather than a skiing Tony the Tiger, may not seem like real interaction. But even this tiny concession to the active audience, giving them some effect on the message, is seen as a major breakthrough in TV, where the audience has been treated as totally passive and totally unknown, except in specially constructed research settings (see Chapter 9).

The Web allows for a kind of participation, if by participation we mean endless choices. But most of the attention to the medium has focused on the possibility of simulating presence. The rapid development of browsers like Netscape and Internet Explorer has gone with the development of plug-ins (software the user downloads to work with the browser) such as Shockwave, Real Audio, and Real Video, that allow for movement and sound (see WORLD WIDE WEB for terms). As with the development of cinema and television, the technology is directed at giving the sense that the viewer is there in the scene, not sitting here looking at the screen. The science fiction of William Gibson (*Neuromancer* (1984), *Virtual Light* (1993), *Idoru* (1996)) and others sets out the possibility of virtual reality, in which the subject enters another place, time, and experience. This is promised on the Web, at least as a goal, by sites that give us the Virtual Car, the Virtual Frog, the Virtual Science Laboratory, or the Virtual Bathroom (a men's toilet in Rochester, NY).

Often it seems that what is needed for the sense of presence is just one more improvement in the amount of information that can be transmitted, so video conferencing can work with higher resolution, and complex animation run smoothly without dropped frames. But what is missing is the sense that another person has something of themselves invested in the interaction, what the sociologist Erving Goffman (1967) calls 'face'. It may be that complex graphics can give us the fleeting visual sense that we are there ourselves, but it is only with this sense of face that we will think the other person is there for us. Market traders are aware that once people get close to them, joining the crowd, they have made a sort of commitment that can be converted to sales. They can't be away in a click. For classic studies this rich sort of interaction, with fascinating examples, see a trilogy of books by Erving Goffman (1963, 1967, and 1971), and for a collection of recent linguistic studies from a variety of academic approaches, see Duranti and Goodwin (1992).

medium – In general terms, media are the means of converting a communicated message for transmission. This may sound more like a piece of equipment than a social institution, but the definition reminds us that the people and institutions around this conversion serve an important function of selecting and packaging (see Fiske (1982), Meyrowitz (1994), Thompson (1995), Lull (1995), and Curran and Gurevitch (1996) for more detailed theoretical consideration). By this definition, advertising appears in all sorts of media, from golf-ball holes to concert tickets to the Internet. There is also a more popular definition, in which 'the media' come to stand for all sorts of social pressure, largely through broadcasting and the press. But it is useful to unbundle this very general usage, and ask just what each medium can do.

In the definition usually used in the advertising business, there are just five media: press, radio, television, and cinema, as well as outdoor ads such as posters. These are the media on which traditionally an advertiser pays a commission to an agency (see AGENCIES). Other media are possible – exhibitions, direct mail, door-to-door leafleting – but they are handled in different ways, and usually treated separately (see INTEGRATION). This division of media arose over the years as agencies started by placing ads in the press and then gradually incorporated new media in their remit. Thus when ad people talk about media, they mean something both broader than the popular conception (not just the press and TV) and narrower (not posters inside on bulletin boards or new media like the Internet).

poster – The term is used in the UK to cover outdoor advertising in general; in the US the general term is 'billboard'. This is confusing, because in the UK the word 'billboard' is sometimes used for a small poster, the size used outside newsagents' shops, while in the US a 'poster' suggests a small advertisement, the size used for movie theatres. The terms for different sizes vary in each country as well. In the UK, the double crown is the smallest size, used in front of shops. The illuminated 40 inch by 60 inch signs on the sides of bus shelters are *4-sheets*, and the standard road-side poster, 10 ft by 20 ft, is a *48-sheet*. Very large posters, double this size, are *96-sheets*, the largest standard size. US posters have different names, but similar sizes: a US *30-sheet* is about size of a UK *48-sheet*. The key distinction is between posters large enough to be read by passing cars, and the smaller posters intended for pedestrian traffic. Posters are usually sold in packages to cover different client needs: for instance, a set of 4-sheets near supermarkets, or a set of sites in one region.

These terms cover the posters in regulated sites, called *hoardings* in the UK. Of course many concert posters or political posters with short lives are pasted up without permission on boarded up shop fronts or concrete walls. This practice is called *fly-posting*, and it enrages the owners of out-door media because it undermines the value of what they have to sell: legally regulated and thus restricted space. (I have taken these terms from Jefkins (1994) and Bernstein (1997).)

promotional culture – Andrew Wernick (1991) has argued that the rhetoric of promotion characteristic of advertising has been extended throughout our culture, to such spheres as education, politics, and even one's sense of being an individual person. He points out the many ways that institutions once seen as having their own bases of authority now compete against each other, and address clients, customers, workers, and supporters as free agents who want to maximize their choices. Keat, Whiteley, and Abercrombie (1994) collect essays tracing the effects of consumer-orientation in such fields as religion, art, policing, and higher education. The ubiquity of such promotion seems to support the idea that it constitutes a major cultural shift. This assumes that the promotion goes all the way through organizations: a university that promotes itself will also be changed in its practices of curriculum development, teaching, and grading (Fairclough 1994).

But even organizations devoted to promotion of products as their main purpose, such as ad agencies, software firms, or car companies, apparently develop complex internal cultures, in which not all efforts are directed at the corporate goals. And it is still unclear to what degree an audience discounts all efforts at promotion, even those wrapped as non-promotional, such as anti-ads, sponsorship of the arts, or apparently personal direct mail.

For me, the most powerful demonstration of promotional culture is in the Walt Disney cartoon *Hercules* (which, like all Disney cartoons, was promoted with a whole range of lucrative toy and fast-food tie-ins), where the hero's rise and fall, in the movie itself, is traced in the sales of Hercules figurines. Kids are already sophisticated enough to know about, and mock, such tie-ins – while still buying the lunch box.

public – The *Oxford English Dictionary* gives one definition of *public* as 'That is open to, may be used by, or may or must be used by, all members of a community.' This is the sense I use when I contrast the public space of posters with the private, domestic space of magazine consumption (Chapter 6). In many areas of life, the distinctions between the public and the private are breaking down; for instance, ads may deal with personal issues, and may use forms of address usually restricted to personal interaction (Fairclough 1992). Note that the dictionary definition relies on there being a community to which the sense of the public can be linked. So, for instance, an art museum may be public, in the sense of being open to all members of the community, but may in fact be used only by one segment of the community. To take another example, there is not one general public that is affronted by Benetton ads, but many local communities that may respond differently to a picture of a black woman with a white baby, or a nun kissing a priest.

There is another, related sense of *public* as the forum for civic action and responsibility: 'Of, pertaining to, or engaged in the affairs or service of the community.' John Corner (1995) has suggested that the public in this sense may be constituted in part by the media, and in particular by television, as Benedict Anderson (1981) suggested that nations derived their sense of themselves as nations from, among other things, newspapers. That is, we see ourselves as people who may make civic decisions about elections, or recycling, or schools, when we are addressed in that way. Again we see what is public, not as given, but as constructed moment to moment. Ien Ang (1991) has contrasted this sense of the audience of broadcasting as a public, with the sense of the audience as consumers, making individual decisions about their preferences for entertainment (see AUDIENCE).

reflexivity – The most general sense of *reflexivity*, as the capacity for reflecting on what one is doing as one does it, is always an issue in social science. The people one is studying are studying themselves at the same time, and social scientists often ask how what they are saying applies to them and their project (Woolgar 1988). But it is also an issue for advertisers, who are more and more aware that members of their audiences think about and discuss the effectiveness of ads, observing the effects of ads on themselves. As the advertiser Adam Lury puts it: 'When you access today's consumer, what they think and what they think you want them to think, are often one and the same' (1994: 96). One response has been reflexive ads, ads about advertising (see Chapter 12).

regulation – Here is a short dictionary of abbreviations (drawn largely from Brierley (1995) and Batra, Myers, and Aaker (1996)).

> AA – The Advertising Association, a lobby group (founded 1924) for the advertising industry as a whole on matters such as regulation.
>
> ASA – the UK Advertising Standards Authority, which receives complaints about print, outdoor, and cinema media (that is, not ITV and Channel 4 or commercial radio).
>
> BACC – The Broadcast Advertising Clearance Centre, which vets scripts of UK TV commercials before they are broadcast.
>
> BBB – Better Business Bureaus, a US network of local business organizations to deal with consumer complaints and demonstrate the effectiveness of self-regulation.
>
> CAP – The Code of Advertising Practice, against which the ASA evaluates complaints against ads.
>
> FCC – The US Federal Communications Commission awards and monitors broadcast licenses, giving it a say in such matters as advertising to children.
>
> FTC – The US Federal Trade Commission, established in 1914, monitors ads for deception and anti-competitive practices, and can impose penalties and require corrective advertising.
>
> IPA – The Institute of Practitioners in Advertising, the trade organization of UK advertising agencies.
>
> ITC – The Independent Television Commission administers the Code of Standards and Practice, the basis for adjudication on complaints about UK terrestrial television commercials.
>
> NAD – National Advertising Division of the US Council of Better Business Bureaus.

strategy – In advertising, 'strategy' is the overall planning of a campaign to achieve specific ends (see Bogart 1990). It comes from the Greek word for 'general', so it implies a top–down view of how things happen. And it carries over from its military origins the connotation that it involves a trick, a device, a single bold stroke. In the culture of the 1980s and 1990s, the word has very favourable associations, a sense of prudent consideration of the future: my university has a strategy for the future, and each department is told it must have a strategy, and the parties in the election present their strategies for education or employment or crime. But it is worth remembering, when you hear the word, that it assumes top down control, and also a certain predictability. This is just what agencies want to be able to promise their clients, but they may be wrong on both counts: they can't control the people in their agency, or predict the responses of the people outside it. Advertising campaigns may be successful or unsuccessful at the level of sergeants and corporals, not generals. Retrospective accounts of campaigns by the advertisers stress strategy (see the annual *Advertising Works*); journalistic accounts of whole campaigns seen day to day (such as Arlen (1980) or Rothenberg (1994)) give an idea of the enormous contingencies along the way.

World Wide Web – The Web is just one set of technologies using the Internet, but it has received much of the attention. From an advertiser's point of view, the key features are that it can serve many users, that messages can incorporate complex files, such as graphics, and that pages are linked in hypertext form. It was developed at CERN, the international research centre in Geneva, to enable high-energy physicists to share the complex data resulting from experiments, by exchanging images as well as texts. When a user asks for a page, the request is sent to the server storing that page. As soon as the user has the page, the connection is broken, and the server is ready to respond to another user. This allows many users to access a server without tying it up.

An ad for a seminar offered by the magazine *Marketing* says this is what one's web designer might say to you: 'Basically, we suggest 40 pages of HTML, with some Javascript and CGI work to create a push element. Is browser backward compatibility an issue, or can we use frames and maybe cascading style sheets?' You may follow all that, but if this sort of jargon floors you, here is an introductory guide to some web vocabulary. More technical and detailed tutorials are available at www.hotwired.com.

> *banner* – an advertisement in the form of an oblong across the page, usually about 468 × 60 pixels, sometimes just giving a message, like a poster, but usually also allowing the user to click and get a link to another site.
>
> *browser* – the software, such as Netscape or Internet Explorer, that enables users to connect to web servers and read what they send. Each new version has enormously expanded capabilities, so designers have to think about *backward compatibility*, the ability of older browsers to continue using the site.
>
> *click-through* – the number of users who click on a banner advertisement and link to the advertiser's site.
>
> *cookies* – programs stored in a browser to track its movements and report this information when the user returns to a site.
>
> *hypertext* – A form of machine-readable data that allows for embedded words or objects to have multiple connections to other

files, instead of all words being arranged in some linear order. Web files are written in Hypertext Mark-up Language, or HTML.

impressions – the number of times users consult a page.

Internet – a set of computer links developed to send messages, including those by e-mail, file transfer protocols (ftp), electronic bulletin boards, and the World Wide Web.

interstitial ads – these ads pop up between pages, allowing the advertiser to use the full screen for animation rather than just the box of the banner.

Java – the programming language widely used for web pages, which allows various computers and operating systems to use the same files; it is now incorporated into most web browsers.

push – technologies that allow a server to send files a user has not explicitly requested (pulled), for instance, sending out only news stories in categories the user has checked in personalizing his or her home page.

search engine – software that contains a list of many web sites, and responds to queries with those sites that use a given term or set of terms. An index, such as Excite, Infoseek, or Alta Vista, compiles this list automatically by searching sites with a spider, a program for following links and listing the words they use. In a directory, such as Yahoo, the sites are compiled by humans who classify them in a tree of possible subjects.

server – the computer that holds the web pages and sends them out on request.

URL – Uniform Resource Locator – The address of a web site, such as http:// www.ling.lancs.ac.uk/staff/~greg.

References

Abercrombie, N., Hill, S., and Turner, B. S. 1988. *The Penguin dictionary of sociology*. Harmondsworth: Penguin.

Alasuutari, P. 1995. *Researching culture: qualitative method and cultural studies*. London: Sage.

Allan, S. 1997. Raymond Williams and the culture of visual flow. In J. Wallance, R. Jones, and S. Nield (eds.), *Raymond Williams now: knowledge, limits, and the future* (pp. 115–44). London: Macmillan.

Anderson, B. 1981. *Imagined communities: reflections on the origin and spread of nationalism*. London: Verso.

Ang, I. 1991. *Desperately seeking the audience*. London: Routledge.

Appadurai, A. 1990. Disjunction and difference in the global cultural economy. In M. Featherstone (eds.), *Global culture*. London: Sage.

Arlen, M. J. 1980. *Thirty seconds*. Harmondsworth: Penguin.

Astroff, R. J. 1997. Capital's cultural study: marketing popular ethnography of US Latino culture. In M. Nava, A. Blake, I. MacRury, & B. Richards (eds.), *Buy this book: studies in advertising and consumption* (pp. 120–38). London: Routledge.

Baker, C. (ed.) 1993. *Advertising Works 7: papers from the 1992 IPA Advertising Effectiveness Awards*. London: NTC.

Baker, C. (ed.) 1995. *Advertising Works 8: papers from the IPA Advertising Effectiveness Awards*. London: NTC.

Barbour, R., and Kitzinger, J. (ed.). 1999. *Focus groups in research*. London: Sage.

Barbules, N. C. 1998. Rhetorics of the Web: hyperreading and critical literacy. In Snyder, I. (ed.). 1998. *Page to screen: taking literacy into the electronic era* (pp. 102–22). London: Routledge.

Barthes, R. 1972. *Mythologies* (Annette Lavers, Trans.). New York: Hill and Wang.

Barthes, R. 1977. The rhetoric of the image. In *Image – Music – Text* (pp. 32–51). London: Fontana.

Barton, B. and Hamilton, M. 1998. *Local literacies: reading and writing in one community*. London: Routledge.

Batra, R., Myers, J. G., and Aaker, D. A. 1996. *Advertising management*. Upper Saddle River, NJ: Prentice-Hall.

Becker, H. 1982. *Art worlds*. Berkeley and Los Angeles: University of California Press.

Becker, H. 1986. *Doing things together: selected papers*. Evanston, IL: Northwestern University Press.

Bernstein, D. 1997. *Advertising outdoors: watch this space*! London: Phaidon.

Bhatia, V. 1993. *Analysing genre: language use in professional settings*. Harlow: Longman.

Billig, M. 1995. *Banal nationalism*. London: Sage.

Blake, A. 1997. Listen to Britain: advertising and postmodern culture. In M. Nava, A. Blake, I. MacRury, & B. Richards (eds.), *Buy this book: studies in advertising and consumption* (pp. 224–38). London: Routledge.

Boden, D., and Molotch, H. 1994. The compulsion of proximity. In R. Friedland and D. Boden (eds.), *NowHere: space, time, and modernity*. Berkeley: University of California Press.

Bogart, L. 1990. *Strategy in advertising* (2nd edn.). Chicago: NTC Books.

Brierley, S. 1995. *The advertising handbook*. London: Routledge.

Channon, C. (ed.). 1989. *20 advertising case histories: second series*. London: Cassell.

Clark, C., and Pinch, T. 1995. *The hard sell: the language and lessons of street-wise marketing*. London: HarperCollins.

Clarke, A. J. 1998. Window shopping at home: classifieds, catalogues, and new consumer skills. In D. Miller (ed.), *Material cultures: why some things matter* (pp. 73–99). London: UCL Press.

Colley, R. H. 1961. *Defining advertising goals for measured advertising results*. New York: Association of National Advertisers.

Cook, G. 1992. *The discourse of advertising*. London: Routledge.

Corner, J. 1995. *Television form and public address*. London: Arnold.

Corner, J., and Harvey, S. (ed.) 1996. *Television times: a reader*. London: Arnold.

Cosgrove, D. 1994. Contested global visions: one-world, whole-earth, and the apollo space photographs. *Annals of the Association of American Geographers, 84*: 270–94.

Crowley, D., and Mitchell, D. (ed.) 1994. *Communication theory today*. Cambridge: Polity.

Curran, J., and Gurevitch, M. (ed.) 1996. *Mass media and society* (2nd edn.). London: Arnold.

Curran, J., Morley, D., and Walkerdine, V. (ed.) 1996. *Cultural studies and communications*. London: Arnold.

Davidson, M. 1992. *The consumerist manifesto*. London: Routledge.

Duranti, A., and Goodwin, C. (eds.) 1992. *Rethinking context: language as an interactive phenomenon*. Cambridge: Cambridge University Press.

Dyer, G. 1982. *Advertising as communication*. London: Routledge.

Ellis, J. 1982. *Visible fictions: cinema, television, video.* London: Routledge and Kegan Paul.

Ettema, J., and Whitney, D. C. (ed.) 1994. *How media create the audience.* Thousand Oaks, CA: Sage.

Ewen, S. 1976. *Captains of consciousness: advertising and the social roots of consumer culture.* New York: McGraw-Hill.

Faigley, L. 1998. Material literacy and visual design. In S. Crowley and J. Selzer (eds.), *Rhetorical bodies: towards a material rhetoric.* Madison, WI: University of Wisconsin Press.

Fairclough, N. 1992. *Discourse and social change.* Cambridge: Polity.

Fairclough, N. 1994. *Media discourse.* London: Arnold.

Falk, P. 1997. The Benetton–Toscani effect: testing the limits of conventional advertising. In M. Nava, A. Blake, I. MacRury, and B. Richards (eds.), *Buy this book: studies in advertising and consumption* (pp. 64–86). London: Routledge.

Fiske, J. 1982. *Introduction to communication studies.* London: Methuen.

Fiske, J. 1987. *Television culture.* London: Routledge.

Forceville, C. 1996. *Pictorial metaphors in advertising.* London: Routledge.

Fowles, J. 1996. *Advertising and popular culture.* Thousand Oaks, CA: Sage.

Fox, S. 1990. *The mirror makers: a history of American advertising.* London: Heinemann.

Georgakopoulou, A, and Goutsos, D. 1997. *Discourse analysis: an introduction.* Edinburgh: Edinburgh University Press.

Gibson, W. 1983. *Neuromancer.* London: Victor Gollancz.

Gibson, W. 1993. *Virtual light.* London: Viking.

Gibson, W. 1996. *Idoru.* London: Viking.

Giddens, A. 1990. *The consequences of modernity.* Cambridge: Polity.

Goddard, A. 1998. *The language of advertising: written texts.* London: Routledge.

Goffman, E. 1963. *Behavior in public.* New York: The Free Press.

Goffman, E. 1967. *Interaction ritual.* New York: Basic Books.

Goffman, E. 1971. *Relations in public.* New York: Basic Books.

Goffman, E. 1979. *Gender Advertisements.* New York: Harper Colophon.

Goffman, E. 1981. *Forms of talk.* Philadelphia: University of Pennsylvania Press.

Goldman, R. 1992. *Reading ads socially.* London: Routledge.

Goldman, R., and Papson, S. 1996. *Sign wars: The cluttered landscape of advertising.* New York: The Guilford Press.

Grove-White, R., Macnaghten, P., Mayer, S., and Wynne, B. 1997. *Uncertain world: genetically modified organisms, food and public attitudes in Britain.* Centre for the Study of Environmental Change (Lancaster University, Lancaster LA1 4YN).

Gusfield, J. 1976. The literary rhetoric of science. *American Sociological Review, 41:* 16–34.

Haskins, J., and Kendrick, A. 1993. *Successful advertising research methods*. Lincolnwood, IL: NTC Business Books.

Higgins, D. 1965. *The art of writing advertising*. Lincolnwood, IL: NTC Books.

Himelstein, L., Neuborne, E., and Eng, P. M. 1997, 6 October. Web ads start to click. *Business Week*.

Hopkins, C. 1923/1966. *Scientific advertising*, reprinted in *My life in advertising* and *Scientific advertising*. Lincolnwood, IL: NTC Books.

Hopkins, C. 1927/1966. *My life in advertising*, reprinted in *My life in advertising* and *Scientific advertising*. Lincolnwood, IL: NTC Books.

IPA, (ed.). 1994. *Papers from the 1994 Advertising Effectiveness Awards* [loose-leaf binder]. London: IPA.

Jefferson, G. 1984. On the stepwise transition from talk about a trouble to inappropriately next-positioned matters. In J. M. Atkinson and J. Heritage (eds.), *Structures of social action: studies in conversation analysis* (pp. 191–222). Cambridge: Cambridge University Press.

Jefkins, F. 1994. *Advertising* (3rd edn.). London: Pitman Publishing.

Jensen, K. B. 1996. Reception as flow. In J. Corner and S. Harvey (eds.), *Television times: a reader* (pp. 187–98). London: Arnold.

Jobling, P. 1997. Keeping Mrs. Dawson busy: safe sex, gender, and pleasure in condom advertising since 1970. In M. Nava, A. Blake, I. MacRury, and B. Richards (eds.), *Buy this book: studies in advertising and consumption* (pp. 157–77). London: Routledge.

Johnston, A. 1988. *Musings on the vernacular*. Berkeley: Poltroon Press.

Keat, R., Whiteley, N., and Abercrombie, N. (eds.). 1994. *The authority of the consumer*. London: Routledge.

Kline, S. 1997. Image politics: negative advertising strategies and the election audience. In M. Nava, A. Blake, I. MacRury, and B. Richards (eds.), *Buy this book: studies in advertising and consumption* (pp. 139–56). London: Routledge.

Knobil, M. and O'Dwyer, B. 1993. *The best ads never seen*. London: Open Eye Publishing.

Kotler, P. 1983. *Marketing management* (6th edn.). Englewood Cliffs, NJ: Prentice-Hall.

Kress, G. 1987. Educating readers: language in advertising. In J. Hawthorn (ed.), *Propaganda, persuasion and polemic* (pp. 123–39). London: Arnold.

Kress, G., and van Leeuwen, T. 1996. *Reading images: the grammar of visual design*. London: Routledge.

Kroll, C. 1997. MPA joins editors to limit advertiser interference. *Advertising age* (September) [from www.adage.com].

Krueger, R. A. 1994. *Focus groups: a practical guide for applied research* (2nd edn.). Newbury Park: Sage.

Lannon, J. 1992. Asking the right questions: what do people do with advertising? *Admap 28* (3) March: 11–16.

Lannon, J. 1994. How they differ from us. *Admap 30* (7) July–August: 30–38.

Lash, S., and Dillon, G. M. 1997. *Detraditionalization*. London: Sage.

Lash, S., and Urry, J. 1994. *Economies of signs and space*. London: Sage.

Lazar, M. 1993. Equalizing gender relations: a case of double talk. *Discourse and society* 4: 443–65.

Lears, T. 1995. *Fables of abundance: a cultural history of advertising in America*. New York: Basic Books.

Leech, G. 1964. *English in advertising*. London: Longman.

Leiss, W., Kline, S., and Jhally, S. 1986. *Social communication in advertising*. London: Routledge.

Levitt, T. 1983. The globalization of markets. *Harvard Business Review* (May–June).

Lewis, R., and Rolley, C. 1997. (Ad)dressing the dyke: lesbian looks and lesbian looking. In M. Nava, A. Blake, I. MacRury, and B. Richards (eds.), *Buy this book: studies in advertising and consumption* (pp. 291–308). London: Routledge.

Lull, J. 1990. *Inside family viewing: ethnographic research on television's audiences*. London: Routledge.

Lull, J. 1995. *Media, communication, culture: a global approach*. Cambridge: Polity.

Lury, A. 1994. Advertising: moving beyond the stereotypes. In R. Keat, N. Whiteley, and N. Abercrombie (eds.), *The authority of the consumer* (pp. 91–101). London: Routledge.

Lury, C. 1996. *Consumer culture*. Cambridge: Polity.

Lury, C., and Warde, A. 1997. Investments in the imaginary consumer: conjectures regarding power, knowledge, and advertising. In M. Nava, A. Blake, I. MacRury, and B. Richards (eds.), *Buy this book: studies in advertising and consumption* (pp. 87–102). London: Routledge.

Mackay, H. (ed.). 1997. *Consumption and everyday life*. London: Sage.

MacRury, I. 1997. Advertising and the modulation of narcissism: the case of adultery. In M. Nava, A. Blake, I. MacRury, and B. Richards (eds.), *Buy this book: studies in advertising and consumption* (pp. 239–56). London: Routledge.

Marchand, R. 1985. *Advertising the American way: making way for modernity*. Berkeley: University of California Press.

Marris, P., and Thornham, S. (ed.). 1996. *Media studies: a reader*. Edinburgh: Edinburgh University Press.

Matellart, A. 1991. *Advertising international*. London: Routledge.

Mayer, M. 1961. *Madison Avenue: USA*. Harmondsworth: Penguin.

Mayer, M. 1991. *Whatever happened to Madison Avenue?* Boston: Little, Brown.

McAllister, M. 1996. *The commercialization of American culture: new advertising control and democracy*. Thousand Oaks, CA: Sage.

McLuhan, M. 1964. *Understanding media: the extensions of man*. New York: McGraw-Hill.

McQuail, D. 1997. *Audience analysis*. Thousand Oaks, CA: Sage.

McRobbie, A. 1994. *Postmodernism and Popular Culture*. London: Routledge.

Meijer, I. 1998. Advertising citizenship: an essay on the performative power of consumer culture. Media, Culture & Society *20*: 235–49.

Meinhof, U. 1998. *Language learning in the age of satellite television*. Oxford: Oxford University Press.

Meyrowitz, J. 1994. Medium theory. In D. Crowley and D. Mitchell (eds.), *Communication theory today* (pp. 50–77). Cambridge: Polity.

Miller, C. 1984. Genre as social action. *Quarterly Journal of Speech, 70*: 151–67.

Miller, D. 1998. Coca-Cola: a black sweet drink from Trinidad. In D. Miller (ed.), *Material cultures: why some things matter* (pp. 169–88). London: UCL Press.

Miller, D. (ed.) 1998. *Material cultures: why some things matter*. London: UCL Press.

Moores, S. 1997. Broadcasting and Its Audiences. In H. Mackay (eds.), *Consumption and everyday life* (pp. 213–58). London: Sage.

Morgan, D. L. 1988. *Focus groups as qualitative research*. Newbury Park: Sage.

Morley, D. 1992. *Television audiences and cultural studies*. London: Routledge.

Morley, D., and Robins, K. 1995. *Spaces of identity: global media, electronic landscapes, and cultural boundaries*. London: Routledge.

Mort, F. 1997. Paths to mass consumption: Britain and the USA since 1945. In M. Nava, A. Blake, I. MacRury, and B. Richards (eds.), *Buy this book: studies in advertising and consumption* (pp. 15–33). London: Routledge.

Myers, G. 1994. *Words in ads*. London: Arnold.

Myers, G. 1998. Displaying opinions: topics and disagreements in focus groups. *Language in Society 27*: 85–11.

Myers, K. 1986. *Understains: the sense and seduction of advertising*. London: Comedia.

Nava, M. 1992. *Changing cultures: feminism, youth, and consumerism*. London: Sage.

Nava, M. 1997. Framing advertising: cultural analysis and the incrimination of visual texts. In M. Nava, A. Blake, I. MacRury, and B. Richards (eds.), *Buy this book: studies in advertising and consumption* (pp. 34–50). London: Routledge.

Nixon, S. 1997. Advertising executives as modern men: masculinity and the UK advertising industry in the 1980s. In M. Nava, A. Blake, I. MacRury, and B. Richards (eds.), *Buy this book: studies in advertising and consumption* (pp. 103–19). London: Routledge.

O'Barr, W. 1994. *Culture and the ad: exploring otherness in the world of advertising*. Boulder, CO: Westview Press.

O'Donohoe, S. 1997. Leaky boundaries: intertextuality and young adult experiences of advertising. In M. Nava, A. Blake, I. MacRury, and B. Richards (eds.), *Buy this book: studies in advertising and consumptions* (pp. 257–75). London: Routledge.

Ogilvy, D. 1983. *Ogilvy on advertising*. London: Pan.

Opie, R. 1985. *Rule Britannia: trading on the British image*. Harmondsworth: Penguin.

Pateman, T. 1983. How is understanding an advertisement possible? In H. Davis and P. Walton (eds.), *Language, image, media* (pp. 187–204). Oxford: Basil Blackwell.

Pennycook, A. 1995. Incommensurable discourses. *Applied Linguistics, 15*: 115–38.

Potter, J. and Wetherell, M. 1987. *Discourse and social psychology: beyond attitudes and behaviour*. London: Sage.

Prendergast, M. 1994. *For God, country, and Coca-Cola*. London: Pheonix.

Preston, I. 1994. *The tangled web we weave: truth, falsity, and advertisers*. Madison, WI: University of Wisconsin Press.

Preston, I. 1996. *The great American blowup: puffery in advertising and selling* (Revised ed.). Madison, WI: University of Wisconsin Press.

Reisz, K., and Millar, G. 1953. *The technique of film editing*. New York: Hastings House.

Richards, T. 1990. *The commodity culture of Victorian England: advertising and spectacle 1851–1914*. London: Verso.

Richardson, K. 1997. Twenty-first century commerce. The case of QVC. *Text* 17: 199–223.

Ritson, M. and Elliot, R. 1995. A model of advertising literacy: the praxiology and co-creation of advertising meaning. Proceedings of the 24th European Marketing Academy Conference. Paris: ESSEC.

Ritson, M. and Elliot, R. 1997. Marketing to generation X: strategies for communicating with 'advertising's lost generation'. Proceedings of the AMA Special Conference: new and evolving paradigms: the emerging future of marketing.

Robertson, R. 1995. Glocalization: Time-space and homogeneity-heterogeneity. In M. Featherstone, S. Lash, and R. Robertson (eds.), *Global modernities* (pp. 25–44). London: Sage.

Robson, C. 1993. *Real world research*. Oxford: Blackwell.

Rothenberg, R. 1994. *Where the suckers moon: an advertising story*. New York: Knopf.

Rothenberg, R. 1998. Bye-bye. The Net's precision accountability will kill not only traditional advertising, but its parasite, big media. Sniff. *Wired* (January): 72–6.

Savan, L. 1994. *The sponsored life: ads, TV, and American culture*. Philadelphia: Temple University Press.

Scannell, P. (ed.) 1991. *Broadcast talk*. London: Sage.

Scannell, P. 1996. *Radio, television, and modern life*. Oxford: Blackwell.

Scannell, P., and Cardiff, D. 1991. *A social history of British broadcasting: serving the nation 1923–1939.* Oxford: Basil Blackwell.

Schudson, M. 1984. *Advertising: the uneasy persuasion – its dubious impact on American society.* New York: Basic Books.

Schudson, M. 1993. 'Afterword' to Advertising, the uneasy persuasion: its dubious impact on American society (pp. 244–60). London: Routledge.

Schultz, D. 1990. *Strategic Advertising Campaigns* (3rd edn.). Lincolnwood, IL: NTC Books.

Sebeok, T. 1991. *A sign is just a sign.* Bloomington, IN: Indiana University Press.

Seiter, E., Borchers, H., Kreutzner, G., and Warth, E. M. (ed.) 1990. *Remote control: television, audiences, and cultural power.* London: Routledge.

Shields, R. 1992. *Places on the margin: alternative geographies of modernity.* London: Routledge.

Shields, R. (ed.) 1996. *Cultures of Internet: virtual spaces, real histories, living bodies.* London: Sage.

Silverman, D. 1993. *Interpreting qualitative data: methods for analysing talk, text, and interaction.* London: Sage.

Slater, D. 1997. Consumer culture and the politics of need. In M. Nava, A. Blake, I. MacRury, and B. Richards (eds.), *Buy this book: studies in advertising and consumption* (pp. 51–63). London: Routledge.

Snyder, I. (ed.) 1998. *Page to screen: taking literacy into the electronic era.* London: Routledge.

Sreberny-Mohammadi, A., Winseck, D., McKenna, J., and Boyd-Barrett, O. (ed.) 1997. *Media in global context: a reader.* London: Arnold.

Steichen, E. (ed.) 1983. *The family of man.* New York: Museum of Modern Art.

Sterne, J. 1995. *World Wide Web marketing.* New York: John Wiley.

Swales, J. 1990. *Genre analysis.* Cambridge: Cambridge University Press.

Talbot, M. (forthcoming). Strange bedfellows. In Andrews, M. and Talbot, M., *All the world and her husband: women in twentieth-century consumer culture.* London: Cassell.

Thompson, J. B. 1995. *The media and modernity: a social theory of the media.* Cambridge: Polity.

Thornbarrow, J. 1994. The woman, the man, and the filofax: gender positions in advertising. In S. Mills (eds.), *Gendering the reader* (pp. 128–51). Hemel Hempstead: Harvester Wheatsheaf.

Thrift, N. 1997. 'Us' and 'them': re-imagining places, re-imagining identities. In H. Mackay (eds.), *Consumption and everyday life* (pp. 159–212). London: Sage.

Tolson, A. 1996. *Mediations.* London: Arnold.

Turner, G, and Pearson, J. 1965. *The persuasion industry.* London: Eyre and Spottiswoode.

Vestergaard, T., and Schrøder, K. 1985. *The language of advertising.* Oxford: Blackwell.

Vidal, J. 1997. *McLibel: burger culture on trial*. London: Macmillan.

Visser, M. 1989. *Much depends on dinner*. Harmondsworth: Penguin.

Watson, J., and Hill, A. 1997. *A dictionary of communication and media studies* (4th edn.). London: Arnold.

Wernick, A. 1991. *Promotional culture: advertising, ideology, and symbolic expression*. London: Sage.

Wernick, A. 1997. Resort to nostalgia: mountains, memories, and myths of time. In M. Nava, A. Blake, I. MacRury, and B. Richards (eds.), *Buy this book: studies in advertising and consumption* (pp. 207–23). London: Routledge.

Williams, K. 1998. *Get me a murder a day: a history of mass communication in Britain*. London: Arnold.

Williams, R. 1974. *Television: technology and cultural form*. London: Fontana.

Williams, R. [1961] 1980. Advertising: the magic system. In *Problems in materialism and culture* (pp. 170–95). London: Verso.

Williamson, J. 1978. *Decoding advertisements: ideology and meaning in advertising*. London: Marion Boyars.

Winship, J. 1980. Sexuality for sale. In S. Hall, D. Hobson, A. Lowe, and P. Willis (eds.), *Culture, Media, Language* (pp. 217–23). London: Unwin Hyman.

Woolgar, S. (ed.) 1988. *Knowledge and reflexivity*. London: Sage.

Index